From Smalltown, U.S.A., to glamorous Hollywood . . . she became the star that millions love —and she paid the price

Lucille Ball has been bitten by a porpoise and a penguin, had her nose set afire, turned into a living chocolate bar, and been made to sail down a flight of stairs on skis. As hilarious off the screen as on, she's one of the great clowns of our century. But her life is scarred by turmoil—and filled with passion, ambition, and heartache. Now best-selling author Charles Higham traces with sensitivity and candor the life of Lucille Ball—and vividly reveals not just the tragedies and triumphs of this beloved comic, but her world: Hollywood!

Discover the truth about:

- The eccentric grandfather who gave her love and hope . . . and nearly wrecked her career
- Her wild, runaway years as a starstruck teen
- Jealousy, tears, and passion—her too-hot-to-handle love for Desi
- Her stormy real-life relationship with *I Love Lucy* co-stars Vivian Vance and William Frawley
- Desilu Productions—the Hollywood empire that made her a millionaire and ruined her marriage
- Love the second time around—her happiness with Gary Morton
- Desi, Jr.'s forbidden romance and battle with drugs.

AND MUCH, MUCH MORE!

The Real Life of Lucille Ball

ST. MARTIN'S PRESS/NEW YORK

LUCY: THE LIFE OF LUCILLE BALL

Copyright © 1986 by Charles Higham

Library of Congress Catalog Card Number: 86-3672

ISBN: 0-312-90919-5   Can. ISBN: 0-312-90920-9

Printed in the United States of America

First St. Martin's Press mass market edition/December 1987

10 9 8 7 6 5 4 3 2

To Bruce Paddon,
Best of Personal Trainers

· ACKNOWLEDGMENTS ·

$\mathcal{I}$am grateful to the following people who helped me to obtain the facts for this book. Howard Davis and Anthony Slide undertook the heavy task of the research into written materials, and Mr. Slide interviewed certain of Lucy's associates. Miles Kreuger was especially helpful on Lucy's musical career. In Jamestown, New York, Anna C. Waite proved extremely helpful in matters of Lucy's childhood and upbringing, aided by Kenneth C. Munson of Wyandotte, Michigan. The historical societies in both towns were very good sources.

I have drawn from interviews with Lucille Ball, John Erickson, the late Busby Berkeley, the late George Raft, the late Kay Harvey, the late Harry Warren, the late Dorothy Arzner, Frances Mercer, Katharine Hepburn, Fred Astaire, the late Henry Fonda, Rudy Behlmer, the late Broderick Crawford, Pare Lorentz, the late Erich Pommer, the late Ernst Matray, George Abbott, John Hall, the late Jack Oakie, George Sidney, Henry Hathaway, Jess Oppenheimer, Harry Ackerman, the late Tay Garnett, Herb Sterne, Bob Carroll, Madelyn Pugh Davis, Ralph Levy, the late Karl Freund, the late Groucho Marx, Marc Daniels, Cam McCullough, William Asher, Rex Reason, Vincente Minnelli, the late Walter Winchell, the late Hedda Hopper, Cornel Wilde, the late James Mason, Kaye Ballard, Melville Shavelson, and Jim Bailey, who was especially helpful on the recent years. I am also especially grateful to Victoria Shellin, who did an excellent job of typing a difficult manuscript, to Jack Caravela and Carol E. W. Edwards, and to Toni Lopopolo, my friend and the kindest and most considerate of editors.

$\mathcal{M}$y first debt is to Lucille Ball herself, who on three separate occasions over the years granted me interviews in which she discussed herself and her problems with an unsparing and sometimes disconcerting honesty. Whereas most stars, aided by their powerful press agents, tend to create a picture of happiness, warmth, family solidarity and even sainthood, Miss Ball didn't hesitate to state harsh facts and express strong opinions. In numerous articles across the years, including some of her own authorship, she has spoken out with startling frankness about both herself and her two children, in a way which perhaps no other figure of her stature in entertainment has ever done. These truthful, if sometimes disturbing, revelations have formed a basis for the research in this book, and are brought together here for the first time. In their zealous desire to protect her, in their eager flattery, fan magazine columnists have tended to render Lucy inhumanly and impossibly gracious. Her gritty, feisty, abrasive, intelligent, edgy character is far removed from that perfumed picture.

I saw her first at her office in the 1960s, where she was rapidly going bananas over countless executive problems that were plaguing her, not to mention the difficulties of sustaining the unequaled inventiveness, wit and style of her *Lucy* shows on television. She puffed away at cigarettes in an almost unbroken chain, filling the ashtray with stubs through the afternoon until they formed a small, toxic white mountain. She insisted she didn't inhale any of them, and when she picked up a particular example of the weed, she puffed her cheeks out like a fish to prove that that was where the smoke was. When I ventured to suggest that some of it might be making its way down her throat, she let out a cloud of smoke in my face, intending to establish by this that none of it had filtered into her lungs. Although never seeming to be funny, talking of just about everything as a funeral director would describe a newly arrived corpse, she was in fact as hilarious off-screen as on, describing with great relish a series of illnesses and accidents that would tax the power of a dozen Jobs. Short of describing a plague of flies or locusts, or being trapped in a log cabin with wolves at the door, she could scarcely have presented a more vivid picture of a life seemingly composed of mishaps. She said she had been bitten by a porpoise, a chimpanzee, a goat, and a penguin. She said she had been gored by the head of a bull, and that an alligator had once taken such a fancy to her leg that it tried to take a bite of it. She described being immersed in a vat of wine, experiencing her nose catching fire, turned into a living chocolate bar and made to sail down a flight of stairs on skis. I forebore to ask her why she never used doubles for these stunts.

I recall meeting Miss Ball on the set of "Here's Lucy," as it was then called, sometime later in the 1960s, in which she had to do the very thing she had just complained of only days before: dealing with an imitation aircraft. She was playing Lucy as a skydiver, having taken it into her head to attempt to skydive in person, not with the benefit of several hundred feet of empty air, but with a thirty-foot drop onto a hard cement studio floor. If the fall were not satisfactorily broken, it could have been curtains for the rest of the season. The actor Rex Reason was her companion in this enterprise: Despite his appearance of a six-foot linebacker, he looked more nervous than she did. He hesitated in the harness, looking gingerly at the floor below, while Miss Ball expertly sailed earthward. A minute later, she was back with him on the swaying plane model, planning, with loud instructions to the crew and director, to do the jump again as she felt she hadn't done it awkwardly enough the first time. The audience would scarcely have noticed, convulsed as they would have been by laughter, but she had to make it perfect. Again and again she plunged; again and again she returned. So it went on the entire afternoon, until the ideal comic effect was achieved. But in between, many of the set crew were cursing under their breaths, wiping their sweaty foreheads and clearly wishing they were somewhere else.

This kind of perfectionism, care and dedication, even obsession, this concern for quality in a medium not noted for it, was typical of Lucille Ball. Some years later, I caught up with her again, this time on behalf of *The New York Times*. She hadn't changed. In her first words to me, not having remembered me, of course, from the previous meetings, she spoke to me like a relative or close friend, unhesitatingly discussing her recent physical ailments and further accidents without the slightest preamble or even a good afternoon. She was on the set of *Mame* and in the midst of shooting the very difficult Christmas dance number when I visited with her. She described how she had gone blue from head to foot the night before when her esophagus gave out. She gave a complete account of her medical symptoms, the medication used to treat them, and the outcome in her present shaky condition. She talked about her hatred of making a musical, which reminded her of her ordeal of doing *Wildcat* on Broadway, in which she kept collapsing during the run until finally the producers had to close the show and she personally had to hand back a fortune in ticket returns. And as she talked about being encased in a king-sized cast after breaking her leg skiing, shattering it with the handle that raised and lowered the hospital bed, getting entangled in a complicated vacuum cleaner hose, which wound around her like the coils of a snake, or plunging out of a fake airplane on the set in a badly rigged parachute harness, I realized that she enjoyed relating these catastrophes and to interrupt for a second would be equivalent to sneezing in church. On the set of *Mame*, she was grim and fiercely determined as ever, riding herd on everyone, demanding the immediate attentions of a woman whom she glumly described as the Mad Hatter (the milliner in charge of her twenties headgear in the movie). Nothing escaped her brilliant eye: not a flaw in the period decor, not a move in the choreography of her friend Onna White, not a detail in the lighting. She knew every light in the studio by name, and could correct them with a word. The nominal director, Gene Saks, was clearly willing to give her her head, and the tension caused by her perfectionism was something for which he was prepared. It was as instructive to watch her work on this picture as it would have been to have seen somebody inscribe the Lord's Prayer on the head of a pin. Peerless as a mistress of the comedic arts, unrivaled as a television executive, matchless as a first lady of the Box, Lucille Ball could only be described as a genius, but a genius whose personal life was dogged by misfortune, and whose difficult, often tortured nature and ill-fated marriage to Desi Arnaz provided an ironical contrast with her daffy, happy small screen life. One could only feel compassion for her, knowing that she, who made more people laugh than almost anyone else, had little reason to laugh in her own life.

She is to this day the most famous woman in television. Mention the name of this great star to people as far apart as the Philippines, Alaska, South Africa, Iceland, or Japan, and it is likely that they will know who she is. There will be a smile, a chuckle, an outright laugh of recognition; to millions, she represents the American housewife, her image suggestive of goofy, manic charm and an essential sweetness of character—the world's most lovable klutz. Her glum, clownish seriousness is one of her greatest gifts as a comedienne. Wide-eyed with surprise in the midst of chaos, the world confirming her worst paranoid imaginings as it surrounds her with constant threats, handicapped by her own clumsiness, consumed with ambition to do impossible and extravagant things, mistress of the double take, she is one of the classic clowns in the tradition of Chaplin, Stan Laurel, Buster Keaton, Harold Lloyd, and Jack Benny. Neither Carol Burnett, expert though she is, nor Lily Tomlin, nor Joan Rivers has reached quite the pinnacle of Lucy. Most comedians I have met are just as gloomy off-screen as one would expect: I remember Jack Benny picking miserably at a salad, complaining about the insufficient serving of cottage cheese. Even beloved Bob Hope and Jimmy Durante fretted over the changes that were taking place in show business and the world. Anyone seeing Jack Lemmon offguard in a studio commissary, as I have done on many occasions, would see a sad face, prematurely old, and haggard with seeming despair. It will be hard to forget having lunch with a tired-out Walter Matthau during the shooting of *Hello, Dolly,* or listening to him describe in words of four letters and one syllable the, to him, unpleasant antics of Barbra Streisand. Nor will I forget how Miss Streisand herself came from doing a brilliantly comic sequence in *Funny Girl* to her dressing room to grumble coldly to me about the behavior of everybody on the set. She was no more pleased when, after she complained that it was difficult for her to express anguish in a scene while running along a pier with two suitcases, the director William Wyler (or so studio scuttlebutt had it) put bricks in the suitcases. None of these talented people suggested that spending an evening with them would be a riot of laughter and relaxed fun.

Lucille Ball is the supreme example of what Katharine Hepburn once told me was the essence of comic art: waiting for a custard pie with an expression of someone attending a burial. Laughter in the face of misfortune on the screeen or an awareness that life is funny is the end of any comic. If they were not so grim about life, they could not hope to act that grimness so successfully in the movies. Thus, the audience screams with laughter: we are seeing someone whose misfortunes are more extreme than our own, and we can escape from our own problems in the pleasant experience of seeing a prat-fall and a tumble downstairs. It was a secret learned by actors from the beginning of the theater, all the way back to the Commedia Dell'Arte and by Chaplin, Buster Keaton, Harold Lloyd and all the other great ones in the movies.

An element in Lucille Ball's success is that millions of Middle Americans identify with her. Born in a small town in the Eastern heartland, child of a somewhat eccentric *You Can't Take It With You* family, she has always been devoted to puritanism, one-man-at-a-time romanticism, Mom, the stars and stripes and apple pie. She loved only two men, the underrated Desi Arnaz and Gary Morton, her two husbands, and this has endeared her to countless women. Very much of her generation of upright, downright, pre—World War I upstate New Yorkers, she has never stained her personal reputation, thus securing the admiration of the conservative middle class, while her seeming inability to cope with day-to-day living has endeared her to just about everyone who has found it equally problematic to handle daily problems. For the character of Lucy, life is a continual struggle, albeit a comic one; that the real-life Lucy has had her torments only makes her public feel more affectionate toward her.

At time of writing, Lucy, to the delight of her countless millions of fans the world over, is preparing the production of a new "Lucy" series at ABC, to co-star her old friend and colleague Gale Gordon. It is planned to air in September; the producers are her veteran writers Madelyn Pugh and Bob Carroll, who have also written the pilot and the first few episodes. Aaron Spelling, multimillionaire creator of *Dynasty*, *The Colbys*, and *The Love Boat*, is executive producer; and shooting is to take place in July at Warner Hollywood Studios. As in the old days, the show will be done in front of a live audience. No more auspicious moment could exist for the publication of a new biography.

$\mathcal{L}$ucille Ball's family symbolized America's progress from the agrarian age to the era of industry, the telegraph and the telephone. Her great-grandparents on her father's side, Clinton and Cynthia Ball, were farmers in Fredonia, New York; in 1890, they moved to the rural community of Busti, southwest of Buffalo. Busti had been the scene of early settlements in the region, where the landowners had lived in log cabins amid forests of maple and fir. Clinton and Cynthia had made money buying and selling property; they bought a fine, beautifully restored farmhouse set on a hill with a road running below it from Sugar Grove to Chautauqua Lake at Crescent Creek. The Balls were popular and successful in Busti, enjoying their rural existence and raising several children with stern but loving care.

Their second son and fifth child, Jasper, who was restless and bored with life on the farm, became excited by the idea of the newfangled invention known as the telephone. Inspired by the pioneer example of Alexander Graham Bell, he persuaded his father, Clinton, to finance him in establishing the first telephone exchange in Busti. This was in 1891, only one year after his parents bought the farm (Clinton died in 1893). People came from nearby Jamestown and Celoron and other towns in the area just to see Jasper, as he with great enthusiasm operated the primitive switchboard. He would gladly give the time of day to any caller who came through the board; a private conversation was quite impossible with Jasper eavesdropping, and anyone making a telephone call would only criticize Jasper if he was very daring, as Jasper would cut people off at any moment if he heard the critical words.

Jasper was married to Nellie, daughter of the well-paid superintendent of the Brooks Locomotive Works in Dunkirk, New York; thus, telephone money married train money, and the result was that the young couple was able to build a homestead, a farm rivaling Clinton's, which boasted one of the largest apple orchards in New York State. Unfortunately, Jasper was more expert at running a switchboard than at cleaning the flues in his house, and the property burned to the ground in 1906. Jasper promptly built another farm, installing the electricity and telephone wires himself, and, restless and energetic, suddenly left the company in the hands of colleagues and took off for Missoula, Montana, where he started another firm, with a correspondent company in Anaconda, near Butte. He had five children; his second son, Henry, then in his late teens, shared his father's enthusiasm for telephone work and learned the business from the ground up by acting as an electrical lineman for Jasper.

Putting telephones through Montana in those days was pioneer work. The state, with its mountainous territory and severe winters, called for strong nerves in its telephone men. Jasper, Henry, and the other men had to beat their way through the teeth of blizzards, leaning hard against the sleet and pushing against the wind. Icicles hung from their mustaches; they had to carry shovels in front of their faces to allow them to breathe. The Montana snow packed hard as marble, and at distances of a mere twelve feet, the Ball team couldn't see each other. They had to follow their course by watching the tops of telephone poles that stuck out from the snow levels.

At times, linemen would be found half frozen to death. The transmission lines were conveyed over storm-blackened wilderness, following the old trapper or cow-punching routes.

There was always the danger that feet would be frozen, hands burned by the electrical current, or eyes blinded by snow, but Jasper's team was extremely resourceful. They could start a fire in a hard hat with a match, a candle, and shavings, and they could make a snowshoe from willows. Sometimes, when they laid the wires on the snow, the wires were frozen solid. At times, the wind would take out miles of poles no sooner than they had been planted, and washouts, snowslides, and block-ades would disrupt the connections for months at a time.

Several men were assigned to each section of the telephone lines. They made their daily inspections in relays, or sometimes in shifts if there was a short section; they worked a twenty-four-hour schedule, regardless of weather, because the slight-est break due to snow or ice or fire or heavy rain could mean a loss of business between the East and West Coast, or between individual towns, that could cost thousands of dollars. Often, the team would have snow up to their waists as they struggled through drifts, with gales sweeping down on them from the hills, guided only by the sharp glittering of the wires overhead. When breaks occurred—when the wires fell down under the weight of frozen sleet or the poles were snapped off by the rush of gales, or floods undermined them—Henry and the other members of the telephone patrol sometimes worked three or four days at a time without sleep or food. The copper wires stuck to their hands like white-hot steel. The spurs on their boots ate into their half-frozen feet. Climbing the poles involved perfect coordination, muscular strength, sureness and confidence; a slip could mean a possibly fatal fifty-foot fall to the earth; touching an electrical wire that ran along the tele-phone cable could kill instantly.

Jasper grew weary of the work; he returned to Busti and then to Jamestown shortly before his granddaughter Lucy was born, while Henry kept to the job and his base in Anaconda, headquarters of the famous Anaconda Copper Company, which supplied much of the wire the Ball Company used. Henry lived first at 300 Hickory Street, and then at 120 West

Park Avenue; both apartments were located on thoroughfares filled with the sound of clanking streetcars and the cries of street vendors. He was tall, slim, well knit, classically handsome. Anyone meeting him on patrol would have observed that he was carrying a kit weighing over fifty pounds. Over his shoulder was slung a coil of wire, plus climbing spurs, steel-tipped leggings used for scaling the poles. Around his waist hung forty pounds of pliers, nippers, wrenches, and other tools. In the pockets of his coveralls were stuffed testers and battery coils; in rough weather, he wore oilskins and heavy leather boots.

In August 1910, Henry went east to marry the pretty and lively Desirée (DeDe) Evelyn Hunt, daughter of Frederick and Florabelle Hunt of 38 Hall Avenue, Jamestown. The wedding took place on August 31 at the bride's parents' home. The Reverend Charles D. Reed, pastor of Calgary Baptist Church, presided over the elaborate service attended by 140 guests.

The ceremony was performed in front of a fireplace decorated with golden glow and sunflowers. Miss Bertha Gifford at the piano played the bridal chorus from Wagner's opera *Lohengrin* as the couple entered the room, "Oh, Promise Me" during the service, and Mendelssohn's "Wedding March" at the end of the ceremony.

Blanche Ball, Henry's sister, acted as bridesmaid. Desirée wore a gown of white lambsdown, with lace and purple trimmings, and carried a shower bouquet of sweet peas. There was a large reception after the wedding; DeDe received many gifts of silverware, china, cut glass, furniture, and linen. It was the biggest event of the season; the couple had no honeymoon but left at once for Anaconda so that Henry could resume work for Jasper's company while Jasper remained in Busti.

Energetic, lively, charming, and intelligent, DeDe adored her good-looking husband; she was lost in admiration of his strong, slim physique and masculine charm. His bravery fascinated her, though the work he was involved in often terrified her. In November 1910, while they were in Anaconda, just twenty-five miles from Butte, sometimes going to the larger town for shopping or visits to the theater, DeDe became pregnant. In the tradition of the time, DeDe wanted to have her baby in her hometown, and the couple returned there briefly. In the meantime, Jasper and Nellie had moved to 117 Royal Avenue in Jamestown, and DeDe insisted Henry take a house not too far away, at 123 Stewart Avenue. Henry continued his work as lineman under less grueling conditions. He was paid $3 a day and a box lunch, a decent sum for those days, when many in America were lucky to earn that much money in a week.

No sooner was Lucy born, on August 6, 1911, than Henry and DeDe and their child moved back to Anaconda, where they took an apartment on noisy, dusty Commercial Avenue in the downtown section. Lucy's first impressions of life were of the cramped, flat, ugly little town dominated by the Anaconda Copper Company's smoke-belching chimneys of blackened brick. The constant clanging of the streetcar was the dominant sound of her babyhood. Her mother's tension over Henry's dangerous work was another feature that influenced Lucy. Throughout her life, from childhood on, she was extremely tense, nervous, sensitive, and vulnerable, filled with anxiety and fear. Because Butte, as ugly and commercial as Anaconda, was the commercial center of that region, Lucy for many years believed she was born there, an understandable conviction that led many journalists to accuse her of inventing her birthplace. A number of magazines reported inaccurately that she had decided that Montana was a more romantic place to be born than New York State, and thus created a fantasy of a "Western childhood."

When Lucy was one year old, the family moved to Wyandotte, Michigan. The reason is unknown, but it is probable that the all-consuming Bell Company, snapping up one local telephone system after another, had consumed Jasper Ball's struggling enterprises in its path, and was offering experienced linemen better wages in Michigan. Located a few miles south of the industrial center of Detroit, Wyandotte was attracting many telephone men at the time, paying them up to $5 a day, and Bell was advertising extensively for help in the Middle West and the East. Henry went to work for the Michigan Telephone Company, which had been recently formed and had already been infiltrated by Bell interests that were planning to absorb it at a later date. Working on the lines at Wyandotte was hard during the winter months, but not nearly so hard as it had been in Montana.

Wyandotte, like Anaconda and Jamestown, had recently changed from a rural town into a grim industrial center. A blast furnace and a rolling mill, the Bessemer steel factory, and imposing glass and saltworks had caused Wyandotte to boom. Smoke still smeared the sky Lucy saw. Her parents rented the back apartment of a large wooden house at 126 Biddle Avenue from a carpenter, Joseph Daniel, and his wife Elizabeth; the Daniels had three children, Marceline, Olive, and Steven. Joseph and his wife were genial, friendly souls, and, friends say today, grew fond of the Balls. The view from the windows of the $10-a-month Ball apartment looked out on a lawn with fir trees, rose bushes and a white fence, Joseph's carpenter shop, and an alley followed by more trees and frame houses. Zeltha Mills, a childhood friend of Lucy's and of the Daniels', who married Joseph and Elizabeth's boy Steven, remembers Lucy as a baby, her seriousness and her glumness, which made people laugh then as much as they would laugh at Lucy Ricardo years later.

Nearby Detroit offered little comfort to the eye or spirit. Its bleak industrial force loomed over everyone's lives. But Wyandotte was pleasanter than the big city to the north. The town had a handsome location a small child could enjoy. The Detroit River ran through it four miles wide and Lake Erie was not far away, with its rocks and beaches, and boating and fishing on weekends. In the humid summers, a pleasant breeze from lake or river gave Wyandotte a coolness and freshness that brought many from Detroit, and its wide streets, lush trees, and fresh air and sunshine made Wyandotte, for all of its heavy industry, a decent place to raise a child.

The greatest drawback was the water. Unlike Jamestown and Anaconda water, which were noted for their purity, Wyandotte water was contaminated. Every effort by local citizens' councils to improve the problem had met with indifference by the city fathers. Sternly warned by medical authorities when they moved in, Henry and DeDe had to boil and filter everything, and Lucy's milk, once she was past the breast-feeding stage, had also to be boiled. The greatest threat to citizens of Wyandotte was typhoid fever, which periodically swept through the town and through Detroit itself. In the early teens of the century, only men in the armed services received compulsory inoculations, and citizens, though constantly urged to volunteer for the doctor's needle, didn't always comply. The Balls were among those who ignored the suggestion.

Meanwhile, Jasper had been traveling around, visiting with his four other children, Clint, Mabel, Maude, and Blanche, and their spouses. He eventually moved to Florida, where he continued his farming activities. In Wyandotte, in the house on Biddle Avenue, Lucy was a bright and cheerful child, prattling away about everything, irrepressible in her energy, and constantly acting out tiny theatrical scenes with her dolls. It was when she was three years and six months old that she first became aware of death.

Everything seemed to be going well in the young family. Biddle Avenue, with its trolleys going up and down, and pretty awnings over the shop fronts and shade trees, was a secure roost for the child, and DeDe was pregnant again. But then, horror descended from a clear sky. Henry began to suffer from severe headaches, lassitude, and sleeplessness, and broke out into a fever sweat. Since he had always been the picture of physical fitness, his illness came as a shock to DeDe and frightened Lucy to tears. His temperature rose and fell alarmingly, reaching its peak in the night hours, and when a physician was called, DeDe learned the terrible news that Henry was suffering from typhoid. Since, clearly, she had been always very careful about boiling the milk, water, and anything else that might be contaminated, it was assumed that Henry must have weakened and eaten ice cream, a seldom recognized dangerous cause of the disease at the time.

There was no cure for typhoid in those days. It would be twenty-five years before antibiotics were developed. The Balls had to be quarantined immediately. Neighbors looked askance at the house and passed it at a distance with fear and trembling. There had only been three other cases of typhoid reported in the last five years in Wyandotte and the thought of a possible outbreak was terrifying. The Balls were ostracized from that moment. A notice was put on the door that read: "Keep Out—Health Authorities." This rejection and forced isolation was appalling to DeDe and had a deep influence on Lucy, almost certainly causing her a feeling of rejection later in life and perhaps inspiring a desire to make people accept and love her, a desire that consumes all entertainers.

In the second week, Henry's temperature rose to 104 degrees. Though he had been able to move about awkwardly and languidly at first, he finally had to take to his bed. He was miserably uncomfortable, restless and hot, his cheeks flushed and his pulse accelerated. His tongue was covered in whitish fur; sores appeared on his lips. His stomach was distended; he was stricken with diarrhea and discharges; rose-colored spots broke out all over him; there were bluish patches on his body and thighs. He was in a state of mental confusion and delirium. His body wasted, and his limbs twisted and jerked; at last, he weakened fatally, stricken with toxemia and final debilitation. He died on February 28, 1915.

It is hard to imagine four-months-pregnant DeDe's state of mind at the time. Not only was there the disgrace of quarantine and the horror of her husband's early death, the man she loved with all her heart, the protracted misery of seeing him die, but there was also the fear Lucy and her unborn baby might catch the fever. Her fears were groundless. DeDe was strong and did not break down when Henry passed away; she pulled herself together and made arrangements to return the body in its pine coffin by railroad boxcar to Jamestown. Lucy said later that, even though she was only three and a half, she would never forget any detail of the house as the family prepared to leave it following Henry's death. The deal furniture, rolltop desk, the table with its tablecloth, the flowers, and even a bird that flew through the window that day and became trapped, its feathers whirring, stayed with her, she said, for a lifetime. However, Zeltha Mills, now Mrs. Daniel, recalls differently. She says that Lucy at her age had no idea her father was dead, didn't even understand what death was, and that in fact Zeltha ran into her in the neighborhood grocery store the following day and was astonished to see Lucy buying a doughnut for her father.

With the whole Ball clan present, and DeDe's family, the Hunts, also in attendance, Henry was laid to rest in a solemn ceremony at Lake View Cemetery, Jamestown, on March 4, 1915. The Reverend Frank Stoddard of Busti, best friend of Jasper Ball, presided. The effects of a father's or mother's death on a child of three are severe even though the child is not fully aware of what has taken place, and Lucy's extreme edginess and nervousness throughout her life may have resulted not only from the quarantine order but from this early and shocking deprivation by an illness the nature of which she could not possibly have grasped. No doubt the desire to escape from the grief surrounding her as a child drove her into further playacting, daydreams, a desire to escape into other people's identities through acting out scenes with her dolls.

DeDe and Lucy moved in with DeDe's parents, who had a house on Eighth Street in Celoron, a suburb of Jamestown, and here DeDe's baby Frederick was born on July 3, 1915. Fred Hunt's father, Reuben Hunt, had been a member of the Ninth New York Volunteers in the Civil War; he and his wife Eveline Frances had for some years managed the popular Brooklyn House Hotel in Brooklyn Square, Jamestown. Florabelle Orchutt was a maid at the hotel when Fred met her and married her at Sinclairville in 1889. Both Fred and Florabelle were "characters," and Lucy adored them as much as her own mother.

Fred C. Hunt was fat, balding, imposing, and dignified. A gold watch-chain stretched across his ample stomach and a pipe, well chewed and filled with his favorite Prince Albert tobacco, was clenched constantly between his nicotine-yellowed teeth. He liked to wear an ancient brown cardigan with buttons missing. His suits, though often shiny, were usually of the best materials; however, they never fitted well, with the result that his ample stomach and love handles swelled over his too-small trousers, and his jacket was usually much too tight at the shoulders. He liked to sit at the upright piano, with the music scores propped up on the rest, playing and singing popular vaudeville tunes in a lusty but insecure baritone voice. When he wasn't playing the piano, he was busy at any one of a dozen different occupations, though he was officially listed in the local city directories of the period as a mail carrier. He kept losing jobs because he was always trying to whip up labor activism, being an enthusiastic follower of the teachings of the Socialist Eugene Debs and fascinated by the activities of the Wobblies, the labor agitators of the time. He was regarded as a harmless eccentric by Florabelle and DeDe and the other members of the family, but Fred was deadly serious about his leftism.

He carried out his principle of share-and-share alike by dividing his meager salary to the last nickel between himself, his wife and daughter, and by freely giving the products of his thriving vegetable garden in the backyard to the poor, entertaining a regular stream of the unemployed at the garden gate. He rejoiced in telling such lies as "The first Hunt in America was a Texas horse thief," and he enjoyed discussing his family origins, dragging out for all visitors a family tree that showed him to be part French, part Irish, and part English. He encouraged Lucy to interest herself in music, and was delighted when DeDe gave her piano lessons as soon as she was able to sit up at the keyboard. The family atmosphere was strict but loving. Florabelle's brothers as well as Lucy and little Fred with DeDe, Fred Hunt's brothers and sisters, and Jasper Ball's family would all visit for Sunday dinner, salivating at the thought of DeDe's rhubarb pie with whipped cream—brought from her house in a box.

The most important influence on Lucy's (and her brother Fred's) early years was Celoron Park, one of the finest amusement areas in the United States at that time. Its boardwalk, with a ramp going down into the lake as a children's slide, the Pier Ballroom, roller-coaster, bandstand, and a stage where vaudeville, concerts, and regular theatrical shows were presented, made Celoron Park a dreamworld for a child. Lucy was among the many kids who worshiped the big, red-faced Jule Delmar who managed this exciting place, and she could hardly wait for her next visit to the park, where the spun-sugar stands, with their pink, shiny clouds on wooden sticks, the coconut shies, shooting galleries, and colorful fortune-tellers' booths were fascinating. There were freak shows, the Fat Lady, gypsy palm readers, donkey rides and a hundred other attractions for young and old. When a primitive blimp or airship sailed overhead, thousands would rush in to watch, and if one of the not infrequent tornadoes wrecked the roller-coaster, or toppled some of the stands, crowds would jam the roads in their flivvers and Model Ts to see the effects of the damage.

Lucy would make the journey with her family on foot or by electric car, while some of the clan came in from other towns on the famous Red Stack Steamer, named for the color of its funnel, which crossed the lake each day and twice on Sundays.

The wonders of Celoron Park increased as Lucy grew older. In 1917, when she was six, America entered into World War I, but although the streets of Celoron were filled with troops marching off to war, Lucy was barely aware of them; none of her immediate family was affected, and Celoron Park was still the center of her attention. The Phoenix Wheel, installed that year, and featured originally at the Atlanta Exposition, carried her, along with two hundred others, through the air, illuminated with 350 colored lights stretched all over its 167 feet of height. As Lucy soared or dipped in the car, she enjoyed a grand view of the lake and the maple-treed streets around.

She especially liked the Zoological Garden, with its birds, snakes, tigers, bears, and the Shetland ponies on which she rode with other children on Sundays. There was an electrical fountain at the center of the park; it shot up water with colored lights playing on it in the tints of a rainbow. There was an electrical column with 250 colored bulbs, a bathing pavilion, toboggan and camelback rides, a merry-go-round, and a house that when you sat in it it turned upside-down, so that you found yourself sitting on the ceiling. There was also a dancing pavilion on the lake, as well as a roller-skating rink.

Orchestras played the year round, headed by the Celoron Gold Band playing dance music for the young girls and their straw-hatted beaux. Lucy and her mother loved the vaudeville shows, which featured oriental dancers, comedy duos, blackface comedians, eccentric dancers, minstrels, magicians, and harmonica and banjo players. They also went to the "penny flickers," which showed movies with Charlie Chaplin and Buster Keaton, and melodramas with long-haired vamps, square-shouldered heroes, and dainty heroines who waved from the garden gate as their young men went off to war. Lucy's favorites were the serials, especially *The Perils of Pauline*, starring Pearl White, in which the heroine was tied to railroad tracks as an express rapidly approached, clung to cliffs with raging torrents just below, or struggled to escape a locked room as a fire swept through a house, always being saved at the last moment by the hero or her own ingenuity—as Lucy and the other children jumped up and down and clapped their hands with glee. In the airless, dusty theaters, freezing cold in the winter and suffocatingly hot in the summer, with their smell of plush and their litter of discarded ice cream cartons, Lucy found a magic world of escape from reality.

An always imposing presence in Fred Ball's Eighth Street household was Florabelle's brother Edward Orcutt, who lived first in Cleveland and then Chagrin Falls, Ohio, and who was always bragging about the "beauty of Chagrin Falls." He kept his money in his shoes at night because he didn't trust the banks. Henry's sisters Maude, Mabel, and Blanche frequently came by, and so did Florabelle's brothers William and Henry, from Kinmundy, Ohio, and Charlotte, New York, respectively. The house was seldom quiet, and at most times it was filled with people from morning to night.

By the time Lucy was eight, in 1919, she was known as an extremely hyperactive child. She was especially afraid of gypsies, who set up their camp on the edge of Celoron under the maple trees every summer. It was said in Celoron that the gypsies would kidnap local children and take them off to their campgrounds; parents would, so the tale went, have to give them a silver dollar to make them return the infants they had kidnapped. Lucy came home one day with a terrifying story. She insisted that the gypsies had whisked her off to their camp but that she had screamed so loudly that they had been forced to let her go. This unlikely charge threw everyone in the household into a paranoid state.

Lucy was always the child who cried wolf, living out in her own life the fantasies of the melodramas she saw on the screen. In her imaginary universe, she was always, with theatrical relish, either threatened by or subjected to terrifying mishaps, and in real life she was always twisting her ankle, tripping over footstools, or suffering from some childhood disease. Chicken pox, measles, mumps, and all of the other children's ailments for her assumed the proportions of the San Francisco earthquake. She was center-stage in the family, making sure that everything revolved around her, the budding child star.

Once when she was nine, she was sitting in Fred Hunt's swivel chair at the rolltop desk, poring over a history lesson he was giving her about the massacre at Little Big Horn and spinning fantasies in her head about the battle, when she glanced up and saw a tradesman looking through the window. In her imagination, that man turned into a ferocious Indian, and she screamed so hysterically that the family had great difficulty calming her down.

She began to get hold of magazines with stories about theater personalities, including the popular theatrical journal *The Green Book*, with its photographs of vaudevillians and musical personalities, including Julian Eltinge, the female impersonator, John Bunny, the fat stage and screen actor, and Nora Bayes, the actress singer who was famous for "Shine On Harvest Moon." The sepia-toned pages of theatrical journals excited her, and she had visions of going on the stage. Both DeDe and Fred and Florabelle Hunt encouraged her, no doubt thinking privately she had little chance of success. They sent her to the Chautauqua Institute of Music to study singing, piano, and dancing in 1920.

That same year, DeDe fell in love with and married thirty-five-year-old Ed Peterson, a tall, sturdy, rather brusque Swedish-American, who was a sheet-metal assembly-line worker. DeDe was taken by his massive shoulders and masculinity, but neither Lucy nor her kid brother Fred liked him, and, like most children, they were still clinging to the thought of their dead father and resented this newcomer into the household. Unlike Henry, who was keen on physical fitness and had high moral standards, Ed was a heavy drinker and had a weakness for gambling. He took it into his head to move with DeDe first to Wyandotte and then to Detroit, where she had lived with Henry. He obtained a job in a factory there.

Possibly fearing the effect of his drunken behavior on his children, unpredictable DeDe made the difficult decision to leave her growing children behind. But instead of allowing them to stay with Fred at Eighth Street, where at least they were comfortable, she foolishly deposited them with Ed's parents, a bleak Swedish-American couple, who disciplined them cruelly. In fact (Lucy said later), she was considered by them so uncontrollable they put her on a dog chain attached to a

wire clothesline used for hanging laundry and left her there
for hours at a time. Sometimes her brother Fred would take
the risk and unchain her, only to be punished for it. At other
times, Lucy would hear a salesman at the door when her step-
grandparents were out and walk as far as the chain would
let her, pleading over the wooden fence with the hawker
to set her free. Occasionally, a man would vault the fence
and release her (she could not reach the catch herself) whereupon she would vanish for the entire day.

Hating the Petersons, Lucy managed to persuade her
mother to come back after only a few weeks. Ed and DeDe
moved into Fred's house at Eighth Street, and at last Lucy and
Fred, Jr., were released from their bondage with the Petersons
and could rejoin their beloved grandparents. But no sooner
had this seeming happiness been restored than another sad
event took place that increased Lucy's paranoia about the
cruelties of life. Florabelle fell ill of cancer of the uterus in 1921
and she suffered such excruciating pain that at the end even
morphine could not give her relief, and her cries of agony filled
the house, horrifying everyone, especially the hypersensitive
Lucy, who cried from morning to night. At the time, Lucy was
working for a blind man, leading him through the streets for
fifty cents a week, and attending school with more energy than
scholarly ability.

When Florabelle died on July 1, 1922, at fifty-five years of
age, Lucy was desperate. Forbidden to go to the funeral for
some unknown reason, she escaped from the house and followed the procession at a distance, crying uncontrollably.

· CHAPTER 2 ·

$\mathcal{A}$fter Florabelle's death, Lucy was inconsolable. She sobbed constantly, and no one could control her. Yet again, she escaped into a dreamworld, pretending to be someone else to escape the reality of disease and death. Sometimes the eleven-year-old girl imagined she was a glamorous woman called Sassafrassa, who was a mixture of the silent-screen comedienne Mabel Normand, Pearl White (of *The Perils of Pauline*), and the foreign vamp Pola Negri. At other times, recalling that her first home was in Anaconda, and remembering all the tales of the Wild West she had heard or read about, she fancied that she was Madeleine, cowgirl heroine of Zane Grey's novel *The Light of Western Stars*. Madeleine was born in Butte, which made Lucy identify with her.

After Florabelle's death, to relieve DeDe, Lucy and Fred and some young cousins helped make beds and cook, and Lucy caused ripples of laughter when she bought a hat with pennies saved from helping the blind man and stood at the sink wearing it, with all its feathers, when she did the washing up. More than ever, she insisted on seeing every play that opened in the area, screaming and crying if she was not allowed to go. She had a crush on the matinee idol James Rennie, whose dark, saturnine good looks and elegant figure fascinated her. Ed Peterson, whom she in many ways disliked, now encouraged her to perform. He belonged to the Shriners, and he arranged for her to act, dance, and sing at Shriner conventions. In 1923, he and DeDe took her to see the celebrated monologist Julius Tannen, who was performing on the Chautauqua circuit. Tannen was a big star of his era, and he would later be associated as an actor with Preston Sturges, the brilliant director/screenwriter, in movies during the 1930s and 1940s. Orphaned in boyhood, raised by the New York Hebrew Orphan Asylum, Tannen was famous for inventing the curtain speech later delivered by George M. Cohan, whose life story was told in the musical *Yankee Doodle Dandy*, which goes: "My father thanks you! My mother thanks you! My sister thanks you! And I thank you!"

With a solemn long face like a cartoon stockbroker, pince-nez balanced on his nose with a long black ribbon, and a ponderously serious manner, Tannen always wore a well-cut business suit. He delivered stories and quips with witty, pertinent, yet sadly uttered references drawn from the pages of current newspapers. He usually made slighting references to himself, which delighted the less sophisticated audiences of the day. Typical of his lines were: "I feel about as welcome in this place as a wet goat"; "These paper cups make me feel I'm drinking out of a letter"; and "A lady has the right to be as homely as she pleases, but this one abuses the privilege." Today, these one-liners may seem rather flat, but delivered in Tannen's funereal manner, with a long face and coolly effortless timing, they evidently seemed funny. Lucy was thrilled by Tannen. As he stood before his audience with a table beside him holding a lamp, a pitcher, and a glass of water, she was dazzled. She told me, "Tannen was magic . . . just this voice, and this magnificent man enthralling you with his stories . . . his intonations . . . which I never, never forgot! He changed my life. I knew it was a very serious, wonderful thing to be able to make people laugh and cry, to be able to play on their emotions . . ."

Inspired by Tannen, Lucy auditioned for and obtained a

role in a local musical revue given by the Masonic Club. She whirled across the stage in a wild apache dance, but her partner threw her so violently across the boards that her shoulder was dislocated, and she went home sobbing and greatly exaggerating her pain. For the rest of her life, she had trouble with that shoulder. And yet, her ambition burst out again. She took a bus to New York despite the fact she was only twelve and a half, and actually obtained a job in the chorus of the big Shubert musical *Stepping Stones*, starring the famous Fred Stone. (Most sources say that she made her debut on Broadway in 1927, but *Stepping Stones* opened in 1923 and ran until 1925.)

Lucy was fired from the chorus for incompetence (and perhaps because her true age was discovered); she returned to Celoron and Eighth Street, by no means chastened, and ready for more excitement. She bobbed her hair, bought a raccoon coat, and started wearing vividly colored cloche hats. At the age of fourteen, she was tall for her age, excessively thin and leggy, manically overenergetic, reacting with wild excitement or despair to everything. Friends remember her plunging into every conceivable kind of activity, including ice-skating, tobogganing, canoeing, swimming, and horseback riding. She was often at Harvey and Carrie's Drug Store on Third Street to enjoy the sodas, and she haunted the Winter Garden, Palace, and Shea's movie theaters. In 1925, she at last (and quite reluctantly) entered Celoron High School, where she began organizing a dramatic club and school band (of which she was the conductor and arranger), and began directing and starring in plays and musical shows. She was a sensation in *Charley's Aunt*, Brandon Thomas' famous old comedy, playing the man who pretends to be a woman, a surprising turnabout from the usual performance of the role by a male. She designed and even carried in the scenery, found someone to lend her a printing press to run up posters and programs, and sold the tickets. But soon she became bored with school and ran away on a train, getting off for no particular reason when it stopped at Newcastle, Pennsylvania, where she got a job washing dishes.

While still in school, sometimes she would walk out of class to fetch some water from the cooler and simply not return; she would walk for miles, talking to anyone who would listen about her crazy plans to go on foot all the way to New York City, which was hundreds of miles away. On one occasion, she ran off with her cousin Cleo, and another time she took Fred, Jr., with her. Brought home screaming and crying, she consoled herself by setting up her grandfather Fred C. Hunt's chicken coop as a stage in the backyard and dressing up in old clothes from the attic to give a performance. Lucy's principal, Bernard Drake, realized she would never make a scholar. Meanwhile, Fred Hunt continued to work as mailman, carpenter, vet, barber, and quack doctor, while Ed Peterson, still drinking heavily, worked on the assembly lines at the factory. DeDe had to eke out the family income by selling hats in a millinery shop.

There was another tragedy when Lucy was almost fifteen years old. The closest friends of the family were Axel and Jenny Anderson, to whom Jasper and Nellie Ball had sold their property in 1917 before moving to Florida. Axel ran a calf-raising and truck-farming operation. On July 12, 1926, this sturdy Swedish-American cranked up his tractor, which he had accidentally left in gear, and was crushed to death by it. Axel's death upset the whole family, and Jasper and Nellie came back from Florida for the funeral.

In 1926, Lucy worked pulling sodas in Walgreen's Drug Store and sold dresses at the Lerner Dress Shop; at weekends she was a barker at Celoron Amusement Park, screeching at everyone to buy hot dogs and popcorn until she lost her voice. She grew closer to her grandpa than ever. He would insist that she and her brother get up early in the morning to see the dawn, and at night gaze into the sunset, remembering everything they saw. Seldom bothering to work in those days, he would sit in the backyard whittling, or making seesaws for the playground, or doll houses, sleds, or tree houses, or a frame for an illuminated text of Kipling's "If," which hung next to the parlor kerosene stove, a poem he liked to recite to young Fred as a set of principles for his approaching manhood.

Losing her job as a soda jerk at Walgreen's because she forgot to put the banana in a banana split, Lucy enlisted, with her mother's support, at the John Murray Anderson/Robert Milton School of the Theater and Dance at 128–130 East Fifty-eighth Street, New York. With its imitation Georgian front, fancy wrought-iron gates, the foyer's beautiful parquet floor, and antique wing chairs and tables, the school had a look of grandiose elegance and importance. John Murray Anderson had been a leading theatrical producer in America and Europe for many years. He had originated *The Greenwich Village Follies*, the Irving Berlin *Music Box Revue*, and the musical entertainment known as the *League of Notions*. Robert Milton's outstanding Broadway career included the direction of *He Who Gets Slapped*, *Outward Bound*, and *The Dark Angel*. Others on the faculty were equally noted: David Burton; James Light, who had co-directed Eugene O'Neill's *The Hairy Ape* and *The Emperor Jones*; Frederick Stanhope, of *The Blue Bird* fame; and Robert Bell.

The school was conducted with the utmost seriousness: No absence from class was permitted except for illness; no fees were returnable; and students were not permitted to answer back to their instructors. The dramatic course, the main feature of the school, boasted such teachers as Christopher Morley, Robert Edmond Jones, Don Marquis, and Channing Pollock. There was a musical-comedy course, in which Martha Graham taught dancing, and there was a motion-picture acting class, in which students had to pass a screen test; the class was limited to thirty. There were classes in scenic and costume design, playwriting, and stage direction and management, with autumn and spring terms of five months each and a six-week summer term. The tuition was very expensive for those days: $350 for drama, $390 for musical comedy, $500 for motion-picture acting, $270 for scenic and costume design, $180 for playwriting, and $350 for stage managing. The school's star pupil was Bette Davis, who dazzled the other students in scenes from plays. Lucy, on the other hand, was a hopeless hick at the school. She was petrified, ill at ease in the atmosphere of serious dedication, hated New York City, and was terrified by the teachers, especially Robert Milton, who looked at her awkward, leggy, frozen manner and big, blank, deadpan eyes and deliberately made fun of her in front of the other pupils. Very often, he mocked what he called her "middle-western" accent; he also made mincemeat of her attempts to perform. Sometimes, feeling very nervous and shy, she would stand at the back of the class and watch Bette Davis on the stage. Lucy was paralyzed with fear, and after six weeks Robert Milton wrote to her mother and told her that Lucy's presence there was a waste of time and money and she should go home immediately. She did, and spent the last weeks of June sulking in the house.

July 3, 1927, was her brother Fred's twelfth birthday. It was also the eve of the Fourth of July, and fireworks were exploding all over Celoron, with everybody in a festive mood. Grandfather Fred Hunt decided to have a Fourth-of-July-Eve party for some of the neighboring children, as well as a visiting girl from a neighboring town, twelve-year-old Joanna Ottinger. He suddenly seemed to lose his reason. He had bought a .22-caliber rifle, and foolishly gave the gun to the children, loaded with actual bullets, to practice with in the backyard. Many of them had never seen a gun before. Fred fired some shots at a tin can, then Lucy followed suit, and finally Joanna picked up the gun. At that exact moment, the eight-year-old son of the next-door neighbors, Warner Erickson, ran out from his own yard into the line of fire. Joanna was firing; the bullet from her gun went through Warner's back, lodging in his left lung. He fell to the ground, bleeding and screaming, and paralyzed in his lower limbs, back and arms.* Fred Hunt was horrified; he, Fred, Lucy, and Joanna rushed forward to do

* He died at the age of thirteen, still a cripple.

what they could. At the same moment, the young Erickson parents emerged, hysterical with rage, and charged Grandpa Hunt with having deliberately ordered Joanna to fire at and kill their son. Police were called, and a harrowing ordeal followed as Lucy, her grandfather, and DeDe, who came running out of the house, were grilled about the event. Warner was rushed to the Jamestown General Hospital, unable to move.

Einer Erickson, the boy's Swedish-born father, swore out a complaint at the office of his attorneys, Carlson and Alessi, charging deliberate and willful orders to kill had been given and insisting that he be paid $5,000, and be fully compensated for legal, hospital, and doctors' fees. Murder charges were not pressed but Grandpa went to prison until the trial took place. The trial was an ordeal for all concerned, since the children, Lucy included, had to give evidence. Although the shooting was an accident, Fred Hunt's gross negligence was appropriately punished. Einar Erickson could not be awarded the full amount, since the entire capital of Fred Hunt was just a few hundred dollars, and his only asset was the house. The house was sold at auction and bought by the highest bidders, Zurh and Bernice Faulkner, for $2,602.32 on September 14, 1928, leaving the family homeless until they were able to find a modest apartment at 20 East Fifth Street in Jamestown. It was a devastating shock to everybody and the local ostracism that followed increased Lucy's feelings of paranoia and nervousness about everything in life.*

After the shooting episode, Ed and DeDe and Lucy drew closer together. One of Ed's sisters, a girl named Lola, went to work as a nurse, and DeDe again sold hats. They all moved into a small cottage in Jamestown with Grandpa, but again there was tragedy as Lola died of cancer in the house. Lucy returned to New York to try to get work in vaudeville.

She was not successful, and instead struggled as an artist's

---

* For years, Fred Junior was falsely named in magazines as the one who fired the shot.

model on Columbus Circle, posing as the Chesterfield Cigarette Girl, and living at the Hotel Kimberly at Seventy-fourth Street and Broadway. Later she worked for dress designer Hattie Carnegie, who in a few years and with very limited capital had emerged from obscurity, becoming one of the most influential figures in the New York world of *haute couture*. Hattie specialized in well-tailored costumes; her East Fifty-seventh Street salon was attended by many celebrated women. At that time, Constance and Joan Bennett, prominent on the stage before their big screen careers, would frequently shop at Hattie's. For some reason, Miss Carnegie decided that Lucy resembled Joan Bennett, and so, although she didn't have the same measurements or appearance, Lucy modeled clothes for Joan. She even dyed her hair platinum blond to match Miss Bennett, who remembers her to this day as eager, highly strung, tense, and vibrant.

Lucy says that one day, while walking across the floor in a new costume, she felt severe pains in her legs and fell to the floor in agony, in front of the astonished customers and staff. Hattie Carnegie was kindness itself; she insisted that her own physician see Lucy, of whom she was very fond. The doctor told Lucy the condition was serious, and suggested that she go over to the Schuster Clinic on 113th Street, as she had the first signs of rheumatoid arthritis, quite rare at her age of seventeen. Professor Schuster said to her that he was experimenting with a new pregnant-horse serum and wondered if she would like to be the guinea pig; grasping at straws, she agreed, screaming theatrically as the needle plunged into her. She credited this treatment for having saved her from being permanently invalided with the disease. However, she still had to go home and give up her career as a model, spending part of her time in bed, part of it in a wheelchair, her legs so contorted that she had to have twenty-pound weights on each foot to straighten them. Such were the primitive methods of the time. For two years, she was in constant pain, and wondered if she would ever be able to pursue an acting career again.

Lucy's best friend in those days was a Jamestown hair-dresser, Gertrude Foote, known familiarly as Footie. Shy, nervous Footie was far different from the edgy, emotional and yet strong and ambitious Lucy, but they had much in common. When Lucy decided to return to New York and go back to work for Hattie Carnegie, Footie asked if she could go with her. Lucy was delighted. Footie resigned her job with the hair-dressing salon, and the two girls went by bus to New York City, checking into the Hotel Kimberly.

Back with Hattie Carnegie, Lucy once again worked exhaustingly long hours, and even at night, to be able to afford better clothes. She was consumed with ambition; now, at almost twenty, she had lost her awkward, leggy look and was strikingly attractive. Her hair was dark brown, almost chestnut, and her huge, surprised staring eyes were an intense, blazing blue. Hattie Carnegie had taught her perfect posture, and her figure, despite her previous illness, was almost ideal. However, her shoulders seemed a little square and sturdy for a woman and her long-legged stride seemed a little masculine also. Tough, resilient, and brittle on the surface, Lucy was as sensitive, volatile, and easily depressed as ever. She was very attracted to Latins, and when she dated, it was often Italian boys, one of whom bought her a fur coat. She continued at Hattie's for three years, into the Depression; she was among the few models Hattie didn't let go when the business situation became constrained.

Her favorite at Hattie Carnegie's was Rose Roth, a diminutive woman who was a talented designer. One day when the two were together, Rose ran into a friend of hers, Sylvia Hahlo, who was an actors' agent. Sylvia, who had been impressed with Lucy at various fashion shows, said without warning, right there on the street, "Lucy, how would you like to go to California?" "What would I do there?" Lucy asked her. Sylvia told her that James Mulvey of the Samuel Goldwyn office in New York had instructions to find a number of models and showgirls for the film *Roman Scandals*, starring the comedian

Eddie Cantor. They would be added to the galaxy of beauties known as the Goldwyn Girls, who were hand-picked for their looks and statuesque bearing, and were very popular at the time. Lucy hesitated; and while she did so, she was offered a part, a tiny, one-day job as a walk-on, in the film *Broadway Thru a Keyhole*, a story of the New York nightclubs based on the romance of Al Jolson and Ruby Keeler. Sylvia insisted on rushing shots of Lucy in the film to Goldwyn, whose representatives in New York immediately overcame Lucy's doubts and signed her to a contract. But when Goldwyn ran the tests in Hollywood, he didn't like Lucy at all. By contrast, the dance director Busby Berkeley, who had been hired to choreograph the film, was taken with her and insisted Goldwyn hire her. If it hadn't been for Berkeley, Lucy might never have come to Hollywood. She didn't discover until later that her break also came because one of the mothers of the twelve girls chosen to go to the Coast had refused to allow her daughter to appear in a Hollywood movie.

Although some accounts picture Lucy as shy and nervous at the thought of going to Hollywood, nothing could be further from the truth. She was excited by the prospect of appearing in a film, even though she was merely to be a slave girl, a figure in Eddie Cantor's dreams. Busby Berkeley, tough, driving and inspired, convinced her she had enormous possibilities, and she found him stimulating and exciting. Kay Harvey, a movie actress and model who met her at the time, was impressed by her steely determination, her sheer will to succeed; she had seldom seen such drive and relentlessness in anyone. She says, "Lucy in those days, even if she was a Goldwyn Girl, was actually a plain Jane, blessed with nondescript brown hair, white skin, and a high-energy drive. She actually appeared to enjoy a fight. . . . When she wasn't working on the picture, she would hang around the set, trying to secure better parts for herself. Betty Grable started out at the same time; Betty could sing, or rather pretend to sing, quite effectively, but Lucy couldn't, and that hurt her and made her feel inferior.

I remember that we all used to go to the Brown Derby on Vine Street together. Betty was not only more talented than Lucy, but she had a mother who smothered her with every kind of pressure to succeed. Trying to imitate her, Lucy went blond again; but later, her hairdressers advised her to go red, a vivid red or orange. Only Clara Bow, the silent star, who had recently suffered a nervous breakdown and was definitely on the skids, had red hair at that time.

"Many of us young kids used to meet at the home of Moe Morton. He was a close friend of George Raft, and Raft's buddy Mack Gray. Moe was a charmer and enjoyed having dancers and starlets like Lucy and Betty and me around for drinks and gossip."

Lucy dated Mack Gray. Gray was a bodyguard-companion to George Raft. Raft was a front man for the Mafia in New York, and owed much of his career to his mob connections. An incident occurred while Lucy was dating Gray. When a diner at the Brown Derby restaurant in Hollywood made a crack about Raft, Raft and Gray suggested the man step outside. Gray grabbed the man from behind and pinned him while Raft broke his nose. On another occasion, Raft clashed with Gray. In the El Royale Apartments on North Rossmore Avenue in Hollywood, Raft pointed his gun at Gray and told him to dance in front of him. As Gray obeyed, Raft shot a bullet into the floor to make Gray jump. The bullet went through the floor and hit the wall of Mrs. Jack Warner's apartment below. On another occasion, while Raft was staying with Gray at the Waldorf-Astoria in New York, Raft had a fight with his girlfriend, the actress Marjorie King. In Gray's presence, Raft went to her closet and cut up all her clothes with a large pair of tailor scissors. When he was dating Betty Grable, Raft had Gray bring her an expensive fur coat. When she turned it down, he laid it out on the doorstep like a doormat.

Mack Gray was an aspiring fight manager. Lucy used to go with him to the fights every Friday at the Hollywood Legion Stadium. Lucy became a great friend of Raft also. He lent her money, responding to her pleas that she was flat broke, and he allowed her to ride in his limousine with a chauffeur. Years later, she tried to repay him, but he wouldn't hear of it. Lucy befriended Virginia Pine, one of Raft's romantic interests. Often, she would go out with Virginia, to places like the Trocadero Nightclub on Sunset Strip. The evening would begin well, but it would rapidly deteriorate into a fight. One night, the four went to the mansion George had built for Virginia out of his screen earnings. All four were chatting comfortably in the living room when suddenly an argument erupted. Virginia, in a fury, began smashing the thousands of dollars' worth of perfume bottles George had given her. Lucy said later, "George was burning up inside, but he just sat there quietly, seemingly calm, saying nothing. When I got up enough nerve to go to Virginia, her bedroom looked like it had been hit by a hurricane. And the room reeked of perfume for months."

Kay Harvey appeared with Lucy in *Roman Scandals*. She says, "I came on the set one day to find 'Queen Lucy,' as we called her, riding on a beautiful brown horse. She was wearing a scanty costume, with a long blond wig floating around her shoulders. The crew dubbed her Lady Godiva as she elegantly rode that poor, tired horse back and forth before the cameras while we were being lighted for a shot." Kay Harvey remembers that while Lucy was riding around the ring, she accidentally almost crushed a chorus girl who fell under the horse's hooves.

Roman Scandals, directed by Frank Tuttle, was a vehicle for Eddie Cantor, the manically energetic, bug-eyed Goldwyn star who had become established on the stage with Flo Ziegfeld. *Roman Scandals* was a loose version of George Bernard Shaw's play *Androcles and the Lion;* the story involved Cantor's improbable appearance in ancient Rome; he, as an unsuccessful delivery boy, dreams of his transference to the age of the Emperor Valerius, played by Edward Arnold. Cantor becomes the emperor's food-taster, a dangerous job at the time, when virtually every meal could very well be laced with poison. Much of the comedy stemmed from an elaborate satire of the Roman court, more seriously treated that year by Cecil B. De Mille, whose elaborate spectacle of Nero's Rome in *The Sign of the Cross* was equally successful at the box office.

Lucy appeared with the Goldwyn Girls in a comic version of an imperial harem of kept women, dancing with long-legged emphasis in the number "Keep Young and Beautiful" by Al Dubin and the ever-reliable Harry Warren, creators of *42nd Street*. In another number, "No More Love," sung by the irresistible Ruth Etting, Lucy and the other girls appeared as slaves, and in a third number, "Build a Little House," she was attractively featured in a modern number. In one scene, she appeared with some alligators that swarmed in a pool. One bit her. "But," she said years later, "its teeth were out that day."

Always glum and serious, Lucy proved to be the butt of jokes in the dressing room. She could not join in the crude, raucous, often obscene conversation of the Goldwyn Girls, with its emphasis on male perfidy, double-crossing and sexual blackmail; she was probably thinking she would rather be somewhere else and the Hollywood she had dreamed of was far from being as desirable as it might seem to a former soda jerk from Jamestown. She was not exactly miserable, but she was not excited either.

She was no more pleased with her next picture, the stunning *Blood Money*, directed by Rowland Brown, in which she appeared briefly as the girlfriend of Chick Chandler, a well-known character actor of the time, in a racetrack scene. She was loaned to United Artists for a tiny part as a chorus girl in the Constance Bennett picture *Moulin Rouge*; Miss Bennett, who had often visited the Hattie Carnegie Salon with her sister Joan to see Lucy modeling, did not remember her, and that cut the sensitive girl to the quick. She appeared as a dancer in *Nana*, based upon the novel by Emile Zola, which was directed by Hollywood's only woman director, the mannish Dorothy Arzner. The star was the lovely and talented Anna Sten, whose career Goldwyn was ruining by trying to turn this fine Russian actress into a pale imitation of Marlene Dietrich. Lucy took little or no interest in the picture, despite its fine photography and elegant decor; nor did she care for her tiny part in *Bottoms Up*, directed by David Butler, *Hold That Girl*, *Bulldog Drummond Strikes Back*, or *The Affairs of Cellini*, starring Fredric March and (again) Constance Bennett. Goldwyn recalled her for *Kid Millions*, another Eddie Cantor vehicle as crude as its predecessor. Being a member of the 1934 Goldwyn Girls was certainly an honor of a sort, but Lucy remained indifferent. In *Kid Millions*, directed by Roy Del Ruth, Cantor played a numbskull who inherits $77 million, the price of a treasure stolen from an Egyptian tomb; in Egypt, Cantor becomes involved with the daughter of a sheikh and, while riding a camel, commits the sin of kissing her, which marks him as an infidel. Lucy appeared in several numbers, including the opening routine, "An Earful of Music," starring Ethel Merman, whose voice, startling as a ship's siren, threatened to shatter the eardrums. Lucy also appeared in a bizarre phallic fantasy of melting ice cream in which the girls become figures in an extravagantly erotic Busby Berkeley musical wet-dream. A bizarre but spectacular number was "I Want to Be a Minstrel Man," in which the girls wore blackface.

Although Berkeley was a sadist who constantly put the make on his girls, treating them as though he were a Marine Corps sergeant in boot camp, Lucy, with her sharp instincts, still responded to his guidance. She wasn't sophisticated enough to understand the implications of what he was making her do. Wanting to escape from being a Goldwyn Girl, she was irritated by everyone's failure to understand her talent. Looking carefully at her face in these films, it is easy to see her impatience and frustrated ambition.

She wanted very badly to go to Columbia, the studio that specialized in knockabout comedies. She felt that she could expand there. And she realized that her days were numbered with Goldwyn. Indeed, during *Kid Millions* she had difficulty maintaining the discipline expected of her, and became more and more erratic. The whole cast was allowed five-minute breaks even by Busby Berkeley, to smoke or go to the bathroom, and invariably Lucy was late returning. While the stars were punctually on set, an assistant would be calling through a public-address system repeatedly, "Miss Ball . . . Miss Ball . . . on set, please." Finally, the genial George Murphy, song-and-dance man, drew Lucy aside. He said to her, "Honey . . . I don't understand you. One of these days they'll fire you." And she replied, "That may be true, but one thing you can be sure of. They'll know who I am!"

What she could actually be sure of was that she would be fired. Nobody had any time for such temperamental behavior in a mere Goldwyn Girl. She left—for a still worse situation.

· CHAPTER 3 ·

*L*ucy went for an interview at Columbia, where its notoriously foul-mouthed boss, Harry Cohn, was rapidly building the studio to prominence from Grub Street origins through a handful of gifted directors, most notably the great Frank Capra. The casting director looked her up and down, observed her newly blond hair, staring blue eyes, and dead-serious expression, and decided on the spot she would be perfect as "a dumb broad." But instead of being cast in a feature, she was thrown into a short. Her first appearance at the studio was in a twenty-minute farce, *Perfectly Mismated*, starring a Ziegfeld star, the rubber-legged, whining Australian-born comedian Leon Errol. Lucy's part consisted mainly in being leered at by Errol.

In 1934, she found a modest frame house at 1344 North Ogden Drive in Hollywood, borrowing the $65 down payment from George Raft. She reached rock bottom at Columbia in *Three Little Pigskins*, starring the Three Stooges, whose idea of comedy was tweaking noses with large crunching sounds, upsetting paint pots over other people's heads, crushing toes with boots, slamming doors on fingers, and poking fingers into eyes. Never gifted with much of a sense of humor despite her gift for comedy, Lucy read what passed for a script and discovered that the first direction in it required her to have a large lemon meringue pie squashed vigorously into her face. No sooner had she recovered from the pie than she was thrown down on the floor and somebody shot seltzer up her nose. She wondered if she should return to Jamestown. Matters improved a fraction when she appeared as a telephone operator (shades of Jasper Ball!) in Frank Capra's *Broadway Bill*, a pleasant comedy about horse racing, and she was just visible in *Jealousy, Men of the Night,* and *The Fugitive Lady.*

Despite her dating several men (according to Kay Harvey, she had a number of beaux at the time), Lucy was miserable. She told me in 1965, "In the true sense I was alone in Hollywood. I didn't belong to anyone. I was unhappy. One night I went on the roof of my house to think over what was the matter with me. I decided that I wasn't doing my part in the world, and, as Columbia had just given me a stock contract to do bits, I decided to share this good fortune. Straightaway I went out and wired my mother DeDe, my grandfather Fred Hunt, my brother Fred, and my cousin Cleo to leave Jamestown and come out to Hollywood." She had warned them that she had no career to speak of, and that she was still poor; but they instantly packed up everything and moved. Fred, senior, had by now overcome the scandal of the injury of the child Warner Erickson, who had died in 1933.

Lucy sent the fares for everyone, but was relieved to learn that Ed Peterson would not be coming; he and her mother were now divorced and he was running a nightclub at Bemus Point, Lake Chautauqua. No sooner had the family settled in, with huggings and kissings and parties and outings to see the odd, ugly little city of Hollywood, than Columbia decided to disband its entire comedy team and move on to more prestigious films. Once again, Lucy was let go. ("One night," she said later, "at six o'clock—boom! I was on the streets, saying, 'What happened?' Nobody knew. They just—got rid of everybody.")

Lucy ran into a friend, Dick Green, who said that there was a call for a showgirl at RKO, with a salary of $50 a week. She had already been to several studio casting departments in vain, appearing only once, and then briefly, as a chorus girl in the film *Murder at the Vanities*. RKO needed her to play a model in a fashion-show sequence in the Fred Astaire/Ginger Rogers film *Roberta*; RKO gave her a standard seven-year contract that was to establish her as a name. She liked the Astaire/Rogers picture and even though her part called for nothing more than parading through an interminable fashion-show sequence in ostrich feathers, she realized that to appear in one of their films was an honor. She looked good in the sequence, standing out even among the many attractive women who surrounded her.

RKO was a happy studio. The atmosphere in the dressing rooms was buoyant, lively, and cheerful. Of all the Hollywood movie companies, RKO was run with the lightest hand. Fear, the staple of the industry, was scarcely present there. And with such figures as Astaire and Rogers dominating the lot, it was not surprising that everyone felt carefree and part of something glamorous, exciting, and enjoyable. Katharine Hepburn had just arrived from New York and was causing much delighted comment: on her wearing slacks, almost unknown for women at the time, her lavish gifts to the crew, and her habit of having picnics on the set, with hampers of food and expensive silverware. The new director George Stevens was much talked about, and the young, forceful Pandro S. Berman, who was in charge of production, bringing his inspired touch to the entire studio operation, was very popular. Studio scuttlebutt had it that Berman dated Lucy at the time.

Lucy's chief RKO rival was Betty Grable, who was emerging at the same time and was a more gifted dancer than Lucy. According to Kay Harvey it was to compete with Grable that Lucy began dyeing her hair red; she stopped yawning her way through scenes and developed herself as a player. She was a flower clerk in the Astaire/Rogers *Top Hat*; she played a tiny part in *The Three Musketeers*; and she turned up as the daughter of a rich couple in *I Dream Too Much*, known jocularly in the industry, because of the star Lily Pons' voice, as *I Scream Too Much*. She often had to travel by train on publicity junkets—

to New York, Chicago, and other parts of the country—and hated these trips. Most of all, she hated her bit in *The Three Musketeers*. She said later, "It was shot in the town of Calabasas. I was wearing eighteen petticoats, and hot velvet, and a hat, and a comb, and there wasn't a tree around, and the heat was unbearable. I said to anyone who would listen, 'That's it. I've had it. I've had it. I'm not going to work as a showgirl or a background anymore. *Good-bye!* I can't stand the heat. I can't stand the heat. Get me a wagon or a dog-cart. Anything. I'm going back to the studio.'"

She walked into RKO and told the casting director that she wouldn't do it anymore. She could not continue; she didn't care what they did to her, but she was not going to go "ever, ever, ever into the Valley, in the sun, again!" The casting director laughed, reminded her of her contract, and immediately afterward sent her back to the Valley in another picture, wearing a fur coat and hat, in an open car that was like a traveling oven, with a Great Dane that dribbled all over her face. She wanted to scream as everyone laughed out loud at her discomfiture, and she grumbled and shouted and made faces. The Lucy the world knows was born.

The family on Ogden Drive was as closely knit as ever. However, Grandfather Fred proved to be a problem. Over the years, in the wake of the shooting incident, and in the wake of his irritated departure from several jobs, he had moved from socialism toward communism. His idol was, as always, Eugene Debs. Indeed, Debs' career became an obsession of his in the depths of the Depression.

Born in Terre Haute, Indiana, in 1855, Eugene Debs died in 1926. He had left school at fourteen and worked in railway shops and as a locomotive fireman. Convinced that unionization along craft lines was a mistake, he formed the powerful American Railway Union, which opened its ranks to unskilled workers as well as skilled. The great Northern Railroad strike of 1894 ended in victory for Debs' union. Following a strike against the Pullman Company and subsequent violence, Debs

spent six months in jail for contempt of court. In 1897, he
formed the Social Democratic party of America, which became
part of the Socialist party of America, formed in 1901. In 1918,
he was convicted and sentenced to ten years in prison for
denouncing the war in a speech in Ohio. While in the Atlanta
Penitentiary, he received almost a million votes as candidate
for President against Warren G. Harding.

Because Debs had been sympathetic to the Bolsheviks in
the Russian Revolution, Fred Hunt felt that his whole family
should subscribe to Communist party policies. On March 19,
1936, not knowing what she was doing, Lucy, along with her
brother and mother, actually registered with the Los Angeles
County Registrar of Voters as intending to affiliate with the
Communist party in the 1936 primary election. On June 16,
she signed a sponsor certificate on behalf of Emil Freed, Communist party candidate for State Assembly in the 57th District.
On September 15, Freed appointed her a member of the State
Central Committee of the Communist party.

Years later, during the McCarthy era, this decision was to
cause Lucy a devastating public exposure and the threat of
professional ruin; she always claimed that she only registered
in order to please her imposing grandfather. Many evenings
were spent listening to Grandpa in his ottoman chair by the
bay window of the house overlooking Ogden Drive as he
talked about the glories of Eugene Debs. Sometimes noticing a
pedestrian passing by, Fred would race down the lawn to but-
tonhole the stranger and insist that he become a Communist
on the spot. Fortunately, the pedestrians he cornered regarded
him as nothing more than a foolish old eccentric and did not
report him as subversive of democracy to the authorities. Very
oddly, at that same time that she was officially subscribing to
communism, Lucy had become a pupil of the woman who, in
the 1950s, was to become the chief bell ringer of the extreme
right wing in Hollywood, pointing an accusing finger at many
liberals, which led to their professional destruction under the
blacklist. This was the formidable Lela Rogers, mother of Gin-

ger, who guided her daughter's career with such determination that she even kept a record of Ginger's every movement during the course of a day and could give her exact location to anyone who asked.

Lela was a tough coach as well as a staunch right-wing extremist; had she known that Lucy had registered with the Communists, she would probably have dismissed her from her sight permanently. Instead, she guided her with considerable, if rather mechanical, expertise, teaching her above all something she really didn't need to be taught—that she should always remain completely deadpan in the most comic scenes, because the audience would laugh more if she didn't smile. There is no question that Lucy was ideally suited to this kind of approach: Her wide-eyed look of blind confusion, her solemn, gloomy mouth, and her way of staring straight ahead as though mesmerized were perfect for a comedienne who was the butt of all the jokes. And indeed her look of concern came from her actual problems at home, including Grandpa Hunt's alcoholism. It didn't help matters when he warned the black maid that she was being exploited by the ruling classes, nor were fresh-faced delivery boys too delighted (since, like most Americans, they had executive ambitions) when he would shout at them, "You strong young working men are the salvation of the world."

Often, in those years, Lucy would go out with the up-and-coming young star Henry Fonda, double-dating with Ginger Rogers and James Stewart, who were also keeping company. Fonda and Stewart shared a house in Brentwood. Ginger and Lucy would spend much time in front of their mirrors at RKO, putting on eye shadow, mascara, lipstick, and rouge on principles taught them by Mel Burns. Sometimes they went over to Brentwood for the double date, where Fonda would cook the dinner, and while Ginger taught Fonda and Stewart to dance the carioca, Lucy would wash the dishes. After dinner, the four liked to go to the Ambassador Hotel's Coconut Grove in the Wilshire District and dance to Freddie Martin's band all night, ending up at dawn in Barney's Beanery on Santa Monica Boulevard, just east of La Cienega, which exists to this day.

Lucy managed to obtain a leave of absence from her contract at RKO when, probably to escape the problems at home and the monotony of her local career, she tried and succeeded in obtaining a role in the stage musical *Hey Diddle Diddle*, which was bound for Broadway. The cast included the former silent star Conway Tearle, as well as Keenan Wynn, Alice White, and Martha Sleeper. The production had a woman director, Anne Nichols; Lucy was cast as Julie Tucker, a screen extra sharing a Hollywood apartment with two other girls. By all accounts, she acted with considerable expertise, earning just under the $100 a week she was getting at RKO. *Hey Diddle Diddle* opened on January 21, 1937, at the McCarter Theater in Princeton, New Jersey, in severe winter weather. *Variety* covered the opening, praising Lucy: "Miss Ball fattens a fat part and almost walks off with the play. She outlines a consistent character and continuously gives it logical substance. Has a sense of timing and, with a few exceptions, keeps her comedy under control." The capacity audience of 1,100 greeted the world premiere joyously; the scenes of life in the duplex apartment in Hollywood, with the three girls devising all kinds of situations to get parts in movies, proved to be hilarious, and a succession of bewildered or nervous directors and movie executives tangled in the girls' net was continuously diverting. However, there were problems: Conway Tearle was suffering from an illness that was finally to take his life, and Morris Green, co-producer, had drastic differences with Anne Nichols. Although the production was supposed to open at the Vanderbilt Theater in New York on February 3, in fact to everyone's disappointment, it closed quickly in Philadelphia and after folding in Washington, D.C., it was dropped. Much defeated by this setback, Lucy returned to Hollywood and, by a great stroke of luck, and perhaps because she had made such a splash in *Hey Diddle Diddle*, found herself cast in a movie of exceptional quality.

The film was *Stage Door*. It was based on a play by Edna Ferber and George S. Kaufman, and the screenplay was written by Morrie Ryskind and Anthony Veiller. The director was Gregory La Cava. An alcoholic, almost driven out of the industry because of his drinking, he had begun his career as a cartoonist. He was a fine director, but he never saw other people's films and had no idea who was a star and who was not. He made sure that every line of dialogue was tailored to an actress or actor. Pan Berman recalls that making *Stage Door* was a torment. Every day he feared that the director would crack up under the effects of alcohol and the whole picture would be ruined. La Cava was drunk throughout the entire shooting, and at one time he fell off the stage at the Biltmore Theater in downtown Los Angeles while he was shooting a scene.

Before the picture began, La Cava had Lucy, Katharine Hepburn, the star, and all the other girls in the story of backstage life come to the studio and play scenes—not those written, but some they improvised, showing life as they lived it. Andrea Leeds, who was in the cast, says, "He had a script girl take down our conversations and he would adapt these into dialogue. He rewrote scenes from day to day to get the feeling of a bunch of girls together—as spontaneous as possible. He would talk to each of us like a life-long friend. That gave us a feeling of intimacy."

Because she had just played a girl in a lodging house trying to crash Hollywood, Lucy was ideally cast as a similar character trying to crash Broadway. As Judy Canfield, resident of the Manhattan Footlight Club, she was at her best; and she was surrounded by talented people, including the grand old British actress Constance Collier, Eve Arden, who snapped out the acid comments that were to become her screen trademark in later years, and Lucy's friend, spunky Ginger Rogers. Lucy, who was represented now by the agent Zeppo Marx, brother of Groucho, Harpo, and Chico, was paid $125 a week.

She ran into trouble with the studio during the shooting. Gregory La Cava insisted that all of the girls wear their own clothes because he hated films in which the actresses dressed beyond their incomes in life. Lucy was pleased to do this, but then, studio files show, she sent a bill to the studio front office for the use of her clothes. A studio official argued with her strongly when she walked into his office, asking for the rental payment. Jane Loring, Katharine Hepburn's girl Friday, who was the troubleshooter on the production, came in and joined in the argument. Claire Cramer, manager of the wardrobe department, also appeared, and announced she had never agreed to pay rental to Lucy and that her contract provided she supply any modern wardrobe she might have that was suitable for the part. The studio official promised to pay Lucy $50 for the use of her things, but then memoed studio manager Joe Nolan, asking him to tell Lucy that he would not permit any such transaction. He wrote, "I would appreciate it very much if you would handle my end of it with a little diplomacy, as I dislike going back on my word, and yet I think the girl has a terrific nerve to expect us to indulge in any such irregularity." The studio did not pay.

Lucy again collided with the studio when she wanted to make radio appearances on "The Phil Baker Show," but this time RKO yielded, and Pan Berman allowed her to appear.

Stage Door was a hit at the preview, and made history. There had been few films before it in which the characters interrupted each other, talked in natural speech, and acted without any frills. When the cast saw the finished movie, they let out whoops of joy. Indeed, Katharine Hepburn recalled later, she actually cried with laughter and delight as she saw the finished work. But Lucy was glum and silent, unimpressed by her own performance.

At this time Grandpa Hunt clashed with the City of Los Angeles. He was obsessed with a tree that grew outside the house on Ogden Drive, claiming that every time he leaned up against it it moved. This was pure imagination, of course. He summoned the maintenance crew from the City Council, saying that the tree was a menace to pedestrians and traffic. However, the foreman took one look at the tree and decided Grandpa was insane. Immediately, Fred Hunt took an ax and began cutting away at the roots. Inevitably, the tree began to sway. Just at that moment, Lucy arrived, driving a secondhand Studebaker, and there was a gust of wind. It blew the tree over and crushed Lucy's newly bought car. Grandpa stood looking at her as she screamed with misery and rage. "I told you that goddamned tree was dangerous!" he said.

Lucy went on from *Stage Door* to make *Joy of Loving*, with Irene Dunne and Douglas Fairbanks, Jr., directed by the veteran Tay Garnett. Garnett told me, "Lucy attacked each scene as though it were the dog's breakfast. She acted as though her life depended on stealing the limelight from the stars—and maybe it did. She always laughed with me when I told her (and reminded her in later years) that the motion picture censors made me change the title to *Joy of Living*. God, how things have changed! They didn't think loving should be joyous, and were afraid that people would think it was a sex picture."

One of the problems of shooting *Joy of Living* in January of 1938 was that Lucy was very irritable throughout. She had wanted to go to Universal to appear with her friend Andrea Leeds in *Letter of Introduction*, another movie about lodging-house life, which also starred Adolphe Menjou. But RKO refused to release her. She was offered a part with the great Jack Benny at Paramount in *Artists and Models Abroad*, but again RKO was adamant that she couldn't go. She was annoyed that her friend Ann Sothern, cast in *Joy of Living*, had to withdraw because of illness, and she had little rapport with Irene Dunne, who replaced Miss Sothern in the picture. Lucy played Irene's sister in the movie and was required to appear in many scenes with her. The tension was considerable between them.

Stage Door had seemed to promise an interesting career, but *Joy of Living* gave Lucy very little to work on. The part of the temperamental, selfish younger sister, filled with jealousy, may have (according to some) reflected Lucy's own envious nature, but it wasn't a part calculated to make her appealing to the audience. It was only when she appeared briefly in a Broadway musical scene that she was able to make a strong impression. And soon she had to appear (though admittedly in the female lead) in a worthless farce, *Go Chase Yourself*, an instruction she felt like giving to the director himself; not much more could be distilled from *Having Wonderful Time*, in which she appeared again as a jealous girl. However, *The Affairs of Annabel*, with Jack Oakie, in which she appeared as a temperamental movie actress making a prison picture, and involved with kidnappers, did offer her the chance to be, as *The New York Times* said, "one of our brightest comediennes."

At the time, Lucy was dating the polished and skillful director Alexander Hall, later to become famous for his comedy of the supernatural, *Here Comes Mr. Jordan*. Hall gave her some of the secrets of the trade: Through him, and from learning on the job, she was beginning to develop a comedy timing. Moreover, the studio publicity machine began churning out fantasies about her, a sure mark of her increasing importance. She was supposed to have taken up an open-cockpit plane in freezing weather to rescue a stranded schoolboy; she was said to be an accomplished wood carver and to own an imitation flower shop. She was alleged to be an avid reader, "preferring biographies." Such nonsense was staple for the period.

Making seven or eight pictures a year was a grinding, grueling routine. While she was shooting one picture, trying hard to make sense of the absurd situations and meaningless, shallow dialogue, she had to read the part for her next movie —on the set, while waiting for her call. She had become more jaded than ever, and when she heard that she was to appear with the Marx Brothers in *Room Service*, she simply yawned. However, the studio regarded it as helpful to her career. RKO had paid $225,000 for the screen rights to the big Broadway hit, and had even managed to borrow the Marx Brothers from MGM, where they were under long-term contract. Lucy's part, despite promises to the contrary, was one of the smallest in her entire career; she simply played an actress in a play which the

Marx Brothers are trying to put on, helping the brothers verbally seduce a producer to support them in their enterprise. However, she was glad to be able to watch her illustrious peers who were still at the height of their popularity. Their timing, repartee and skillfully engineered knockabout were an inspiration to her. But nothing inspiring could be gleaned from her next movies, *The Next Time I Marry*, *Annabel Takes a Tour*, *Beauty for the Asking*, and *Twelve Crowded Hours*. She was somewhat desperate when she heard that she had been chosen to test for the role of Scarlett O'Hara in *Gone with the Wind*. It is hard to imagine more absurd casting. Clearly, asking her to come in and test was nothing more than part of a cruel publicity stunt; she had to go through the humiliation of taking lessons in southern speech from voice coach Will Price. Walking from the parking lot to producer David O. Selznick's office, she was caught in a sudden rainstorm without an umbrella and appeared before him drenched to the skin. She was so nervous she literally sank to her knees during the reading. Selznick burst out laughing at the sight of her.

· CHAPTER 4 ·

*I*n 1938, Lucy, now twenty-seven, was more miserable and isolated from people than ever. RKO was treating her badly; part after part was worthless, dredged up from the bottom drawer of movie cliché characters. She said later that she was "very happy to be the queen of the B's," but in fact those who remember her at the time confirm that all she could think about was breaking loose from her contract and trying to find an opportunity at another studio. She began the year with a new manager, Arthur Lyons, who managed to perk her up a little with his unconquerable optimism and fast line in smooth talk; but soon, she found herself dumped into *Beauty for the Asking*, directed by Glenn Tryon, in which she played a beauty-shop proprietor who develops a face cream and becomes a major success, a story based upon the career of Helena Rubenstein. Kate Cameron of the *New York Daily News* praised the performance, saying, "Miss Ball rises high enough above her material to remind us that she is of the stuff that stars are made of." She appeared in *Twelve Crowded Hours*, in which she starred opposite Richard Dix, a story of crime and illegal gambling in a big city. In *Panama Lady*, arguably her worst picture, she was a cabaret entertainer stranded in Panama City; although critics admired her performance, and Wanda Hale in the *New York Daily News* said the picture was a "minor triumph" for her, she was bored to distraction by the entire concoction. She obtained some relief from *Five Came Back*, a story about an airplane, the *Silver Queen*, which crashes in the jungle; among the passengers were a professor and his wife, a secretary eloping with her employer, a gangster's son and his henchmen, a political killer, and an FBI man, and the girl played by Lucy, a hard-bitten former prostitute. The collection of stock characters and familiar story were given considerable life and excitement by the screenwriters and the director, John Farrow (father of Mia Farrow), a loud-mouthed, brutish Australian who sadistically ill-treated anyone who failed to stand up to him. Notorious in the industry for his violent temper and use of foul language (despite his distinguished background as a prominent Roman Catholic who had been given honors by the Pope), Farrow greatly aggravated Lucy, who clashed with him on several occasions during the shooting. Rain delayed the production for several days, the actor John Carradine fell ill, and Farrow's insistence on long rehearsals and lineups proved distracting to everyone. Despite the many irritations of the work—the problem of dealing with Farrow, fending off the crude advances of Chester Morris, and the physical work of the jungle location— Lucy managed to cope. However, she was fretful and sickly during the weeks of production, and at one stage had an unpleasant shock: She was leaning against the trunk of a jungle tree imported to the sound stage, which had supposedly been carefully checked for any possible insect life, when two large black spiders crawled out of a hole and dropped on her head. She screamed uncontrollably, and had to be assisted off the set. Everybody laughed; she was furious.

The film was well received, and Frank S. Nugent in *The New York Times* wrote, "*Five Came Back* . . . is a rousing salute to melodrama, suspenseful as a slow-burning fuse, exciting as a pinwheel, spectacularly explosive as an aerial bomb." Lucy was singled out from the cast for her excellent, gripping performance; at last she had a part she could get her teeth into, and it isn't surprising: The script was co-written, oddly enough, by Nathanael West.

At the time, Lucy remained obsessed with her family—her antic mother, DeDe, her brother Fred, who was beginning to make his mark in the business world, her grandpa Fred Hunt, still manically driven, caught up in the issues of socialism. She dated Broderick Crawford, who was twenty-eight at the time. Stocky, witty, and lively, he was just beginning his career as an actor in 1939. He had made a considerable mark as Lennie in the Broadway adaptation of John Steinbeck's *Of Mice and Men* shortly before Lucy met him, and had emerged as a stalwart second lead in Henry Hathaway's adventure film *The Real Glory*, set in the Philippines during the Spanish-American War. Crawford had a brusque directness and flair, a muscular energy and drive that Lucy responded to, and pictures of them at the time, dancing in nightclubs or enjoying drinks on the patios of hotels, indicate a warm, pleasantly sunlit relationship. However, although they were briefly engaged, the relationship had little chance of lasting; both were consumed with their careers, and neither was prepared for a commitment at the time. Lucy again began seeing Alexander Hall and was amused by his account of directing Melvyn Douglas in drag in the comedy *The Amazing Mr. Williams*, but this revived romance came to nothing. Lucy was still attracted to Latin men, and according to Kay Harvey and others who knew her in those years, she dated several Mexicans, Italians, and Spaniards without ever feeling an impulse to marry any one of them.

One of Lucy's continuing aggravations was the studio's persistent refusal to loan her out. When Pandro S. Berman left the studio to go to MGM, she felt the last chance of achieving anything approaching a major career disappearing. In the year of his departure, 1940, a new executive, George Schaefer, took over. Cultivated, intelligent, and wise, Schaefer dedicated his energies to developing the career of the young Orson Welles, and he also hired the documentary filmmaker Pare Lorentz, who had made two masterpieces, *The Plow That Broke the Plains* and *The River*, to make a story of steelworkers starring Robert Ryan and Frances Dee, *Name, Age, and Occupation*. He had little or no interest in Lucy, who to him was just another contract girl. Under his regime, her career scarcely improved. However, Schaefer did give her one opportunity: He starred her in *Dance, Girl, Dance*, directed by Dorothy Arzner, for whom Lucy had appeared so briefly in *Nana*. As before, she felt uncomfortable and uneasy with Arzner. Straitlaced and puritanical, somewhat naive because of her origins, and lacking in any degree of true sophistication, Lucy was embarrassed by widespread gossip about Miss Arzner's lesbianism, and felt quite uncomfortable when confronted by a severe, well-tailored, crop-haired, mannish woman who barked directions with all the toughness of a John Ford or Henry Hathaway. No doubt Lucy was also tense because Dorothy Arzner was known to have sexually approached more than one leading lady in her pictures.

In *Dance, Girl, Dance*, Lucy also came under the guidance of the producer Erich Pommer, who had once been the all-powerful head of UFA, the great German studio, and had more recently been a partner of Charles Laughton in London, where they founded Mayflower Pictures together. Pommer had singled out Lucy for the part of Bubbles, a nightclub dancer and singer, who, determined to acquire riches through men, emerges as a burlesque performer and stripper in downtown Los Angeles.

Dorothy Arzner, a gifted craftswoman, searched the dance halls and strip joints in Los Angeles for settings for the story; edgy, but determined to do her homework, Lucy, Miss Arzner told me, went with her, exploring the seedy back streets of the city, fascinated and repelled at the same time by its atmosphere. She went to one particular strip joint, the Follies Theater, on South Main Street, with Alexander Hall, observing the bumping and grinding, the brutality of the strippers' lives, and their raw humor. In particular, she watched the locally well-known strippers, who used slow walks in time with the music; she decided to use a faster technique, and she told Ms. Arzner prudishly she would not strip down to her underwear, even if the film censors allowed it. She told the *Hollywood Citizen News* with characteristic modesty in an interview on March 23, 1940, "I'll still be dressed as modestly as a grandmother. Even after I take off my clothes. What I've got is a costume consisting of six dozen pieces of chiffon. I can throw away piece after piece and still not shock the censors."

The shooting was delayed because of pre-production difficulties. Lucy frequently became exhausted during the rehearsals. Ernst Matray, the dance director, pushed her very hard indeed, and at 4:45 P.M. on April 20 she collapsed, and everyone was sent home. Playing dramatic scenes all day long and rehearsing well into the night for the dance scenes wore her out; she was living on junk food, smoking and enjoying cocktails; her precariously balanced constitution kept giving out. However, she managed to give an electrifying performance in the big striptease number, "Oh Mother, What Do I Do Now?"

It was during the making of *Dance, Girl, Dance* that the most momentous meeting of Lucy's life took place. Desi Arnaz was a young actor in town. He was in the commissary one day when he saw her, and she heard him saying to someone that he didn't like her acting and would not want to appear with her as the studio was pressing him to do, in a picture that was being planned for him, *Too Many Girls*, to be directed by George Abbott. Desi Arnaz was the sensation of the New York theater at the time; the studio was in a buzz over his arrival. He was very much Lucy's physical type. Dark, with olive skin, a chunky build, and an eager, energetic, wide-eyed stare, he was the kind of Latin she couldn't resist. Born in Santiago, Cuba, on March 2, 1917, he was the great-grandson of Santiago's mayor; his grandfather had been the doctor assigned to President Teddy Roosevelt's Rough Riders during the attack on San

Juan Hill in the Spanish-American War, and his father had become mayor of Santiago at age twenty-nine, the youngest man ever to fill that office.

Raised as a strict Roman Catholic, Desi was deeply locked into his family; like Lucy's, his folks owned farms; his father was a pioneer in dairy farming and delivering refrigerated milk. Desi grew up to be sturdy and athletic, fond of horses and fishing, bicycling and swimming. At a young age, he was an enthusiastic visitor to the notorious Havana whorehouses, losing his virginity at fourteen. He was a man's man, fond of gambling, chasing girls, and crazy about fast cars. During a Cuban revolution, his home in Santiago was burned to the ground; he managed to escape to the mainland, moving, in traditional Cuban fashion, into southwest Miami, where he worked in an importing company sorting tiles for roofs; and later feeding and caring for canaries. Having a strong musical bent, along with his athletic prowess, he landed a job with a band at $39 a week, as a guitar player and singer. He had a pleasant, sweet tenor voice and had a strong sense of rhythm; he delivered the songs with enormous energy. Boldly expressing a sexuality startling for the time, he used his physique with aggressive emphasis at the microphone.

He moved to New York and joined the Xavier Cugat band, performing at Billy Rose's Aquacade, a conglomeration of showgirls, swimmers, and exotic scenery starring Johnny Weissmuller and Eleanor Holm. Desi was a success, but he was starving on the money Cugat paid him and he had to steal food from hotel kitchens in order to exist. Eventually he began to prosper, rising to a salary of $100 a week. He was a great success at La Conga, a nightclub in New York where his routine stopped the show. He dated the debutante Brenda Frazier, frequented Polly Adler's popular bordello, and became friendly with Richard Rodgers and Lorenz Hart, who recommended Desi to George Abbott, director of their new musical *Too Many Girls*. They wanted Desi for the sympathetic role of Manolito, an antic Latin football player, one of a group of four body-

guards of an heiress and debutante who had certain character-
istics of Brenda Frazier. They felt Desi would be ideally cast as
a football player and that he had the vocal range and style to
handle the part. Exhausted after performing at La Conga till
4:30 A.M., Desi came to the theater one morning and sang a
number for Abbott, whose only comment was "Well, at least
he's loud enough!" Desi overacted his reading outrageously,
because Larry Hart had advised him to, but Abbott still decided
he was good for the part and told him he would give him a
try.

Abbott loved Desi's frantic hamminess. He told him jokingly after the first scene, "For an amateur, you're doing
great!" His conga routine stopped the show again and again.
The black-tie opening-night audience at the Imperial Theater
in New York on October 14, 1939, was enraptured. Immediately, plans were made to bring Desi to Hollywood for the
movie version.

Dance, Girl, Dance was still dragging on when Desi walked
into the commissary that day. Lucy had just finished a fight
scene with Maureen O'Hara, similar to the one in which Marlene Dietrich and Una Merkel had been involved in in *Destry
Rides Again;* her hair was in a mess, and makeup simulated a
black eye. Desi asked George Abbott, "Who's the redhead?"
and was amazed to learn she was Lucille Ball, for whom he
had no particular admiration. When Abbott told him she was
going to play the part of an ingenue in the picture, he thought
Abbott must be kidding. How could this brassy, tough woman,
so obviously experienced, playing so convincingly a strip-tease
artist, possibly act an innocent young girl, heiress to a large
fortune, who needed the protection of a stalwart football
team? He was confusing Lucy with her part: She *was* innocent.

A few days later he saw Lucy again; now she looked stunning in a yellow sweater that showed off her beautiful figure,
and a pair of elegant beige slacks. He was strongly attracted
now and when she went up to him with her bold stride, her
huge blue eyes staring directly into his, challenging him, he

felt excited in spite of himself. "Why don't you call me Lucille and I'll call you Dizzy?" she said to him. He told her his name was not Dizzy. She went on, not changing her wide-eyed stare, "What is it then? Daisy?" He replied, "Daisy is a flower. It's Desi. D-E-S-I." He then, on an impulse, asked Lucy if she liked to rumba. When she said that she had never learned, he asked her if she would like him to teach her how. He took a deep breath and added, "It may come in handy for your part." He proceeded with this elaborate pickup by saying that he was going out with a group of kids from New York to El Zarape, a popular Mexican restaurant on Sunset Boulevard. Would she like to come? She wasn't coy; she accepted at once. That night, they danced together all night until dawn, when he dropped her off (those were different days) safely at the door of her home on Ogden Drive. He was having an affair with another woman at the time, and couldn't imagine getting serious about this tough, snappy, seemingly outgoing but moody girl. He met her again that Sunday, by chance, at the home of comedian Eddie Bracken at Malibu; Lucy was on the beach, playing with a beach ball. Later that evening, Desi's girlfriend left with somebody else. So immediate was the electricity between them that Lucy broke off with Alexander Hall, whom she had been seeing again, and Desi broke with his girlfriend.

Desi was very attractive and Lucy found him impossible to resist. When she was cast in *Too Many Girls*, the outcome was inevitable. She said later, "When Desi drove onto the RKO lot [at the outset of shooting], I was leaning out my dressing room window. He flashed by in a long, gray Buick Roadmaster with a uniformed chauffeur, yet!" Soon after they met, Desi began to call Lucille "Lucy." Desi drove them in the Buick to Palm Springs on weekends, going a hundred miles an hour and terrifying the hypersensitive Lucy. On the way back, she found a way to overcome her fear: She screamed at the top of her voice, alarming motorists who happened to be passing by. When Desi asked Lucy what was the matter with her, she said that Kate Hepburn had told her to scream because it would "exhaust her vocal chords and make her hoarse."

The romance was impassioned and explosive. Making *Too Many Girls* was fun for everyone, and director George Abbott was an inspiration. To this day, he remembers (he is now in his nineties) the electric energy that Lucy and Desi brought to their scenes together. ("I knew they would be inseparable in the future.") Meeting Desi enlivened Lucy's whole existence. She was no longer bored and restless. She began grinding out another picture, *A Girl, a Guy, and a Gob*, produced by the former silent comedy star Harold Lloyd. The story was as silly as the title, and Lucy found it well-nigh unendurable to make it. When Desi moved to Chicago to appear in the stage version of *Too Many Girls*, Lucy would fly there on weekends, often traveling through the night because in those days it took eighteen hours to reach the Windy City from the West Coast. She would join Desi at his hotel, spend the night arguing and making love, and then depart for Los Angeles, only to count the days till she could return to Chicago again.

Desi also performed as a soloist in New York at the Versailles Nightclub, and at the Roxy Movie Theater, where he appeared live before showings of the picture *Alexander's Ragtime Band*. It was impossible for Lucy to reach New York City to be with him. They telephoned each other at great expense and talked for hours on end, painfully longing for each other, fiercely possessive always, questioning each other jealously on every man or woman they met. Desi, in particular, was extremely jealous, and whenever Lucy was not present to answer his calls on Ogden Drive, he was almost hysterical, and she, when she could not reach him in his New York hotel suite, was almost equally upset. When she called she never told him where she had been while at the same time saying to him things like, "What are you trying to do, lay every goddamned one of those chorus girls?"

Desi was angry when he saw a picture in the paper of Lucy

with the handsome mayor of Milwaukee on the promotional tour of *Dance, Girl, Dance*. "You crumb bum, you're screwin' da mayor!" Desi screamed at her over the telephone. Of course, she was doing no such thing. She replied by denying the charge and accusing him of doing the same thing to "every waitress or soda hop in New York." Lucy flew to New York on November 29, 1940. She stayed at the Pierre Hotel with Desi. When a reporter asked her if she had any intention of marrying Desi, she said no, it was out of the question, because their careers separated them too much. As the reporter left the Pierre suite at noon, Desi threw Lucy lustily into bed. Later that day, Desi said to Lucy, "I'm going to marry you tomorrow morning!" She was so astonished, all she could say was, "Where?" He told her, without drawing a breath, "Connecticut. I can get the five-day wait waived there." He said that probate judge Harold L. Nape of Connecticut had promised to make the necessary arrangements; they could drive over the border, get married, and then Desi could play the Roxy the same night.

Lucy said angrily, "What, no honeymoon?" Desi told her the honeymoon would be "in the Roxy dressing room." Later that night, Desi returned after performing at the Roxy. He found her RKO boss George Schaefer in the Pierre suite with Lucy. Schaefer started gesticulating at Desi. Desi couldn't understand what the problem was until Lucy said, "George is trying to tell you something!" "What is dat?" Desi replied, afraid that Schaefer might be disapproving of the approaching marriage. Lucy said, "He's trying to tell you your fly's open. And you're not wearing shorts, yet. George, Desi believes in advertising!"

· CHAPTER 5 ·

$\mathcal{J}$ust before the wedding, *Too Many Girls* was released in New York, at Loew's Criterion Theater. Lucy and the picture received glowing reviews in *The New York Times;* Desi's performance did not. Bosley Crowther described him as "a noisy, black-haired Latin whose face unfortunately lacks expression and whose performance is devoid of grace." But not even this attack by a powerful critic could affect Desi and Lucy's spirits as they drove to Greenwich, Connecticut, on November 30, 1940. Lucy was twenty-nine and Desi was twenty-three. Desi was still performing with his band at the Roxy Theater in New York. According to Lucy, the conversation went as follows:

DESI: We goin' upta Greenich an' get married.
LUCY: I didn't know.
DESI: I tole you las' night between rumbas.

So headlong was their rush to the altar that they had quite forgotten to obtain the necessary Wassermann blood test and even the wedding ring. They took the test barely in time for the noon ceremony at the Byram River Beagle Club performed by Justice of the Peace John P. O'Brien. Meantime, Desi's hard-pressed manager and agent, Deke Magaziner and Doc Bender, tried to get a ring. But all of the jewelry stores in

Greenwich were closed for the weekend; in desperation, the two men went to Woolworth's five-and-dime and bought the cheapest and silliest-looking ten-cent wedding ring imaginable. It was made of copper, and would have turned green over the subsequent years if it had not been coated later in platinum. At last, the wedding took place, but due to the slowness of trains and the long drive back to New York, it became impossible for Desi to return to the Roxy Theater in time for the matinee. Desi called the theater; the manager was appalled to discover Desi was still in Greenwich. The manager said he had a line around the block and what the heck was he going to tell the people. Desi suggested the manager go out and make an announcement of the marriage; the news was sure to bring a cheer, and everyone could come back for the second show. Desi arranged for a motorcycle squad to escort him and Lucy back through heavy traffic down the turnpikes all the way into Manhattan.

The wedding was simple and cheerful, with all the guests in high spirits. The late-night crowd at the Roxy was hugely enthusiastic, thronging outside the doors to greet the couple as they arrived. Desi romantically carried Lucy over the threshold of the dressing room, and they downed quick glasses of champagne. With a nicely theatrical touch, Desi led Lucy onto the stage at the end of his performance. Another theatrical touch came from the management: They had supplied the audience with rice to throw, and the entire crowd, screaming and yelling, bombarded the couple from the second balcony all the way to the orchestra. And somehow, in all of this madness, Desi had managed to call El Morocco, the famous nightclub, and arrange a wedding party in the small hours of the morning. A galaxy of stars of the theater world appeared to wish them good luck, including Richard Rodgers and Lorenz Hart, George Abbott, and the columnist Dorothy Kilgallen. The band played "Here Comes the Bride" as the couple walked in, followed by almost every number Lucy had ever pretended to sing in her pictures.

Lucy and Desi stayed at the Pierre until the end of the Roxy engagement, when Desi obtained a three-picture contract at RKO. The couple boarded the Twentieth Century Limited for Chicago and Los Angeles at the beginning of January 1941. In those days, train travel was luxurious; a red carpet stretched out along the platform at Grand Central Station, and white-uniformed porters stood ready with champagne and caviar. The drawing room consisted of two adjoining compartments, and was flooded with flowers. The dining car, where many of the famous gathered on first-name terms, served fine food with sterling silver services and spotless napery. The lights shone, the menu glowed; fresh trout straight from the lakes was brought aboard at certain points and served to the passengers in the Art Deco Pullman dining car.

It was a delayed honeymoon. Desi kept the other passengers awake playing guitar into the night, singing love songs to Lucy. There was no question that the fiery, impatient natures of the two were in accord. Passionate, highly strung, excitable, humorous, and audacious, they had a great deal in common. Once they were in Hollywood, Fred senior and junior and DeDe gathered around and Desi was as delighted with them as they were with him. Always a good cook, Lucy adopted many of Desi's favorite dishes in the kitchen, including the traditional chicken and rice dish known as *arroz con pollo*. Among the visitors to their apartment in Hollywood was Carmen Miranda, the Brazilian bombshell, who was temperamental, unstable, and subject to fits of depression, but who exuded great fire and charm on the screen. She had just made a sensational debut in *That Night in Rio* for 20th Century–Fox, causing a stir at the studio when she performed her first number without underwear. This example of exhibitionism became the talk of Hollywood; Darryl F. Zanuck, head of the studio, was horrified when he saw the rushes.

But, much as the Arnazes enjoyed those days in Hollywood, problems were shadowing them. Lucy reported to the studio for work on February 24, at $500 a week, but her box-office situation was still wretched. Her manager, Arthur Lyons, was having a fight with Joe Nolan at the studio over getting her even this modest contract. Lucy was upset about the situation and kept fretting about the delay.

Telegrams flew to and fro between Joe Nolan, business affairs chief, and Lyons, all of them indicating that Lucy was getting more and more uneasy about her future at the studio. And her concern was not without cause. It took all of Lyons' efforts to secure her a future. The fact (hidden very carefully by her press agent) was that Lucy was regarded by exhibitors as box-office poison. In March, J. R. McDonough reported to RKO's George Schaefer the results of an Audience Research Institute survey run by the Gallup Poll. The results were shocking. The conclusion was that, although Lucy had appeared in more than thirty-five pictures, 40 percent of all theatergoers said they had never seen her. She emerged with a marquee value equal to that of Maureen O'Sullivan, Maureen O'Hara, or George Murphy; in other words, she was one of the least-known players on the RKO roster in all of the United States. (Lucy's chief popularity, such as it was, lay with theatergoers under eighteen; Gallup revealed that she had recently been placed forty-fourth on a list of sixty Hollywood players. Gallup added: "It is apparent that so far as the great majority of theatergoers are concerned, Lucille Ball is still a more or less unknown quantity. . . . My personal opinion is that she is going to be grievously handicapped by her age. She is already older than sixty-five percent of the theatergoing public (exclusive of children under twelve). Our findings have shown that, as a general rule, theatergoers prefer actresses of their own age."

Only 58 percent of the audience in 1940, Gallup said, was aware that Lucille Ball was the name of an actress at all, and only 33 percent could identify her from a photograph. It was clear, the report added, that however well known she may be in Hollywood and among exhibitors, she needed "more pictures and more build-up" before the theatergoing public became completely aware of her. "Unfortunately the special procedure employed in our Dark Horse study does not reveal any marked symptoms of promise on her part. Perhaps the most encouraging feature of audience reactions . . . is the prevalence of comments to the effect that she is common, cheap, a hussy, vulgar, coarse . . . or cute, a sweet dish, nice shape, sex appeal, just a blonde, and a homebreaker."

The report said, "Such early comments are surely a more healthy sign . . . than the comments we get on certain other personalities to the effect they are great actresses but high-class and high-hat." None of this was calculated to appease Lucy's temper at the time. Nor was she pleased by the nonsense the studio thrust her into, beginning with *Look Who's Laughing*, which featured Edgar Bergen and Charlie McCarthy and Fibber McGee and Molly. Lucy was completely wasted in this absurdity. Feeling bored and restless, she decided that the only way to make life pleasant in her new marriage was to buy a property, not in Beverly Hills, which she could not afford in any case, but in the San Fernando Valley. At the recommendation of the comedian Jack Oakie, who knew the property, she and Desi decided to buy a pleasant house with five acres of grounds in Chatsworth, 20 miles north of Hollywood. The address was 19700 Devonshire, between Reseda and Northridge. The property consisted of a colonial ranch house, a swimming pool, orange trees, and white-painted wooden fences—a perfect place to bring up children.

The Arnazes dreamed of raising cattle and chickens, and of planting a lush vegetable garden, but they were very short of money, and they didn't have sufficient capital to pay a third down on the $14,500 price of the property, which is today worth well over $1 million. The owner, developer William Sesnon, who was looking for the publicity of well-known names to buy his ranch houses, suggested that they put down 10 percent, with ten years of repayments. After Lucy's business manager Andy Hickox and agent Arthur Lyons had been consulted, Lucy was placed on a very strict allowance on her $500 salary and her payments to her family were reluctantly cut, and when Desi agreed to make similar economies, they at last managed to find the down payment of $1,450.

It was a fine house. The kitchen enjoyed north light, with a stunning view of orange trees; the dining and living rooms had glass windows from ceiling to floor, as did the master bedroom, providing a sweeping view of mountains as far as the eye could see. Lucy was busy that summer of 1941 giving a strong feminine touch to the living room, which had motifs of roses and trimmings of emerald leaves in the wallpaper; Desi's mother and DeDe joined to help hang the organdy curtains and arrange the glazed chintz chairs. The atmosphere was cozy, comfortable, and very American. They called the house Desilu.

It was a long drive into town in those days, before modern freeways, and sometimes Lucy would get irritable at the length of time it took to get to the studio. Moreover, the summer heat (air conditioning was not common then) was intense in the San Fernando Valley; several degrees higher than the rest of Los Angeles. Lucy was constantly busy on radio, appearing mostly on "The Rudy Vallee Program." It was during that summer that at least one opportunity to improve her ailing career came along. Damon Runyon, chronicler of New York lowlife, was in Hollywood, planning a screen version of his story "Little Pinks," to star Eddie Albert and Dorothy Comingore, who had just made a splash in Orson Welles' *Citizen Kane*. The two failed to satisfy Runyon in the test, and he decided instead to cast Henry Fonda and Merle Oberon. The studio, however, was against borrowing Oberon from Goldwyn because it was felt she lacked box-office appeal. The director Irving Reis was brought in from Florida to direct the movie, now called *The Big Street*, and Lucy, who was on suspension for refusing to make a film entitled *My Favorite Spy* on loan-out to 20th Century–Fox, was put back on the payroll in place of Oberon. The picture was delayed, because a number of famous people were mentioned in the script and clearances were slow in being obtained.

In the meantime she made *Valley of the Sun*. Set in the 1860s, in Arizona, it was the story of a government agent, played by James Craig, who pretends to be an Indian scout; he poses as an exploiter of the Indians. In reality he is a government agent trying to help them. Lucy is a restaurant owner who is responsible for aiding him in his pursuit of decency in a small town. It was a mistaken effort from the beginning. Unlike *The Big Street*, the movie did not have a good script, and the difficulties of shooting on location in Taos, New Mexico, in that September of 1941 were considerable. The La Fonda Hotel in Taos was pretty, but not air-conditioned, and the heat was intense. Production was delayed when James Craig sprained his left knee, and delayed again when an extra was electrocuted by a cable. Desi's presence was helpful, but even so, working in the desert, with the wind blowing fine silt that irritated Lucy's sinuses and made her eyes water, was a maddening ordeal. Then came heavy, drenching rain, from September 25 until October 3, turning the ground to mud; Lucy and Desi wished they were somewhere else. The director, George Marshall, who had had a great success with *Destry Rides Again*, told me years later that Lucy greatly disliked the script; and when the entire production was shifted to Santa Fe, it proved to be nothing but a major headache. The colorful Indian summer camp south of Taos provided visual relief: some five hundred Indian men, women, and children lived in age-old tepees and one hundred specially constructed willow wickiups were built for the production. The company saw cattle drives on ranches, and covered wagons rolling across the plains, but all this was of strictly limited interest to Lucy. The rain went on and on.

Making cracks about the ineptitude of the title *Valley of the Sun*, Lucy and Desi returned to Hollywood. Desi's career had been bumping along very modestly at the studio. He had made a worthless picture called *Four Jacks and a Jill*, in which he played a dual role as a prince and a taxi driver, an impossible rip-off of 1930s comedies about the rich flirting with the poor;

and he walked through a movie called *Father Takes a Wife*, also making no impression, though his rendition of the famous song "Perfidia" attracted attention.

Desi very much liked Lucy's grandpa Fred C. Hunt, who, though in failing health, still liked to putter around at his carpentry projects in his workshop at Ogden Drive. Fred never stopped telling housemaids that they were victims of capitalism (thus driving them headlong from the house), and haranguing everybody who delivered a newspaper or a milk bottle by listing the evils being done to the underdog. Like a child, he was granted $5 a week pocket money by DeDe, which he usually gave to Sunset Boulevard prostitutes, telling them to take the night off. But eccentric though he was, he proved helpful in building chicken coops, fences, and other things from wood at Desilu. And though his constant flow of semi-Communist talk struck Desi and Lucy as harmlessly amusing, there was a more serious side to it. Lucy's brother Fred suffered from his unwitting association with communism when he went to work for Vega Aircraft on the night shift, and was dismissed without warning. When he asked why he was being discharged, he was told that he was not a good citizen. He decided that his political registration must be the reason. He obtained letters of character and affidavits to try to get his job back, but in vain; the Communist stigma was too strong. Finally, unable to get any employment in Los Angeles, he went to Wichita, Kansas, where he found work in a machine shop. He worked at Beechcraft for some months there, and later at the G and A Tool Company and Swallow Airplane Company. When called up for service around the time of Pearl Harbor, he ran into further trouble, and was deferred again and again.

Fred Hunt, Sr.'s, eccentricity outran itself when he managed to whip up a brief studio strike. He was becoming increasingly embarrassing and senile, but the Ball family ranks closed around him.

Another problem was that after Lucy had turned down several parts at other studios to avoid being separated from

Desi, of whom she was still as possessive as he was of her, there were indications that Desi would be released from his contract at any minute and would have to go on the road with his band in order to make a living. This was ominous. And not only that; Lucy knew that she was only an inch away from her own dismissal by RKO. Her pictures simply weren't making money, and the studio could no longer hang on to her. A new executive, Charles Koerner, who did not admire Lucy, had taken over from George Schaefer, who had driven the studio close to bankruptcy through his policy of making artistic pictures, including *Citizen Kane* and *The Magnificent Ambersons*. Koerner dared not risk continuing to employ anyone who was not definitely box-office, and he was fretful over Lucy's salary, which was now $1,500 a week due to the extreme pressure exercised by her agents. It was clear she would soon have to go. But she would still make *The Big Street*, and one other picture.

• CHAPTER 6 •

$\mathcal{T}$he Arnazes' marriage was close to coming apart after only a few months. Although the couple was very much in love, the separations were proving near-fatal, and even the telephone conversations they cherished, enriching Ma Bell to the tune of thousands, often disintegrated into unseemly squabbles. Desi, with his Latin sense of pride, was driven almost mad when he was addressed in various places as Mr. Ball. (Lucy called him Mr. *Bell*.) His replies were often bitter and hostile.

He took off to Mexico on a State Department tour as part of the Good Neighbor Policy designed to cement North and South America just shortly before Pearl Harbor. On the trip with him were Mickey Rooney, Norma Shearer, Robert Taylor, and Clark Gable, among others. In their three days in Mexico City, the team of stars was a sensation. However, it was at a time when there was considerable Nazi penetration of Mexico City, and there were some demonstrations against the stars.

Lucy flew to New York in December 1941, to be with Desi for a brief period at an apartment a friend had lent them. They were there on Sunday, December 7, when they woke up to the news that the Japanese had bombed Pearl Harbor. Lucy was convinced that the attack would be followed by an invasion of California, and she and Desi rushed back to be with their families. Needless to say, Fred Hunt was delighted by the news, particularly when Hitler declared war on the United States four days later. Fred had been driving everyone crazy by going around saying that Hitler's invasion of the Soviet Union the previous June deserved a proper response from America. All efforts to quiet him had proved futile.

When Cuba declared war on Japan, a week after the attack on Hawaii, Desi, who was a resident alien, was eligible for the draft in one of the United States' domestic services. Instead, he decided to enlist in the Navy. He discovered, however, that due to a technicality, he could not volunteer for service in the Navy, but could only be drafted. His friend and Lucy's, Captain Jackson Tate, an aircraft-carrier commander, did his best to push the matter through the Department of the Navy, but Desi was still not allowed to volunteer. He completed a bad picture to work off his RKO contract, ironically entitled *The Navy Comes Through*. After that, he was finished at RKO.

In the spring and summer of 1942, Lucy at last made *The Big Street*. Lucy was Gloria, a petulant and difficult social butterfly, out for a buck on Broadway, obsessed with money and possessed of the thought that the only reward for true love was "a one-room apartment, two chins and three kids." Gloria decides love is not for her, but her feisty nature gets the better of her when she informs her nightclub-owner boyfriend she is leaving him. He strikes her; she falls down a flight of stairs and becomes a cripple.

With an artful combination of laughter and tears, shrewdness and sentimentality, Runyon pressed the story forward. He showed how, in her plight, Gloria discovered her true friends and was aided by the devotion of Little Pinks, played by Henry Fonda, a much-scorned busboy described by Gloria as "a little weasel." Though the film was occasionally farfetched, not least when the busboy pushes the crippled golddigger in her wheelchair from New York to Florida to show his true love, it succeeded because of Lucy's daringly frank playing of a bitch. Her harsher side, evident to husband and friends, was courageously revealed in her performance, which was played with a jagged edge.

Lucy still regards *The Big Street* as one of her best films. She would always be grateful to her friend Carole Lombard, who had introduced her to Damon Runyon. Clearly, Runyon saw the grating harshness in her nature under the brutal but witty charm.

She was tense and ill at ease about playing opposite Henry Fonda, and knew that she stood in danger of being upstaged by him. She was afraid of the cruelty of the character she was playing, and approached, quite nervously, Charles Laughton, who was starring at the studio at the time; he agreed that he would read the script and give her advice. He read it immediately, then called her at home and asked her to drive from Northridge to Pacific Palisades, where he then lived with his wife Elsa Lanchester. Miss Lanchester recalled years later Lucy arriving, wide-eyed and red-haired, almost hyperventilating with tension, as Charles tried to relax her as much as possible. He told her it was an excellent script and a superb opportunity for her to act, and she replied, "But my part is so bitchy. It's so crude." And Laughton said, "My advice to you is play it. This woman is the bitchiest bitch that ever was. Don't soften it. Play it truthfully." She agreed, and the result was her best screen performance.

Lucy completed her RKO contract with *Seven Days' Leave*, in which she co-starred with Victor Mature, who was an amusing and easygoing companion during the shooting. The story was the old chestnut about an Army draftee who will receive a hundred thousand dollars if he weds a society heiress, played by Lucy, by the end of a seven-day furlough. Lucy acted with awkwardness and exaggeration and finished the picture in a bad temper, aggravated by the fact that she was not at all happy with the circumstances of her brand-new marriage. In the fan magazines, she and Desi were a cheerfully extroverted pair, cleaning out chicken coops, planting and raising vegetables, and leaning on the white garden fence of the ranch as they posed for pictures. But with both their careers in bad shape, Desi had to keep going out on the road with his band, and in the late summer of 1942 he took off to New York for an assignment at the Rumba Casino, where he played to reasonably good audiences while Lucy fretted irritably at the farm, barely consoled by her anxious family. Her brother Fred was equally depressed. After struggling through one awkward situation after another, dogged by his "Communist" past, he tried to finance a skating rink, but this fell through, carrying with it most of Lucy's savings and his own.

In the spring of 1943, Desi and Lucy were separated again. He toured for the Army and Navy Relief Fund, designed to raise money for families of soldiers who had died overseas. The tour became known as the Hollywood Victory Caravan, and included such stars as Claudette Colbert, Cary Grant, Olivia De Havilland, Merle Oberon, and Bing Crosby. The team was received by Mrs. Roosevelt at the White House; it opened with great success at the Capital Theater that night. Lucy fretted constantly that she was not asked to go on the tour with Desi. The reasons why she was not remain obscure and incomprehensible.

However, she had a consolation prize: MGM was determined that she should make a film version of the successful stage show *Du Barry Was a Lady*, by Cole Porter, which had starred Bert Lahr and Ethel Merman on Broadway. At first, Lucy was hesitant, knowing that she couldn't sing or dance; she had hated the vocal and physical matching necessary when she did musical scenes in her RKO films. Up to now, those scenes had only been minimal (except in *Dance, Girl, Dance*, in which she had at least managed a successful striptease), but after Ethel Merman's sensational performance on Broadway, how could she possibly follow in her footsteps?

It was explained to her by Charles Koerner, president of RKO, who was selling her contract, that she would be rehearsed and prepared by the best—by Robert Alton, the musical director, and by Charles Walters, a most able dance director. She would have weeks in which to prepare her part; MGM's lavish operation was a far cry from RKO's meager budgets and rushed, pressured schedules. With her strange streak of diffidence and unease about herself, Lucy still held back, but at last she gave in, taking with reluctance an opportunity that most performers would have given years of their lives for.

Du Barry Was a Lady underwent radical cleaning up from the extremely risqué, bawdy stage presentation. The star, Red Skelton, a hypersensitive, finely tuned man with a broad style and a tendency to mug, proved considerate and thoughtful to Lucy, but the two did not have a deep rapport. He played a hat-check clerk who wins a $150,000 lottery; she played a singer in the same club. When Skelton takes a Mickey Finn, he has a dream in which he becomes King Louis XV, lecherously pursuing Lucy, who wears high, powdered wigs and hoopskirts as Madame Du Barry. The excessively heavy, dire humor of the show and the endless rubbernecking and grimacing of Skelton were a trial; Zero Mostel, the great comedian, was wasted in the part of the nightclub fortune-teller. Nevertheless, given the mood of the times, with everyone desperate for escapism, the picture was expected to be a major success, and Lucy, going glumly through her paces while fretting over the difficult period clothes and the heavy wigs under the hot Technicolor lights, gritted her teeth and reminded herself that MGM was a step up in class.

One scene in particular irritated her. She and Skelton had to jump up and down on an enormous Louis XV period bed. She had to rehearse for hours with a coach, jumping up and down on a trampoline; the bed would later be arranged with special springs. But the constant bouncing made her legs hurt unbearably and caused her nausea. Also, throughout the shooting, she was feeling miserable about Desi's prolonged absence and worrying that he might be having affairs with other women. It was, as always, very tiresome for her to have to mouth exaggeratedly while someone else's voice was matched to her lip movements in the songs. She managed to sustain her spirits more or less by playing poker with her cronies, driving a flashy red convertible, sporting a garish new hair color, and trying on larger and larger false eyelashes.

The studio executives liked Lucy's performance in *Du Barry Was a Lady*, and Louis B. Mayer personally conveyed his approval to her. She suggested he sign Desi to a contract. Mayer went backstage when Desi was appearing in a show called *Ken Murray's Blackouts;* he asked the delighted Desi to come to see him at the studio in Culver City. At the meeting, Mayer said that Desi reminded him of his favorite racehorse, Busher. He was so virile and spirited and frisky. He complimented Desi on his performance, and then called Lana Turner into the office, asking Desi to hold her in his arms and kiss her. Desi enthusiastically obliged. After that, Mayer asked Judy Garland to come in, and Desi went eagerly through the same procedure with her. Mayer liked Desi's impassioned attack on the two women, and decided he could be a "Latin lover" in MGM pictures co-starring them. But then came a blow: He offered Desi a mere $500 a week.

Lucy was being paid over $2,000 a week for *Du Barry*. Desi told Mayer that to be receiving $500 at the same studio was humiliating. Mayer reminded him that his pictures at RKO were no good; Desi agreed, but talked Mayer into paying him $650.

Although this was not good money, and Desi was upset, Lucy was delighted. At least, now that she was embarking upon a career at the studio, she would be able to be with her husband and keep an eye on him. But then came two other blows: She suffered a miscarriage of their first child, and, without warning, Desi was sent by the USO to tour Cuba, and other Caribbean islands. The band played in the backs of trucks in many places, using headlights for spotlights, Army blankets for curtains, and soldiers in drag as chorus girls.

Meanwhile, Lucy was more lonely and depressed than

ever. Although her career was beginning to improve, she found the Chatsworth farm lonely and gloomy after the long drive from the studio at night. Her brother Fred was in Arizona; DeDe was in Hollywood and seldom visited. She tried to suppress her feelings as she began preparing for another musical, *Best Foot Forward*, to be produced by Arthur Freed; it had been a great success on the stage with Rosemary Lane. She got the part because Lana Turner was unavailable due to a pregnancy.

Best Foot Forward was an improvement on *Du Barry Was a Lady*. Crude and garish though it was, it was a lively entertainment, briskly made and full of enjoyable knockabout comedy. Lucy played a haughty, condescending star of the screen whose career is fading rapidly. When she receives an impassioned fan letter from a military-school cadet, she goes to the school as a publicity stunt, in an effort to bolster her flagging popularity. The cadet's girlfriend tries to defeat Lucy, convinced that the cadet has amorous designs on the star.

Among the supporting players were Nancy Walker and the young June Allyson, who emerged with considerable style in the movie. Miss Allyson was an odd combination of girlish charm and insecurity and steely professional toughness and ambition. Destined to be a classic goody-goody on the screen, she had a single-minded forcefulness that was to propel her briefly to the top. Although, as the critic Bosley Crowther said, she "couldn't sing worth a fig," she had ability in conveying a spunky, pushy, brassy charm particularly attractive to audiences in the 1940s.

Miss Allyson's account of her meeting with Lucille Ball in 1943, told in her memoirs published in 1982, is interesting. June says that she was about to give up her career when Lucy urged her to stay on; Lucy, she insists, reminded her of her own early struggles and her failure to be accepted by the John Murray Anderson/Robert Milton School. Miss Allyson writes, "I looked at Lucy and thought of the difference between us— how lonely and frustrated I was and how she had a full life, husband, friends, and everything, and was a star. I wanted to express this, but all I could blubber was 'Yes, but you're tall!' "

It was not until later that June Allyson discovered Lucy's own misery. She was to become a frequent guest of Lucy's at the ranch, hiding out with her new boyfriend (and later husband), the singer and actor Dick Powell. Lucy would often grumble to her about her marriage, saying of Desi, "We're not ships that pass in the night so much as cars that pass in the morning. . . . This is supposed to be married life?"

The whole last five months of 1942 and the first two of 1943 Lucy was occupied with *Du Barry Was a Lady*, and *Best Foot Forward* also took up much of the early part of 1943. It was during the last weeks of the first picture and the first weeks of the second that Desi was chosen for a war movie, *Bataan*, about an Army platoon in the Philippines that bravely defended a bridge.

MGM called Lucy to say that Desi was required immediately for *Bataan*. She tried to telephone him; he was impossible to reach through the War Department, but she finally, after many hours and at vast expense, got through to a colonel who told her that he could be found at St. Thomas, where he was due to perform at Bluebeard's Castle, a local hotel. At last, she managed to get through to the airport in St. Thomas and had him paged. When he came to the phone he was frantic and said, "Lucy, don't tell me. You're dead!"

Lucy replied, "Can't you hear me? I'm alive!"

Then he said, "Mother is dead!"

She assured him he was wrong.

"*Your* mother is dead! The house burned down!"

"Just listen—" she went on.

"You may not be dead, but if you found me here, you must be dying!" he said.

"None of those things. Get your ass back here. You're wanted to star in *Bataan!*"

Robert Taylor and George Murphy were also in the cast of that movie. Desi played a GI who dies of malaria two-thirds of the way through the movie. He got on well with the director, Tay Garnett, who had directed Lucy in *Joy of Living*. The movie was successful and earned Desi the much-prized Photoplay Award for the best performance of the month. But even though Lucy and Desi were on the set at the same time, often one was shooting at night while the other was shooting in the daytime. On weekends, they often quarreled violently, still obsessed with thoughts of the other being unfaithful. Desi had never hidden the fact that he womanized at the time.

Lucy went on to make *Thousands Cheer*, a multi-star movie vaudeville show in which she appeared in a sequence as a volunteer for the WAVES, lecherously examined by an aged Frank Morgan. Then, in May of 1943, Desi was at last called up for the draft. However, just before he was about to leave for bombardier school of the U.S. Army Air Corps he tore some cartilage in his knee during a star baseball game near Riverside, and consequently failed his physical. But so severe was the man shortage that, despite injury to the cartilage in both legs (the other from an earlier accident), he was assigned to the infantry and had to go through basic training, including push-ups and ten-mile hikes with backpacks on grueling obstacle courses. He was hazed by the other recruits because of his Hollywood background and appearance in *Bataan;* fierce-tempered, he beat up several men who insulted him and his wife, and was assigned to latrine duty in consequence. Transferred to another camp after renewed evidence of his leg problems, he became an instructor for recruits who couldn't read or write.

At last, he was able to work with Lucy on something creative: She urged her friends in Hollywood, including Mickey Rooney, Lena Horne, Lana Turner, and Tommy Dorsey, to join the camp shows free of charge, and she herself appeared whenever possible between schedules.

Once again she appeared as a star in the movie *Meet the People*, a version of a stage show that never succeeded on Broadway. The story showed her signing on with a shipyard as a riveter in order to appear democratic. It was an inconsequential picture, but she played her part brilliantly, her klutzy efforts in the shipyard amusingly foreshadowing her predicaments on "I Love Lucy."

At the beginning of 1944, the marriage was in worse shape than ever. Although Lucy had helped Desi in arranging the special camp concerts, their schedules had grown more and more separate and distancing. Desi did his best to overcome the problem by constantly applying for jobs that would give him more time with Lucy, but when he was transferred to Birmingham Hospital as a lay consultant in the San Fernando Valley psychological ward, dealing with difficult cases of men suffering from combat fatigue, the exhausting work kept him from home almost the entire week. Once again, Lucy pitched in, not only in a desire to help the hospital and Desi, but in an effort to strengthen her shaky marriage. She raised funds, along with others in Hollywood, for a swimming pool and a bowling alley for the hospital. She arranged entertainments as often as she could. But still, there were the separations, the quarrels, the differences of opinion, the meaningless jealousies. The Arnazes fought prolonged and bitter battles day and night.

One event that did bring them temporarily closer together was the death of Grandpa Fred Hunt on January 9, 1944. Grief-stricken, DeDe took his remains back to Jamestown, as he had wished. Lucy flew to Jamestown soon afterward, contacting many of her old friends, and recognized a surprisingly large number of fellow schoolgirls and playmates. Popular in Jamestown, she asked for the owners to take her yet again through the house on Eighth Street that Fred had once owned, nostalgically exploring it room by room while the owners gazed transfixed at their famous visitor. At the funeral, she wiped away the tears and stood staunchly as her grandfather's body was lowered into the grave. Asked by local reporters about her marriage, she lied bravely that everything was wonderful.

During those difficult months, gossip-mongers falsely tried

to suggest that Lucy was dating other men. Even when her male cousins escorted her to an opening, the columnists tried to imply that she was having affairs with them. So-called friends called her to say they had seen Desi with other women. When, at an elaborate costume party, Lucy was seen dancing with men, Desi yet again became jealous—more so than ever. There were stories in the press that Lucy had locked Desi out, both at her hotel suite in New York and at their ranch. She grew hoarse calling up columnists or telegramming them, insisting on retractions. Her language was often very blunt and basic as she bawled out reporters, and this treatment, considered undignified in a star, made them even more vindictive.

In September 1944, Lucy, always volatile, and now irritated beyond endurance by the stories of Desi's infidelities that were relayed to her by seemingly everyone, decided to file for divorce, charging "extreme mental cruelty," a convenient cover in those days when studios went to any lengths to conceal indications of possible adultery or other forms of misbehavior in their contracted stars. That Lucy filed on the spur of the moment is clear from the fact that she told none of her friends—any more than she had told them about her wedding. She was so anxious to be rid of Desi that she asked for no alimony whatsoever, and asked that in return "Sergeant Arnaz" would waive his right to postpone trial of the suit until after he left the service. She was due to appear in court on October 15, the delay caused by a backlog in the court calendar. She was seething the whole time, unable to concentrate on scripts she had been sent by the studio, and constantly going over in her mind the thought that, as she told Desi many years later, he must have been "screwing everybody at Birmingham Hospital." When he asked her, at that later date, to whom she was referring, she said, "The bingo girls, the milk girls, and the worst part of it was that it was me who supplied them to you." Presumably, she was referring to girls running the bingo games at the hospital and girls serving milk to sailors on compulsory alcohol-free diets.

On October 14, with the hearing in court set for the following day, Desi called up Lucy and asked her how she was feeling. She replied coldly that she was fine. She wondered what on earth he was doing placing the call at that particular moment, and bore in mind her attorney's warning that she wasn't supposed to talk to him.

Without hesitation, and with cheerful insolence, Latin charm, and sheer chutzpah, he asked her what she was doing that night. Her voice grew colder. "Nothing in particular," she said. "Have you forgotten I'm divorcing you tomorrow morning?"

He asked her again what she was planning to do that night. She said icily she had nothing special in mind. He asked her if she would like to have dinner with him. She shrugged and accepted. Thus, the well-known couple, on the verge of a much-publicized divorce, went out to dinner in Beverly Hills, causing many surprised stares as they did so. The spectators would have been still more astonished if they had known what followed. Lucy and Desi spent the night in bed! At 7:30 A.M. next day, Lucy jumped out of the sheets and announced that if she didn't leave at once she'd be too late for the court hearing. Amazed, Desi asked her why she now wanted to go through with it since they had been so pleasantly reconciled. She told him that the press was expecting her, she had bought a new outfit and a new hat, and she wanted to please the reporters! She told him she would be back in a few hours, and she was, announcing that an interlocutory decree had been granted. During the hearing, she testified: "He was spending too much money. When we argued about it, he became angry and went away. I never saw him for a week. That was a habit of his—going away whenever we had an argument. He always ran out on me rather than stay and talk the matter out. I got no rest at night at all." The brief hearing cost Lucy $2,000. She drove back to the apartment and spent the rest of the afternoon and night in bed with Desi. The couple then announced that the divorce was invalid because if the couple cohabited during the one-year waiting period before the final decree, the divorce had no legality. The entire comedy ended with their returning to the ranch at Northridge, where they were photographed feeding the chickens and taking care of a large, grumpy pig with the distinguished title "Duchess of Devonshire." The Duchess weighed 2,200 pounds and would appear at their bedroom window in the middle of the night, giving out alarmingly loud grunts. Lucy would wake up irritably and say, according to Desi Arnaz's memoirs, "There's your girlfriend trying to get into the bedroom!"

Every effort made to persuade them to sell the Duchess to a slaughterhouse failed, since there was no way they were going to turn her beautiful blubber into pork. Indeed, when she became too difficult to handle, they boarded her at another ranch and paid for her food and lodging. They adored her till the day of her death. She would look at Desi with large, lovelorn eyes, and a huge red tongue would come out and lick him slowly but surely until Lucy would scream with mock jealousy.

The arguments continued at the farm. On more than one occasion, Desi was found sleeping in hotel lobbies because he had arrived too late to get a room after Lucy had locked him out. And her career was not much better than her marriage. Indeed, so short-lived was her starring career at MGM that she was lucky if she could get an interview in *Popular Mechanics*. In fact, when she went to the zoo in Los Angeles, a press agent had to work overtime to interest anyone in photographing her feeding the sea lions.

She was even reduced to supporting actress in a film called *Without Love*, which exactly described her feelings for the script. This was a picture with Spencer Tracy and Katharine Hepburn in which she spent most of her time walking on and off with actor Keenan Wynn, making smart remarks with wide eyes and a straight back, in very well-tailored costumes, while everyone was looking at the two stars. Then came a further humiliation: She was cast in a musical, Vincente Minnelli's *The Ziegfeld Follies* of 1946, in which everybody except Lucy could sing and dance. She was given a long whip and told to stand by a gilded cage and crack the whip over eight chorus girls dressed as panthers.

An incident during the production illustrated her character. A reporter arrived on the set between shots and began questioning her. He was of the old school, with a slouch hat and a cigar, and he addressed all of his questions to her bosom. She got so tired of him not looking at her face as he asked her questions that she suddenly reached down into her bodice and pulled out two falsies, which she had worn as a gag, waving them in his face and suggesting that he take them home as a souvenir. He fled. After years of being deadly serious, a butt of humor and consumed with jealousy, Lucy at thirty-five was beginning to become a touch more sophisticated and mature. She had started to develop the dry humor that typified her later in the "Lucy" series. On one occasion, irritated by the dance director, she turned up on the set in a wheelchair with her arm in a sling, her teeth blacked out and her face covered in bruises, and announced that this was the "result of the direction she was getting." Unfortunately, the story boomeranged in the press and made her unpopular in the white sepulcher of Metro, which was ruled by sanctimonious principles and high-toned pretensions.

Lucy enjoyed inventing gadgets and gags. Along with the director Edward Sedgwick and Buster Keaton, she built a nutcracker the size of an auto engine. It was so complicated that those who put nuts in it were lucky not to lose a finger. Her favorite invention was a device known as a venetian-blind raiser. The contraption would respond to the press of a button when it was desired to raise a blind. As the blind went up, there was a small explosion and a record player ground out "Hail to the Chief," followed by a large picture of Louis B. Mayer, which popped up from the contrivance, much to the annoyance of Mayer, who humorlessly had the entire thing removed from every office in which it was installed. Lucy's reward was for her name to be put below the title in a movie entitled *Easy to Wed*, starring Esther Williams (of whom it was said, "Wet she was a star") and the freckle-faced Van Johnson.

When Desi was discharged from the Army at the end of the war, he too suffered a humiliation; he wasn't cast in the Esther Williams picture. He owed $30,000, mostly to the Internal Revenue Service, and realized that he had no future at MGM. He sought his release, and approached two people he knew, Milton Krasny, head of General Artists Corporation, and the genial Herman Hover, owner of Ciro's nightclub on Sunset Boulevard, to whom he suggested that he form a new band at the club.

Hover, still alive in 1986, though long since retired from the nightclub business, says that Desi was greatly mistreated and misunderstood in Hollywood, and that he knew he would be a sensation at the club. Hover decided to reopen Ciro's with Desi in charge of the rumba band, and everyone in black tie, Lucy, DeDe, and others in the family turned up to celebrate; Lucy gruelingly worked overtime to ensure that everybody who was anybody came to the show. Whatever her feelings of ill temper, whatever her jealousies, she was still in love with Desi, and wanted to help him as much as she could. It was as humiliating for her as it was for him to see the miserable way in which his career had shriveled up at Metro.

The opening was a great success and the crowds were tremendously enthusiastic. Larry Storch, recently out of the Navy, made an impact as one of the vocalists, and so did the duo Dulcina and Amanda Lane.

But still the arguments went on. Desi said later, "Every time we quarreled, I'd throw my clothes in a suitcase and move into a hotel room. The first thing I'd do was to send my clothes out to the cleaners, but by the time they returned Lucy and I would be made up again." So costly were the hotel bills that Lucy and Desi agreed they would construct a guest house behind the ranch, where Desi could go when they had differences of opinion. It was rather like a doghouse, and sometimes Desi's face would be seen glumly staring out of the "kennel" window. He reminded Lucy's mother DeDe (she told a reporter once) of "a spaniel in the rain."

Lucy made a picture on loan-out from 20th Century–Fox entitled *The Dark Corner*. It was a thriller in the mode of *Laura*, a story of crime in high places, with brittle, sophisticated dialogue that hasn't worn well. ("The grass looks tired. As though it has been left out all night.") The movie starred Clifton Webb and Mark Stevens. Lucy played a secretary, without much enthusiasm.

The director was the rough, tough veteran Henry Hathaway, a good journeyman with a no-nonsense attitude to picture-making who expected his cast to behave professionally at all times. Hathaway said years later, "Miss Ball was a friend of Freddie Kohlmar, the picture's producer, and I think that's how she got the job. One morning, she came onto the set late. I had a tracking shot to do, and I needed to do a run-through for timing purposes. I was shocked to see she had the script with her when she was supposed to have memorized her lines.

"I said to her, 'What the hell is that?' And she said, 'I'm not quite sure about the scene.' I told her to at least try to give a reading. And then I found out she didn't even know the lines to start with. She hadn't even bothered to look at the script at all.

"So I said, 'What the hell kind of an actress are you? When you start work in the morning, I expect you to know the fucking scene and what you're going to do. And you're late anyway, for chrissake. Go back in the fucking dressing room, because you're no good to me until you know the scene. We'll sit here and wait for you and when you're ready come out and we'll get started. I can't time it with you standing there reading from the script.' I was mad as hell.

"She looked at me funny and went back in the dressing room, while we all sat there for a whole hour waiting. Finally, she at last came out and we started the run-through. She blew her lines twice. I told her to go back and learn them.

"There was a big ruckus. She went straight up to Freddie

Kohlmar and complained. He came down on the set and I said, 'I don't want to work with people who don't know their lines. I have no patience with them, and I think they're wrong, and you talked me into using her in the goddamned first place. Now I know you used to go with her. You got her the part as a favor to her, but she's going to know her fucking lines or you can take me off the picture. I don't work with people like that.' "

Years later, in 1982, Hathaway ran into Lucy again. "We were at a little place called Skippy's, and she and her husband and a whole bunch of people were having a party. She called out 'Hello.' About fifteen minutes later I felt a hand come around my neck and a head leaned in. And I looked up. It was Lucy, and she said, 'You know, I was a real shit to you. I learned a lot because I expected people who worked for me later to do the same goddamned thing that I wasn't doing. Like I said, I was a real shit, and I'm sorry.' "

Lucy began work on a picture called *Two Smart People*, in which she played a crook involved with a con man, played by John Hodiak. At the same time, Desi was making a picture entitled *Cuban Pete*. Very often, the separations of the couple were so extended that they became virtually strangers. Desi recorded in his memoirs that they would meet at the top of Coldwater Canyon as she was driving from the ranch to Culver City to make her movie at about 5:00 A.M., while he, either filming at night or appearing at Ciro's until 4:00 A.M., was driving past her in the opposite direction. They even made an arrangement whereby they would meet at the top of the canyon at 5:30 each morning, kiss like a couple of teenagers, and exchange reports on the day's or night's work. On other occasions, they would meet at 7:00 at night, also at the same trysting place.

Lucy grew weary of MGM, and MGM grew weary of her. A young producer she liked very much, S. Sylvan Simon, who was at Columbia Pictures, offered her a chance to return to that studio, and MGM was glad to see her go. But before she signed the Columbia contract, she had to appear in two other pictures on loan-out. One of these was *Lover Come Back*, made at Universal, and the other was *Lured*, in which she appeared as an American dancer in London, acting as a decoy for a murderer in foggy, gloomy streets. It was her best picture in some time, but did little for her career. The only compensation was that she earned $75,000 making it. Desi was extremely jealous of George Brent, a famous lady-killer, who appeared with her in *Lover Come Back*, and of George Sanders, another polished seducer, her co-star in *Lured*. He was also jealous of Franchot Tone, the handsome leading man in her first Columbia Picture, *Her Husband's Affairs*, a sharp, intelligent man who had once been married to Joan Crawford. Lucy insisted her interest in these male stars was purely professional. All available evidence shows that she was probably right. Columnist Hedda Hopper wrote in her column, "About once every six months someone notifies me that Lucy and Desi Arnaz are separating. I've learned to doubt the reports, but dutifully check with the personalities involved. Both Lucy and Desi get on the phone; and we have a long, amiable conversation. Doubtless they have their spats, as which couple doesn't. Besides, Lucille is Irish [sic] and Desi is Latin—a combination that occasionally makes for some spectacular fireworks; but it's nothing serious." Her rival, Louella Parsons, noted that Lucy wore a bracelet with the inscription: "My name is Lucille Ball Arnaz. If lost, return me to my master—Desi."

Perhaps in desperation, Lucy, who had always enjoyed her forays into radio, began appearing in a series on CBS, "My Favorite Husband," with Richard Denning. She played a klutzy, slightly crazed housewife who was constantly getting tangled up in kitchenware, dropping pancakes or blintzes on the floor, upsetting the coffee, or losing crucial ingredients to recipes. She played the part with a busy, extravagant speed and freedom far removed from her deadpan screen personality.

The idea for the series came from CBS vice president Harry Ackerman. He had been flying from New York to Los Angeles, and in an effort to relieve the tedium of the journey, had passed the time by reading a comic novel, *Mr. and Mrs. Cugat*. "It was a funny look at marriage between two wildly different types," recalls Ackerman, now an independent producer. Richard Denning was cast as Lucy's all-American spouse, the upright, downright vice president of a bank married to a madcap woman whose capers kept them both in amusingly tepid, if not quite hot, water. Ackerman, who directed the first few shows himself, says, "Lucy was dreadful without an audience, so we had to bring a dress rehearsal audience in to help her with her timing. She absolutely bloomed in front of an audience. She's one of the world's great clowns."

Sometimes the writers Jess Oppenheimer, Bob Carroll, Jr., and Madelyn Pugh, stayed up all night writing a script. Oppenheimer says, "Lucy loved the rewrite until she got to the very last line. Then she said, 'That's no good. I won't say this shit.' Then she threw the script across the room. I walked up to her, put out my hand, and said, 'Good-bye, Miss Ball, I can't say it's been nice working with you.' She started crying and begged me to come back. So I had to give her a good talking to about appreciating how hard people worked for her. And I said I'd come back if she'd apologize to Bob and Madelyn. She did, and we never had a problem after that. She was a terrific sport, always admitted when she was wrong. I grew to respect her."

Oppenheimer mentioned the difficulties Lucy had in the early days of *My Favorite Husband*. He says, "She stuck behind the script. She didn't fully trust her instincts as a clown. I tried to encourage her to ham it up more, to allow a pause for the laughs I was sure she could get. Finally, I told her I was sending her to school one Sunday. I got her a pass to the taping of "The Jack Benny Show." Benny was the master of the silent reaction, which he would hold sometimes for twenty seconds *on radio*. And it worked. Lucy went and saw him, and she told me the next day, 'I never realized what you can do with just a script and a microphone.' From then on, she became much more free, much more daring."

Radio released her. Whereas the movie camera, for all her adeptness, often fazed her, and she frequently had run-ins with the crew and other members of the cast and her directors because of her camera-consciousness, she was totally at ease in the aural medium. In fact, she loved it, and Richard Denning could not have been a more charming co-star. He was relaxed, very professional, good-natured, and easy to work with, an ideal foil for Lucy. The show was fun, and the only thing wrong with it was that Lucy would undoubtedly have preferred that Desi play her husband in it. But he was not thought of as a radio actor; he was Cuban, and racism predominated in the media. Lucy was also too sensitive even to consider pushing Richard Denning out of the show. During a break in the broadcasts, after piling up many episodes, she took off in yet another direction. She decided to return to the stage. Anything would be better than making one dreary movie after another.

She was sent the play *Dream Girl*, by Elmer Rice, a very entertaining romantic comedy about a girl caught up in fanciful daydreams. The screen version was played by Betty Hutton. Lucy was extremely nervous about facing live audiences once more, always a strain for screen personalities, whether or not they had previous stage experience. However, she wanted very badly to have personal contact with her public, and part of her longed for the cut and thrust of stage performance.

However, Lucy was distracted during rehearsals because of an episode that forced her into a lawsuit against the Radio Corporation of America. She had recorded a tongue-twister, in falsetto, entitled "Peter Piper Picked a Peck of Pickled Peppers" as a background for Desi's record "Carnival in Rio." The arrangement was that her identity would not be disclosed, and when RCA made publicity out of the gag, she was very upset. The case was settled out of court.

While in New York, on the verge of the *Dream Girl* tour, Lucy appeared as grand marshal in a torchlight parade that started a fund drive by three thousand women for the new medical center of the New York Infirmary Building Fund.

Though it was pouring rain, Lucy sat in an open carriage for three hours, holding an umbrella and smiling gamely in the light of six hundred torches as the procession of thirty-five floats moved down Fifth Avenue in a blaze of rain-swept lights.

One of her reasons for going to New York at the time and agreeing to rehearse there was that Desi was in town, playing the Copacabana. She was fiercely jealous of the beautiful Copa girls; Desi wrote in his memoirs, "I would (again) protest that I never fooled around with people I was working with. To which she would answer, 'Ha!' But it was true, most of the time, anyway." Which was another way of saying that it was false only part of the time.

Lucy toured in *Dream Girl* through every kind of weather and location for twenty-two weeks, while Desi continued his orchestra tours. Once again, they were forced to talk constantly on the telephone from various places.

There were some nerve-racking experiences on Desi's tour. On the flight from Omaha to Los Angeles on an old prop plane, a DC3 transport with bucket seats, the pilot lost an engine; somehow he managed to fly as far as Los Angeles, when he asked Desi where the city was. As calmly as he could, Desi suggested the pilot contact the control tower at Los Angeles International Airport. The air-traffic controller was astonished when the pilot said he had no idea where Los Angeles was, and asked him who was on board. He replied, "Desi Arnaz and his band." By the time the plane finally got in, everybody on board was in a high state of nervous tension. Lucy was frantic when she found out, burning up the wires hysterically, until at last Desi managed to calm her.

The band appeared with Bob Hope on his radio show in many cities, moving on to play at the Palace Hotel in San Francisco for three months. It was there that Desi featured a singer, Carole Richards, whom he very much admired and who was extremely attractive and talented. Lucy was jealous, especially since her brother Fred was now managing the tour for Desi, and she accused Fred of betraying her by arranging the introduction. She flew in from one of her tour locations to join Desi at the Palace Hotel, and from beginning to end that weekend was a hell of mutual recriminations. He, in turn, would become overwrought when he saw pictures of her in the paper with her cousin Cleo's husband, Ken Morgan. Desi would return home during breaks in the tour to scream at her, and she would fight with him, accusing him of making out with girls on the road. Again he would throw his clothes into a suitcase and move out, but so swift were the reunions that, again, when he would send his clothes to the cleaners, before they were returned he was back in the house.

Lucy's *Dream Girl* tour was something of an ordeal for her. It was physically exhausting, done in one-night stands, often in second-rate theaters in remote places. In Seattle, the cast was stricken with a mysterious virus, forcing the production to close for Christmas 1947. In a typical example of impulsive generosity, Lucy, aware that the production might shut down and the producer might run out of money, paid for the hospital bills and even the wages of the stricken cast; perhaps her other motive was that she was determined to get everybody to the Biltmore Theater in Los Angeles, so that she could perform in her adopted city and show the producers who had wasted her in tedious roles a thing or two. Unfortunately, by the time she reached Southern California, she was suffering from the virus herself, and it was only her willpower that managed to get her through the opening-night performance at the Biltmore on January 5, 1948. The review by the *Los Angeles Times'* Edwin Schallert was favorable, buoying her up tremendously. Schallert wrote:

> Here is a young lady of the films who could, if she would, have a dazzling footlight career. And what is more—though this may be a brash statement to make—she is, in a sense, wasting her talents in pictures. . . . Miss Ball is a striking presence in the foot-

light world. She has efficiency as a comedienne. She
can tinge a scene delicately with pathos. She has
special facility in dealing with sharp-edged repartee.
She apparently never overdoes the sentimental side
of a role . . .

While noting that at times her performance was too broad
and lacking in finesse, Schallert continued, "Definitely, this is
a minor criticism of a very interesting performance given by
the star in a show that has many delightful compensations."
He remarked that Lucy was especially adept in the dream sequences, and he praised her for her curtain speech. However,
she collapsed with exhaustion the following night, and her
repeated absences shortened the run. She was troubled also by
a lawsuit that plagued the Ball family. Her cousin Cleo was
seeking to obtain guardianship of a sixteen-month-old child,
Dennis Schroeder, who had been placed by his parents in
Cleo's care when they arrived from Kansas and had been unable to find a suitable home. They claimed that Cleo and her
husband refused to return the child. The case dragged on until
finally the child was returned to his parents.

Lucy said of the *Dream Girl* run, "I thought I would die and
was wishing I would. I was delirious during one whole matinee. I didn't know I was in the hospital. I went back, but we'd
lost a week then. All the people around town that we wanted
to see the show came, but I wasn't there. We could have run
for weeks, but the show closed shortly after I got back." Many
people canceled their tickets because they didn't believe Lucy
would return to the show, and when she did, it was far too
late.

There were other irritating matters. A thief broke into
Desi's car and stole a gold lapel pin bought as an anniversary
gift for Lucy, set with nine rubies and formed in the shape of a
key, with the words "Nursery Key" on the back. The couple
still did not have a child, and when asked about it, Lucy would
say, "How do you conceive on the telephone?"

Near Rolling Prairie, Indiana, on a journey between Madison, Wisconsin, and Akron, Ohio, the Arnaz Band tour bus collided with a truck in a head-on collision. Several members of the band were injured, including trumpet player Bobby Jones, violinist Charlie Harris, and saxophonist Joe Miller. The driver allegedly had fallen asleep while driving at 85 miles per hour. The band barely escaped with their lives. Desi and the other performers were trapped as the bus burst into flames; it was only through the quick action of the truck driver that they were released—the driver had to use a hatchet to cut open a hole through which they could escape.

Despite Lucy's brief appearance in *Dream Girl* in Los Angeles, Schallert's review did not go unnoticed. Indeed, Paramount, no doubt prodded by Bob Hope, who had always admired her, offered Lucy the leading role opposite him in George Marshall's movie *Sorrowful Jones*, based on a Damon Runyon story originally filmed as *Little Miss Marker*. The teamwork of these two comedians was exciting to watch, and the producer Melville Shavelson still recalls the pleasure he had in seeing them strike sparks off each other on the set. Lucy played a nightclub singer, dubbed by Annette Warren. She acted the part of the sharp-tongued show-business dame to the hilt; she had grown considerably in technique, and unquestionably Bob Hope's effortless skill made her realize she would have to pull out every stop to hold the audience's attention. He, too, was well aware of Lucy's adroitness. She had the talent of seeming to be doing nothing, just standing there, with her back very straight, her eyes very wide, staring, delivering lines with a rasping edge; but her timing was like clockwork, precisely geared to the demands of a sequence. The picture was a hit, earning twice as much money as any other Bob Hope movie at the time, and the fact that this was ascribed in part to Lucy was very encouraging to her and helped revitalize her fading film career. The reviews were favorable. *Newsweek* wrote of her performance, "Lucille Ball, who has played a Runyon doll before (*The Big Street*, 1942), makes as delightful a one as any guy could hope to find between Times Square and Lindy's.'' Reviews like this were compensation for a major mistake Lucy had just made. She had turned down the chance to do the screen version of *Born Yesterday*, which had made a huge star of Judy Holliday on Broadway, in order to appear with Hope. *Time* and *Life* enthusiastically agreed about her appearance in *Sorrowful Jones*.

Lucy went back to RKO to make another picture, *Easy Living*, but it was an inauspicious return; she had little opportunity to shine in the part of a dumb secretary in love with a pro football star played by Victor Mature. In 1949, Desi, back from his long tours, decided to ask Lucy, perhaps in a desperate effort to secure their marriage for the future, if she would agree to a second wedding in the Catholic faith, and, always romantic despite her grave doubts about Desi and the constant misery of her separations from him, Lucy spontaneously agreed. She was very excited when, on June 19, in a church not far from their ranch, Our Lady of the Valley, Father Michael Hurley performed the nuptials. Lucy at last got the opportunity to wear a wedding dress and hat, and this time her mother, brother, cousin, and other family members turned up. The director Ed Sedgwick gave the bride away, and Captain Ken Morgan, husband of Cleo, was best man. Desi's high-spirited mother was matron of honor.

·   CHAPTER   7   ·

*O*n December 8, 1949, Lucy made her television debut on the program "Inside U.S.A. with Chevrolet," scheduled for the *Los Angeles Times* CBS television station, KTTV. She appeared as a dance hostess in a skit written specially for the show, opposite Peter Lind Hayes, who played a Western millionaire. The show was well received, and it gave her the germ of an idea. She had grown weary of the endless second-rate movies she had made, and her constant cheerful chatter and hard-boiled line of repartee disguised with increasing thinness her impatient nature and irritation with everything and everyone around her. She had become so nervous that she couldn't sit still for a hairdresser, and so she had a room built on the farm with permanent-wave equipment, in which she did her own hair and fingernails.

To her friends, who included the Czech actor Francis Lederer and his wife Marion, Eve Arden, Rory and Lita Calhoun, Farley Granger, Bob Crosby, and Priscilla Lane and her husband Joe Howard, she would complain that she had decided she could scarcely endure much more making of feature movies. Her nerves were fraying badly over Desi. She began studying Shakespeare, took up Spanish, painted in oils, specializing in snow scenes, bought clothes but seldom wore them, switched her brands of perfume by the week, and found one of her few consolations in life in her favorite dish, hamburger with raw onion. She was still humorously arguing with Desi over the temperature of their bedroom; he still liked it very hot, and she wanted the window open, even on winter nights, because she was claustrophobic and hated heat.

Columbia treated her as poorly as all the other studios. She was reduced to making a meaningless cameo appearance in a film starring Rosalind Russell, *A Woman of Distinction*. Somewhat better was the comedy *Fancy Pants*, made at Paramount, a reworking of the famous film with Charles Laughton, *Ruggles of Red Gap*, with Bob Hope as the British butler in the sticks. In this new version, Hope was a ham actor forced to pose as a super-correct manservant when he is hired by mistake by a wealthy, crude, nouveau-riche family in New Mexico. Lucy played the heiress to the family fortune who falls in love with the klutzy butler, thereby jilting fortune-hunter Bruce Cabot. During the shooting a horse stepped on her foot and Bruce Cabot, with his cowboy boot, stepped on the other one. She was in the hands of doctors for months.

An unsettling incident took place during the film when Lucy was teaching Bob Hope to ride a mechanical horse. Bob Hope said later, "The thing was seven feet off the floor, and George Marshall wanted it to go faster and faster, for realism's sake. You've heard of runaway horses. This mechanical beast got its AC and DC mixed up and started galloping like a two-year-old in heat. The next thing I knew, I was spread-eagled on the cement floor. An ambulance rushed me to Hollywood Presbyterian Hospital, where X rays found nothing broken but my morale." His doctor bills came to $4,500. Hope suffered from severe back pains for some time. He had to go through months of therapy. That was the last time he ever rode a mechanical horse.

At the time, Lucy decided to test her rather grating singing voice on the stage, and she and Desi, who always yearned to appear together (if only to keep an eye on each other), worked very closely on an act. A friend of Desi's, Pepito, billed as "the Spanish Clown" in vaudeville in the old days, agreed to work out some routines with Desi for presentation on the stage. Lucy and Desi went to San Diego to the grand old Coronado Hotel, a turn-of-the-century architectural folly of great charm, and worked with Pepito around the clock, having a lot of fun with a cello and a xylophone as part of the preparation. It was "real Rube Goldberg stuff," Lucy said later. "Pepito built me this incredible cello. I pulled a stool out of it, a horn, a toilet paper plunger, gloves, flowers, and a violin bow."

Lucy experimented with a fright wig that was rather like a large dish mop. After much preparation, Bob Carroll, Jr., and Madelyn Pugh, who had been writing the radio show "My Favorite Husband" for Lucy, put the sketch together. Desi wrote some lyrics and worked out a rumba routine.

The tour was a sensation. It opened in Chicago and took in New York, Minneapolis, Omaha, and San Francisco. Lucy appeared in an ancient white tuxedo with tails, carrying the cello through the audience. Desi would come and ask plaintively, "What's going on out there?" Then she would say, "Where is Dizzy Arnazy?" in a voice like a man's. Striding onto the stage in a masculine manner, she'd ask Desi if he was Dizzy Arnazy. He'd correct her, and then say, "Look, mister, what do you want?" Lucy would say she wanted a job with the band. He would agree to give her a chance, and as she took the cello out of its case, she'd knock over the music stands, hit some of the players "accidentally," and at last search for a seat. When, aware that his whole orchestra was being thrown around, Desi would ask for her credentials, she would simply frown and fold her arms. Later, she played a trained seal using a xylophone, and during one song, she wore a 1920s whore's outfit, bawling out, "They call me Sally Sweet!"

Lucy's producer/director friend S. Sylvan Simon offered her a slight but attractive screen comedy, *The Fuller Brush Girl*, in which Lucy played a saleswoman caught up with murder and kidnapping, pursued by the cops in a reworking of the screwball comedies of the silent era. There were numerous pratfalls and hysterical chases in the Keystone Kops vein. Lucy was at her most amusing as she fled the police over a series of back fences or made herself up as a grotesque parody of Bubbles, the striptease dancer of *Dance, Girl, Dance*, when forced to conceal her identity in a theater.

Part of her performance consisted of being rolled around in a barrel. She had asked that the scene not be shot after lunch, for obvious reasons. She threw up anyway. In one scene her right eye was affected when a prop exploded and ice-cold air shot into her face, making the eye water uncontrollably. On another occasion, she had to pull the bung out of a wine barrel and be saturated in wine while she tried to plug up the barrel. Since she was supposed to be drowning in wine, she was forced to swallow some in the scene. Wine was forbidden on the set, so the prop man had prepared a horrible vegetable-colored water that tasted disgusting and made her sick. She came down with a severe cold, narrowly escaping pneumonia, after being soaked in the unpleasant substance for hours. Sundays were spent with her physicians, who pumped her full of vitamins and various medications so she could struggle gamely back to the set at 5:45 A.M. the next day. She told the columnist Darr Smith of the *Los Angeles Daily News*, "I'm going groggily through all this for a lousy fortune. You work all your life to get to a place where you're important enough so that people will invite you to vacation resorts for free. You know, you become sort of a part of the landscape. Well, when you reach that point, you can't get out of town long enough to go anywhere but Palm Springs. . . ."

She grumbled on in the same interview, "You'd think on Sunday I'd have a day of rest, wouldn't you? But no, on Sunday I'm recovering from what happened to me on Saturday." Soon after the interview, while filming, she was running a switchboard, she took out the wrong plug and a powdery substance shot into her eye and rendered her momentarily blind. When she fell as she ran across a lawn in a chase sequence, she fractured four vertebrae. Yet, relentless perfectionist that she was, she would never let go until a scene was absolutely right.

There was another problem during *The Fuller Brush Girl*. Normally, Lucy spent the weekends with Desi on a cabin cruiser, but suddenly he kept disappearing to San Francisco, and she was convinced that he was cohabiting there with a woman. Herb Sterne, publicist on the film, remembers, "We were shooting *The Fuller Brush Girl* and there was a convention of Fuller Brush VIPs, and Miss Ball was supposed to be the guest of honor. Naturally, I arranged for her to appear on time; she was supposed to be dressed to the nines.

"However, though she did dress, put on her jewels, and leave her Chatsworth home, she never showed up at the dinner. I was very upset. All of us called the house, but no Miss Ball. And the next day, when she was supposed to be on the set, she wasn't. We decided not to notify the police, because of the bad publicity it would have caused; it would have been all over the papers.

"A week went by, and still no sign of her. No explanation, nothing." Sterne and the other publicists managed to keep the press, which had gotten wind of her disappearance, at arm's distance. They said she was ill, inventing a variety of ailments to explain her peculiar behavior. Then one day, the phone rang in Sterne's office, and it was the airline at Burbank. Sterne says, "They said that she was listed as being on the next flight from San Francisco, and would we want to send a cameraman. I said no, no way. She still didn't call. She showed up the next day on the set, smiling." Sterne asked her, the first chance he got, "How was the weather in San Francisco?" She replied, coolly, "Just great!" And that was the last time the matter was mentioned.

Lucy took off again with Desi on tour and on this occasion she at last became pregnant. She made the announcement in New York, saying the baby was expected in January 1951. In Chicago, she suffered a loss of over $10,000 worth of jewelry in a theft from her hotel suite, including two rings worth $5,000, a pair of gold gypsy earrings, and a platinum mesh choker. Back in Hollywood, she had another unsettling experience. She received threatening letters from a man who had been paroled from San Quentin and was roaming around Hollywood stealing from various stars. Sometime later, she surprised him rifling her dressing room and he fled.

Also in Hollywood, Lucy began talking to Cecil B. De Mille about possibly doing the part of the elephant girl in *The Greatest Show on Earth*. She was not fazed when she read in the script that she would have to lie on the ground with the elephant's foot about half an inch from her face. Impressed with her coolness, De Mille assured her the picture would not start shooting until after her baby was born. However, once more she was stricken with bad luck. She miscarried again, perhaps because of further quarrels with Desi and the strain of the personal appearances. She was heartbroken, wondering if she would ever be able to have a child.

Lucy continued to be miserable with Harry Cohn at Columbia. He refused to give her a decent part in anything. Possibly because of her absenteeism, he had no respect for her, and at last forced her into an absurdity called *The Magic Carpet*. She begged Cohn not to push her into this nonsense, so that she could make *The Greatest Show on Earth* for Paramount, but he refused. She had no alternative but to go ahead, and at least she collected $80,000 as her part of her play-or-pay contract. (In another version of the story, she told Harry Cohn she would never accept less than $80,000 for any movie, and he said, "Okay, we'll put you on a magic carpet.") Publicist Herb Sterne recalls, "The leading man was John Agar, husband of Shirley Temple, who was almost young enough to be Lucy's son. She had no dressing room. There was a canvas dressing room on the set."

In November, Lucy found herself pregnant again. This was a mixed blessing. She would not be able to make *The Greatest Show on Earth* because of the new pregnancy, and she was not feeling well during the making of *The Magic Carpet*. In her moodiness, despite the part of her that rejoiced at the prospect of having a child at last, she spent breaks in shooting, Sterne recalls, huddling on the edge of the set, leaking stories to reporters about how Harry Cohn was mistreating her and what a son of a bitch he was. Sterne says, "So Cohn in his turn started leaking stories to the press about what a bitch Lucy was, but he was not punishing her; she wanted the eighty grand, and she was earning the eighty grand. So she started on me about leaking stories to the press, and I said, 'I am not doing this. This is the second picture I've worked on with you; I wouldn't do this to you; I like you.' 'Well, goddammit, what the fucking hell,' she said, and so forth. She just went ahead and finished the picture.

"Lucy was mercurial. She'd call you a son of a bitch one minute and come and put her arms around you and give you a kiss the next. Very volcanic—I liked her. She was straight-talking, no frills. I started working for her because she raised hell with Harry Cohn and said, 'I want that son of a bitch who works with Rita Hayworth. That Herb Sterne. I want the glamour treatment.' I did my best to give it to her."

Lucy didn't announce her pregnancy until after the picture was over. She phoned Harry Cohn from the set and said, "Harry, this is Lucille Ball, and I just want you to be the first to know that Desi and I are going to have a baby." According to Desi, Cohn answered, "Why, you bitch! Why didn't you tell me before the picture?" Later, De Mille came up to Desi and said, "Congratulations, Mr. Arnaz. You are the only man who has ever screwed his wife, Cecil B. De Mille, Paramount Pictures, and Harry Cohn, all at the same time."

Desi embarked on a radio show named "Tropical Trip," a musical quiz cooked up by Guy Della Cioppa of CBS and producer Harry Ackerman. First prize was a two-week vacation in South America. Desi was drawn to the idea of a show that would cement North and South American relations. In January 1951, with Lucy well along in her pregnancy, the show was begun. Desi used the money to add a nursery that included two bedrooms and a bathroom, and a large playroom, to the Chatsworth house.

The spring of 1951 was darkened by an unexpected tragedy. Lucy told me that her friend S. Sylvan Simon, who was forty-one years old, committed suicide for reasons unknown. However, the official published version was that he succumbed to a heart attack, leaving a widow and two children, a boy and a girl. His death was a terrible shock to Lucy, and when I mentioned his name, she began to cry, then said, looking me straight in the eye, "How could you know that name? It was he who inspired the crazy comedy that led to 'I Love Lucy.' No one ever gave him credit for it. Where have you been all my life?"

And certainly, there was truth in what she said because not only the stage presentation and "My Favorite Husband" but the antic humor of *The Fuller Brush Girl* led directly to the show that would make Lucy and Desi the biggest names in television.

· CHAPTER 8 ·

*L*ucy announced that she would be giving birth in June. She decided that she would not risk yet another miscarriage by going through the strenuous routines and long hours involved in her Columbia comedies. She undertook an exercise program with a personal trainer and vowed she would embark on a career in television, where the schedules called for a conclusion of work in the late afternoon, and where the enclosed studio conditions largely prevented the necessity for strenuous outdoor shooting. She cut personal appearances in theaters to a minimum and insisted Desi stay with her during the pregnancy, as his previous absences had caused her much of the emotional stress that had caused the loss of two babies. She tried to tell herself that he was no longer an excitable playboy, and had settled down; and she took off with Desi and Louella Parsons to Del Mar, where they played canasta and relaxed. The psychological trauma of recently losing a second child was overcome by the prospect of another.

For some time, she tried to find a way to incorporate her career with Desi's, but the racial prejudice against him as a potential leading man was still strong, and this in itself was an irritation to her. Now that she was thirty-nine years old, her personality had changed. Although she didn't have much money and her career was quite undistinguished, she had, on the brink of middle age, acquired a steely will. She was no longer the haughty, cool, sleek figure who modeled well-tailored, box-shouldered 1940s costumes in garish colors in one MGM musical after another; nor was she the daffy, air-headed charmer of the Columbia comedies. Never gifted with much of a sense of humor, for all her sensational comedic gifts, never one to enjoy life much, she had now become strong, resolute, and determined to a degree. She was direct and positive in purpose. When she made up her mind to do something, that was it. Desi, more informal, relaxed, and warm-hearted—Latin—found her an increasingly severe taskmistress in the house, fanatically tidy, calling all the shots, and emphatically running the show. Firmly and with her usual blunt realism, she decided that if she continued her career on present lines, it would surely collapse within a short period of time and she would be forced to either retire or make the impossible gamble of attempting a career on Broadway. The alternative, of course, was the still-primitive medium of television.

Television had gotten off to a sporadic start in the years before World War II, when people would watch fan-shaped screens on expensive mahogany consoles that brought them flickering gray images of badly presented newscasts, sporting events, and primeval comedy shows. The war had suspended television, outside of some experiments, and in the late 1940s, much opposed by the film industry, which correctly saw that it would be swallowed up by the competition, this hybrid form of visual entertainment, not exactly art, not exactly photographed radio, and not exactly movies, either, struggled to obtain a foothold in the American home. The earliest figures to emerge in television were Milton Berle, known affectionately as Uncle Milty, whose grinning, throwaway routines concealed a hard core of sophisticated expertise; Sid Caesar and Imogene Coca; and Howdy Doody. All were accompanied by deafening laugh tracks and most were kinescoped, giving them a curious, canned, lifeless feeling when seen today.

Lucy and Desi conceived the idea of developing the essential matter and style of "My Favorite Husband" and of the Columbia comedies in the new medium. The effect of this would be to give Desi a job, since his part would be written as that of the Latin husband of a daffy WASP housewife. It was clear that since they were comparatively young, the couple would need older foils in the form of a couple well into middle age. The writers of "My Favorite Husband," Jeff Oppenheimer, Bob Carroll, Jr., and Madelyn Pugh, assisted by Lucy's agent Don Sharpe, who played a creative part, joined to develop the characters, the conflicts, and the comedic antics of the couples Lucy and Desi had conceived. The writers drew also from the vaudeville act that the Arnazes had presented in the Middle West, and Don Sharpe, who also acted as go-between, negotiated a deal with CBS to try to develop a pilot. Harry S. Ackerman, West Coast director of CBS network programs, encouraged the couple to move ahead. However, William S. Paley, chairman of CBS in New York, was not in the least interested in the idea. He felt that neither Desi nor Lucy was a sufficiently known national name, that it would be difficult for the public to accept a Latin leading man, and that in every way the format proposed was unsuitable to television and would be useless in the ratings.

It is true that at the time it would have taken extraordinary foresight to have predicted that anything whatever could come of such a plan. It took a great deal of persuasion for Ackerman to induce Paley to show even a flicker of interest. (In his memoirs, Desi Arnaz ignores these problems with Paley, and suggests that Paley immediately decided to make the pilot, without much persuading.) Whatever would happen, Lucy was determined not to give up her plan. She felt it was the only way to save her marriage. She couldn't endure another week of separation from Desi while he was on the road. In view of the fact that there was so much reluctance at corporate headquarters in New York, it was quite clear that she would have to get the proposed TV program off the ground herself. Everyone warned the couple that they would be committing professional suicide and would go broke on TV. But one night, Lucy said later, she had a vivid dream that her friend Carole Lombard, killed in a plane crash in 1942, came to her saying, "Honey, go ahead. Take a chance. Give it a whirl!"

She and Desi called the company they now formed Desilu. They put their heads together and discussed how they would do the show. They decided to film it live in the studio with an audience—not kinescope it. CBS immediately reacted against the idea, and even the sympathetic Harry Ackerman had his doubts. Lucy explained that she wanted to be able to keep the shows for her children, like home movies, for the indefinite future; they told her that kinescope was the only acceptable form. She objected to that because kinescopes, which usually were of poor quality, tended to be thrown away or burned by the studios. For this reason, she had never been able to see an earlier appearance she had made on television with Ed Wynn. Once again, in meetings with the executives, she was told that she was asking the impossible; furthermore, she was told that a live audience in the studio was out of the question. It would be too difficult to control, there might be hecklers or people acting out of order, and the laughter might not be there at all. Becoming more and more irritable, she pointed out that "My Favorite Husband" had been done in front of a live audience. She also brought up yet another point that distressed the CBS brass. She said that, although she intended placing the show in a Manhattan setting, in fact she would not make it in New York because she wanted her children to grow up in California, where the life was healthy, and because she was not prepared to give up the farm at Chatsworth. This was the last straw, and she was told to forget the whole idea immediately. At one CBS meeting, an executive snapped at her. "This is not what we have in mind, Miss Ball!" And she replied, "Then forget it!" and stormed out.

There was no alternative. Lucy and Desi would have to find capital, hire studio space, and embark on the pilot themselves. They had not the slightest idea whether the show would make it. Lucy, highly strung and tense as ever, was in a bad state of nerves as work began on the pilot script. She and Desi borrowed $5,000 (some sources say $8,000) from General Amusement Corporation, the agency for which they had toured in vaudeville, and they scraped up a matching figure from their meager savings. They had been spending close to every cent, and after paying their taxes, they had not, contrary to public opinion, a great deal left over. Indeed, if need be, they would have taken a second mortgage on their ranch to support the venture.

They worked very closely with their team of writers. It was clever of them to hire Bob Carroll and Madelyn Pugh, not only because of the experience these two had in putting together the scripts for "My Favorite Husband," but also because they were not married to anyone then, and had a lighthearted, satirical, and observant view of the institution of wedlock. Jess Oppenheimer, who had written the "Baby Snooks" radio series for Fanny Brice, drew some elements from that show for the "Lucy" concept, saying today, "The interesting thing was that even though the characters Fanny and Lucy played were essentially alike—both were very childlike—Lucy's playing of the same situation was so radically different, you'd never have thought they had arisen from the same idea."

The first script was not the basis for what finally emerged, although there was some discussion on the format of the two couples living together in New York. In the pilot, Desi appeared as himself, and Lucy as herself. A talented director, Ralph Levy, was hired to direct; he had worked with Lucy on "The Ed Wynn Show." Oppenheimer and the other writers struggled to adapt Desi's and Lucy's theatrical techniques to this different medium. In one sequence, Lucy walked around her living room wearing a lampshade to prove she could be a Ziegfeld Girl. This, more than any other moment in the pilot, was prophetic of Lucy's constant dressing up as her television self. The pilot was shot at Studio A at Sunset Boulevard and Gower Street in Hollywood, and, despite every effort, it proved impossible to film it within their budget unless it was kine-scoped. One scene took place in a living room and the other in a nightclub. At the end of March 1951, Don Sharpe picked up the finished kinescope and flew it to New York to look for a sponsor on Madison Avenue. CBS had made it clear: No spon-sor, no deal.

Sharpe took the pilot from office to office. Few could dis-tinguish between the sounds of a live audience and canned laughter, and seemed not to be interested in the fact that the show was exceptionally fresh, lively, and amusing. At least six agencies turned down the pilot before Sharpe brought it to the Milton Biow Agency, whose major client, Philip Morris ciga-rettes, was looking for possible changes in its sponsored TV programs following unsatisfactory presentations of radio's "Truth or Consequences" and Horace Heidt's "Youth Oppor-tunity." Watching the pilot in his screening room, Biow found it awkward and weak, but he saw the potential of a Ball-Arnaz teaming that could be funny and popular, provided that a full personality was worked out for each. Sharpe advised him that writers were already at work on such a concept, and Biow began to think perhaps there could be something in this. He decided to ask the advice of his friend Oscar Hammerstein II, lyricist of *Oklahoma!* and *Carousel*, and Hammerstein sat back and laughed like a child when he saw the material. He agreed with Sharpe that it would be possible to build a convincing human-comedy series around such an enjoyably dizzy couple. Encouraged by this response, Biow decided to act. He called Sharpe and said, "If Lucy and Desi are willing to go along with Oscar's idea, I think I can interest Philip Morris." Sharpe sug-gested that Biow fly to California and meet with Lucy, Desi, and the writers. Biow acted at once. At a meeting with all concerned in Hollywood he told them that if they could create characters along the lines Sharpe had mentioned, he would be able to move at once. It was April 1951, and Lucy was seven months pregnant.

In the wake of Biow's departure, Lucy and the writers, with

Desi contributing many ideas, began to work out details of the characterizations. Madelyn Pugh recalls that when some of the ideas were brought to Lucy, she was wary, dubious, and even challenging, but once she was convinced, she wouldn't change a word in the concepts. She worked like a road mender, spending long hours on ideas that could be stockpiled in a think-tank for unlimited future use. Idea after idea was recycled from "My Favorite Husband" and either scheduled for immediate use or put on the back burner. A trick address was worked out just in case anyone should claim that the show was invading their privacy. The two couples were to live in a brownstone at "623 East Sixty-eighth Street, New York." Actually, there was no such postal address; the house would have been located in the East River. The characters of Lucy and Ricky Ricardo were a struggling couple: Ricky was a bandleader earning $150 a week at the Tropicana; Lucy was a housewife obsessed with dreams of stage and screen stardom. The foils were the Mertzes, a more humdrum couple: Fred was obsessed with baseball, and Ethel was always fretting and worrying about household problems. The relationship between the two couples would be humorous, sometimes harmlessly hostile, usually friendly, or teasingly familiar. Very often, audience identification would be obtained by having the two wives gang up against the two husbands, or vice versa.

The character of Lucy was obsessed with ensuring Ricky's eternal love, often posing in sexy outfits or as a vamp to secure his continued interest in her, but she was also shown trying to outwit him in her climb to success in show business. Foolish, vain, klutzy, and basically sweet, she was always shown in exaggerated situations, humorously trying to put one over on the female competition, wherever that might be found. Ethel was a compulsive eater, spending too much time in the kitchen, while Lucy was always dieting to be ahead of her. One of the elements the writers worked out was the theme of disguise: Lucy and Ethel would dress as country bumpkins with blacked-out teeth, hair like dish mops, and Daisy Mae dresses straight off the rack; or at other times as vamps, in clinging evening gowns with long cigarette holders. It was decided from the beginning that the two couples would act dead serious even when they were clowning outrageously. Above all, Lucy was adamant that her character would not resemble in any way the sort of person she had played on the screen. She did not want to act like a person that she had portrayed in *Without Love,* delivering wisecracks and walking out on the punchline, closing the door; nor did she want to be dressed up, dripping with jewelry and furs, or acting in the grand manner as in *Du Barry Was a Lady* and *Easy to Wed.*

Along with wanting to develop a definite pattern, a system of working that would be cheaply presentable in a modest set or two, Lucy felt it would be necessary to create an appropriate camera technique. She remembered Karl Freund, known affectionately as "Papa," one of the big names in German cinematography in the era before Hitler. Plump, jolly, and very talented, Freund had made a great deal of money from patenting an exposure meter that was in use throughout the world. He had retired from the screen in 1951. Lucy had enjoyed working with him on *Du Barry Was a Lady* at MGM, and she and Desi called him at his home in the Hollywood hills to discuss his coming back to work with them. Reluctant at first, he eventually warmed to the idea and, always inventive, thought out a technique that would in fact revolutionize the television industry.* Just as he had worked out for motion pictures the process shot and the back projection that saved money by giving audiences the impression they were present in different locations while watching studio-made films, and the exposure meter that had brought massive changes in cinematographic techniques, Freund devised the idea of shooting

---

* According to some versions, Freund was in Washington, D.C., at the time, working with the government, and Desi had the idea of shooting with different cameras. Freund was opposed to the idea, saying it was impossible. Finally, Desi challenged him by suggesting that the impossible was what Karl Freund could do. Then Freund came back and found the solution.

the "Lucy" television show with three cameras, known as multicam. Up to then, each scene was filmed in separate shots to get more than one angle, but in Freund's approach, the three cameras would shoot all the action at the same time. Thus, Lucy and Desi and their editors could watch the shows at night as though they were making a movie, and put together the very best shots. Reaction shots, double takes, and mugging could be timed to a fraction of a second to "milk" the audience to the limit.

Now came the question of the name of the show. William Paley and the other executives at CBS were adamant that Desi must not appear in the title. They even wanted it to be called "The Lucille Ball Show" co-starring Desi Arnaz. Lucy was furious and told CBS she would take the show away from them once and for all and go to the other networks. They yielded slightly and said they would call it "The Lucille Ball and Desi Arnaz Show." Again, she was angry and upset. It was shocking to her that Desi's name would be put last; she simply couldn't face up to his lesser star status. Finally, someone came up with "I Love Lucy." Lucy at first felt this wouldn't work because the critics might say, "We hate Lucy." But then she thought, as she said later, "People would know that the 'I' was Desi. That gave him first billing. And then, how could you go wrong with the word 'love' in the title? I decided to go with it—after exactly half a second."

Yet again, CBS suggested they should make the show in New York, and once again the Arnazes turned the idea down. It was decided that they would make thirty-nine episodes for the 1951–52 season, at a cost of $19,500 per episode. Filming the show would ultimately save money since it would make it possible to distribute it to the largest possible audience. The couple agreed to take a $1,000 cut on the $5,000-per-episode fee, in return for owning 100 percent of the shows. CBS agreed. Some years later, they were to sell the shows back to CBS for $4.5 million. One of the reasons CBS made this arrangement was that the network was convinced that the filmed shows would be a failure and so would the series. Freund worked out a skillful camera technique. This successful cameraman had to accept union scale to stay within the Arnaz budget. Because of his wealth from his personally patented light meter and lenses, he accepted the arrangement.

Now the Arnazes had to find somewhere to make the show. Even at this advanced stage in their preparations, they had no studio. They thought of using the Earl Carroll restaurant and nightclub, but there wasn't room for three or more cameras on the stage, and the audience couldn't get in close enough to watch the players. They thought of getting hold of a small theater in Hollywood similar to that used in the Groucho Marx show, "You Bet Your Life." Groucho Marx's format, very cramped indeed, had no visual appeal: It simply involved Groucho sitting or standing and making rude remarks to contestants while the cameras were static, like those in early sound films. If Desi and Lucy were to move the cameras around as they planned, they would need a much larger theater; also, since they were going to use full-scale motion-picture cameras, they had to have enough height to allow for boom shots.

Finally, in the middle of a night, Desi sat up with an inspiration. He announced that he would make the show on a motion-picture soundstage for the first time in history. Lucy pointed out that the studio would never allow 300 people in to watch the show being made because of fire and health laws; there was always the danger of fires on soundstages because of the hot lights, and since the studio doors had to be closed firmly or even locked to prevent outside noise from airplanes or passing traffic, people could be trapped and killed in the event of a conflagration. Desi wouldn't take no for an answer. After constant discussion with Lucy, and investigating the problems of filming with an audience in a movie studio, he determined that if all the conditions of a normal theater were met, they could get away with it. A sprinkler system would have to be supplied, three exit doors, and seating arrangements that would allow for immediate evacuation. Furthermore, the soundstage would have to be on a city street so the Fire Department could get to it quickly. And two firemen would have to be present at all times during the filming.

Lucy, Desi, Karl Freund, and other friends searched the city from one end to the other until at last they found General Service Studios Stage 2. It was ideal in every way, since it could accommodate several sets, allow room for the cameras, place an audience firmly in bleachers and provide elaborate sound and electrical equipment. Only the floor was a major problem. It was wooden, and, ripped apart by the camera equipment of over thirty years, it was full of potholes and uneven planks, on which people could trip and fall or where camera tracks and dollies could jam. The studio was on Selma Avenue in a sleazy residential district in the heart of Hollywood. Desi went in person to see the head of zoning in downtown Los Angeles; he was told the whole thing was impossible because the crowd waiting to get in would swarm all over the block, creating noise and traffic obstruction, and besides, the screams of laughter and the bursts of applause from the studio would upset the neighborhood. Desi had already received a similarly negative response from the Fire Department. But Desi would not be stopped. He told the zoning man he would talk to every single person who lived nearby and ask them point-blank if they would object to what he had in mind. The zoning man said their approval would have to be in writing. Desi went from door to door and everybody agreed not to create problems for him. However, he had to promise to soundproof the wall that stood adjacent to Selma Avenue. He also promised that special guards would direct the audience, control its noise, and herd the people in and out with a minimum of trouble. Within a year, Desi bought every house on the block to prevent any further problems, giving each of the owners a handsome profit.

Contracts were drawn up with General Service Studios. Desi and Lucy were surprised to find that the owners, George and James Nasser, were on the edge of bankruptcy. They were very pleased to make a deal, but pointed out that they were about to lose their property. It seemed the whole thing might fall through. Desi asked the Nassers how much they would need to pay off their creditors and the answer was $50,000. The Arnazes didn't have anything like that amount of money. They would have to sell their home to obtain it. Fortunately, Harry Ackerman at CBS came up with the cash, and as a result the Arnazes secured a good rental deal and saved the Nassers financially as well.

The next question was casting. Lucy and Desi had to find an ideal pair to play Fred and Ethel Mertz. And while they were still looking, another production matter arose: Lucy gave birth. Her first child, Lucie Desiree, was born on July 17, 1951. Lucie was beautiful: Delivered by Cesarean section, she weighed 7 pounds, 6 ounces, and was 21 inches long. Desi rushed out and bought a blue Cadillac to celebrate and to take his wife and daughter back to Chatsworth, and to the new nursery, where he sang the baby his own song, "There's a Brand New Baby at Our House," which became quite a successful recording.

While Lucy was still in bed, she was on the telephone every day with Desi, figuring out who could play Fred and Ethel. The character actor William Frawley, a short, fat, grumpy man, without much charm or warmth, had met Lucy on and off over the years. He had boldly called up and said, "Do you need a good actor to play Fred?" Desi promised to consider him. He and Lucy discussed his sour puss and gruff, grinding voice and felt he would be perfect. But CBS was dubious. And so were both the advertising agency and the sponsor. They were worried that because Frawley was an alcoholic he would be undependable. However, Desi felt more and more convinced they had found their Fred as time went by.

One thing in Frawley's favor Desi found on researching his background was that Frawley had had experience in vaudeville. Born in 1887, he had begun as a clerk for the Union

Pacific Railroad in Omaha, Nebraska, and had joined a musical, *The Flirting Princess*, in Chicago. With a piano-player partner, he had sung, in just the right mode, the famous song "Melancholy Baby" all over the country on the vaudeville circuits, and later developed a technique of grim-faced, hilarious monologues that made him widely known and respected. In pictures, he usually played curmudgeons with considerable flair. A confirmed bachelor, he lived with his sister at the Knickerbocker Hotel on Ivar Street in Hollywood, where he spent every evening watching or listening to sportscasts.

Desi met with him at the well-known, well-worn Nickodell Restaurant on Melrose Avenue, with its wooden booths, basic American menu, and subdued lighting. Desi told Frawley he was concerned about stories that Frawley was an alcoholic. Frawley, according to Desi, said, "Well, those bastards, those sons of bitches. They're always saying that about me. How the hell do they know, those bastards?" Desi told him he didn't care whether he drank or not, but everything was riding on the success of the show, since he and Lucy had given up their careers for this terrific gamble, and he couldn't make any mistakes. He knew Frawley was the only person in the world to play Fred Mertz, but he had to be assured that Frawley would cut out drinking. Desi said, "If you screw up, you will be fired and blacklisted throughout the industry." In spite of this, Frawley ordered up drink after drink at lunch, and Desi began to get tense; but he needn't have worried. Frawley laid off the Scotch for the whole length of production and never missed a day's work in all the years of "I Love Lucy." He had no interest in anything except supporting his various sisters and going to the games or the fights. He would never give up a weekend or a night when the ball games were on the air. Therefore, he was perfectly cast as the ultimate middle-American type, as much of a national symbol as the hamburgers and hot dogs he loved. He never cared how he looked, was perfectly content with his large belly, and grumbled all the time at schedules, the hot studio lights, and Lucy's perfectionism.

Now came the question of matching Frawley's Fred Mertz to the perfect Ethel. "Thank God for Vivian Vance," Lucy said years later. Marc Daniels, hired to direct the first season of "I Love Lucy," knew Vivian and admired her. Soon after he got the job of directing "I Love Lucy," Daniels recalls, he was anxious to impress the Arnazes that Vivian would be the ideal choice. He insisted that Desi and Oppenheimer should accompany him to the La Jolla Playhouse near San Diego, where Vivian was appearing in *The Voice of the Turtle* by John Van Druten, as an acid but good-natured second-string figure to the leading actress, Diana Lynn. Desi was delighted with her performance and said to Daniels at the first intermission, "I think we've found our Ethel." Daniels went backstage to see Vivian and told her the good news. But the actress responded adversely, saying that she wasn't interest in getting mixed up with television since she was going to do a movie at Universal. Daniels shouted at her, "You goddamned idiot, take the job! It's going to be a great series! I've seen six or seven scripts already and the pilot!" Vivian held back, very uncertain. However, she finally agreed.

Vivian Vance's background was quite different from that of William Frawley. She was born in Kansas in 1912, and had always been in legitimate theater, starting with the Jerome Kern/Oscar Hammerstein musical *Music in the Air* and later replacing, at a moment's notice and with great success, Kay Thompson in the show *Hurray for What!* under the direction of the young Vincente Minnelli. She was successful in *Anything Goes* with Ethel Merman, *Red Hot and Blue*, and *Let's Face It* with Danny Kaye and Eve Arden. The fact that she had stage experience was crucial in her appearing in the theatrical format the Arnazes had devised. The only problem was that, once she was hired, William Frawley took an instant dislike to her. He said to Desi after grumblingly meeting with her, "Where the hell did you find this bitch?" They clashed when a scene was prepared in which the Mertzes would sing and dance in a crazy nightclub routine with Ricky. Vivian infuriated Frawley by telling the choreographer that she was sure Frawley couldn't dance. He shouted at her that he had been soft-shoeing in vaudeville since he was five and that before long he'd be teaching (referring to the choreographer) "Old Fat Ass how to do the fucking thing." In turn, Vivian was annoyed because, in their preparations, Frawley would only read his own part, whereas the other actors naturally read all the parts. He hadn't the slightest interest in her dialogue, and it was as much as he could do to be polite to her or pick up her cues. All this time, Lucy, busy with her newborn child, hadn't met either Frawley or Vivian Vance, and had to take everybody else's word for it that they were perfect.

$\mathcal{T}$he three writers had the staggering task of preparing thirty-nine first-season episodes for "I Love Lucy" in less than three months. This meant a total of nineteen and a half hours of material, or about twelve hundred pages of dialogue and situations, and all of this with Lucy a brand-new mother and Desi, a brand-new father, already a basket case. The pressure was insane, and no doubt explains to some extent why Lucy underwent a change of character at the time. She now became more fiercely driven, all-consuming in her emphasis on quality, on perfection itself. She became her own creation, in a sense; not malign or evil, but a hypersensitive stickler for standards. In the tiny dimensions of television, a version of road-company vaudeville or traveling road-company sitcom, "I Love Lucy" was to set the tone for the new medium's comedic approach for decades. The pressure she brought to bear seemed to bring out only the best in the team of Marc Daniels, Karl Freund, Lucy and Desi, Oppenheimer, Pugh and Carroll, production manager Al Simon, art director Larry Cuneo, editor Alan Jaggs, assistant director James Paisley, and camera coordinator Maury Thompson. The first "I Love Lucy" episode was prepared and put onto film in four and a half days. Marc Daniels scheduled his initial rehearsal for Monday, September 3, 1951, a day of sweltering California heat. General factotum Lou Jacoby took care of all the crucial janitorial tasks, including filling the water coolers, arranging for doughnuts and coffee, and setting up chairs. The democratic attitude of all concerned, in which no one was more important than anyone else, made the "Lucy" teamwork magnificent. Rehearsals began with Lucy meeting Vivian Vance for the first time. They liked each other instantly despite many differences and fights during the years of work that followed. When Lucy went on "Good Morning America" in 1983 to talk with David Hartman about her life, she wept at the mention of the late Vivian Vance's name.

The first episode was entitled *The Diet*. (It was actually shown third, but shot first.) The reason for its selection was that the makers correctly believed that dieting was an obsessive concern of millions of Americans and that any teleplay of that name would be sure to seize attention. In the story, Lucy reverted with good humor to the condition she was in just before giving birth to her daughter; padded out to make her seem to be twenty-two pounds overweight, she pretends to be a victim of excessive amounts of junk food. Word comes that a singer appearing in Ricky's nightclub will be leaving the show, and Lucy takes it into her head to replace the girl. In an absurdly funny scene, Lucy goes to an audition, and despite her size is told she can take the floor as a new act on condition she sheds twelve pounds in four days. She is seen jogging (an oddly prophetic touch), but when climbing on the scales is horrified to discover she is only five ounces lighter. That night at the evening meal, she miserably bites on a celery stick while her husband and the Mertzes stuff themselves with a heavy meal. Finally, she is so desperate for food that she snatches a chunk of meat from the slavering jaws of the Mertzes' dog. At last, she has only five hours left in which to lose the last five pounds. So she contrives to buy a kind of torture chamber filled with steam, locking herself in and almost suffocating until finally the weight is soaked off her. No sooner has she finished her song than she faints from lack of food.

It was a very funny idea, with a strong appeal to an incalculable number of American women, and the technique sprang from taking an identifiable situation and stretching it to the limits of what was possible and just slightly beyond. Lucy's solemnity, her determination to diet, added to the amusement of the approach; and the fact that she tackled every rehearsal grimly, constantly puffing at cigarettes, had everyone in stitches, almost to the point of annoying her. From the very first day of rehearsal of that first classic program, Lucy toiled like a construction worker. The noise level was shattering from actual construction during the work; the studio was being re-modeled and sets were being put together for future episodes while the rehearsals went on. Everyone's nerves were on edge in the turmoil. Desi was going crazy. He would be halfway through a humorous scene in which he was expressing dismay at Lucy's dietary plans, when an assistant would come up to him on the set and tell him that he had to make a crucial executive decision. Even as the rehearsals continued, questions kept arising: How exactly would the permanent sets of the Ricardo and Mertz apartments look? And how could movable walls or windows be used to allow fluent, free-wheeling shoot-ing instead of endless static setups with people walking up and down to the chalk lines?

September 6 was the day when the actual filming of *The Diet* would begin. Sleepless, exhausted, Desi and Lucy were discussing details with Marc Daniels just an hour before shoot-ing was scheduled to start, when a Los Angeles Health and Welfare Department officer turned up without warning. Much to Desi's fury, the man said it was impossible to film the show that night. He told Desi there would have to be two bathrooms, a men's room and a ladies' room, for the audience, and there was no ladies' room "within the proper distance." Desi went bananas. He asked the studio manager to arrange a bathroom for the ladies. When the manager returned, he said, looking extremely awkward, "I have bad news." "What is it?" Desi snapped. "The only bathroom we can use that is close to the audience is Lucy's. The one in her dressing room."

This would mean that all the women in the audience would be parading in and out of Lucy's dressing room, which was the only place in which she had a moment of privacy. Jess Oppenheimer said incredulously to Desi, "We're about to go on and do our first show and you're looking for a *bathroom?*" Desi recalls that he replied, "Yes. We're supposed to supply a place for the ladies to pee in, but it's in Lucy's personal bathroom." Nothing would stop Lucy. She announced that if that was the only bathroom they could use, they could darn well use it, and let's get on with the show.

The delay over all this red tape meant that the selfsame studio audience was becoming extremely restless at the entrance, where they were waiting to go in. They were munching popcorn, swilling Cokes, and talking much too loudly. Desi went out front and began to usher them in, telling them about the historic event they were about to witness: the first time a television play of this sort would be performed for three cameras. He told them not to worry about the many distractions that would take place, including the constantly moving cameras, and he even gave them a lecture on Papa Freund's techniques, promising them, to general laughter and applause, that they wouldn't have their view blocked by the cameras. He told funny stories learned from his friends in vaudeville, and then ceremoniously introduced the cast one by one, with Lucy coming in last. According to him, he delivered the line as she appeared: "Here's my favorite wife, the mother of my child, the vice president of Desilu Productions. . . ." Then he added with good humor and considerable emphasis, "My favorite redhead, the girl who plays Lucy, Lucille Ball!" Lucy came in, kissed a reluctant William Frawley, who comically screwed up his face, and a more receptive Vivian Vance, and then said to Desi, "How ya doin', you gorgeous Cuban?" and blew kisses at the crowd. All this was to the tune of the "I Love Lucy" theme song, played by Desi's band. Lucy's and Desi's mothers were both present.

The history-making performance began. The audience was

hysterical with laughter as Lucy struggled with her outsized stomach, tried to squeeze into the size 12 dress left behind by her predecessor in the nightclub, struggled with the pooch for the meat, and then at last emerged triumphantly at her first performance in the club. At the end, the applause went on and on, and the Arnazes had to take several bows.

There was an unfortunate aftermath. On Monday morning, the group looked at the actual film, anxious to see if it was as funny on screen as it had been in the studio. However, there was a technical problem. The performance had been delivered like a stage play, without a single interruption, and at a pace not entirely suitable for television. It was decided to have breaks in the performance during which time the band would entertain or Desi would provide gags. This way, it would be much easier to control the pace and allow for makeup or clothing transitions and for the commercial inserts.

The team plunged into another episode, entitled *The Girls Want to Go to a Nightclub*. It was another theme with which millions of people could identify—the family quarrel. It is the eighteenth wedding anniversary of the Mertzes. Grumpy Fred Mertz wants to go to a boxing match, and Ethel wants to go to a nightclub. Lucy sides with Ethel and decides to go separately with her to the Copacabana. The men announce they will go to the fights separately and take with them two glamorous dates. Lucy and Ethel disguise themselves as hillbillies, with blacked-out teeth, spotty faces, and garish gingham clothes. Finally, Ricky and Fred realize that these crazy dates are not hillbillies but their wives. All four go off to a boxing match.

In a third episode, yet another highly identifiable theme was used: the fear of women that their husbands are no longer attracted to them and they must find some way to restore their love life after years of physical and sexual boredom or separation. Ethel suggests that Lucy read a new self-improvement book that tells lonesome wives how to turn their existence into a perpetual honeymoon. The first suggestion the book contains is that the wife should put on a sexy dress at breakfast time.

Lucy turns up looking very glamorous for the morning meal, but Ricky doesn't flicker an eyelash and goes on reading the paper. Encouraged by the book to "be a pal," Lucy pitches into a poker game with Ricky, Fred, and their partners; without even trying, she wins the game, thereby infuriating Ricky. Then advised by the omniscient doctor-author to surround her husband with childhood memories, Lucy redecorates the apartment with Cuban furniture, chickens, a large mule, and palm trees. Ricky is horrified as she does a Carmen Miranda routine. But at last, amused and touched, he kisses her.

Before the debut of "I Love Lucy" on television, Desi wanted to test the show on another kind of audience. He ran *The Diet* in a theater in Riverside, near Los Angeles. The audience laughed just as much as its studio counterpart, and he was able to give Lucy good news. In the following days, Desi worked at insane speeds, doing post-production, firing editors and replacing them, preparing new scripts, rehearsing and filming other shows, editing the music, trying to time shooting schedules so as not to run too much over the thirty minutes of actual projecting time, working until midnight on the cuts, running footage through Moviolas, and battling all of the countless technical problems in which he had involved himself. He would often arrive home at 2:00 A.M., go over the accounts, make out checks (they still didn't have enough money to justify a business manager), and worry over such things as floors, sprinkler systems, dolly wheels, seats for the audience, and overall budgets. He managed to trim the budget from $95,000 for the first show to $60,000 for the fourth—well over the agreed $19,500 per episode. Yet, despite every effort, the team was almost $250,000 over budget by the time they were ready to go on the air. The studio was going crazy, and leading executives were placing bets that the show would lose half a million dollars in the first year.

With everyone on edge, and CBS boss William Paley feeling very much the worse for wear in New York, "I Love Lucy" finally debuted on Monday, October 15, 1951, at 9:00 P.M., up against the popular show "Lights Out." All through the afternoon preceding the telecast, the team had been reading and discussing the script for *The Seance*, in which Lucy succumbs to the craze for astrology and numerology, and gets involved with spiritualism and a Ouija board. They were so caught up in their work that they almost forgot to watch the program. Incredibly, there was no television set in the studio; not even in an office. Lucy began trying to figure out how she and Desi could make the thirty miles back to the ranch in Northridge in time to see the episode. Finally, Marc Daniels' wife Emily invited the gang to see the show at the Daniels' house in Laurel Canyon. She whipped up some food in the few minutes they had before the program began, but they were all so excited they forgot the dinner.

Only William Frawley was absent; that curmudgeon went home to his hotel instead to listen to the fights. Nobody in the gang laughed once during the half hour, as they stared at the small gray screen transfixed, tense, uneasy, looking for technical errors. Only Vivian Vance's husband Phil Ober reacted with a loud, rather tiresome laugh, which did not amuse the others. The video reception was bad; the show looked as though it had been filmed under water (the Philip Morris commercials glittered and shone brightly). Everyone got out of bed early next morning to read the trade reviews. Lucy read, to her surprise, that one columnist said she had the bluest eyes in existence, despite the fact that the show was in black and white. The reviews were generally good. *Variety* wrote: "As story-line comedies go, it is the better part of appreciation not to ask yourself too many questions and just go along with what transpires on your screen." *The New York Times* said: " 'I Love Lucy' has the promise of providing a refreshing half-hour of video entertainment. . . . Although a poor second act spoiled the first show, the basic characterizations are sound enough to go on to better things, provided the situations are not permitted to get completely out of hand." Amazingly, the big brass at Philip Morris suddenly decided they didn't like it. The president, O. Parker McComas, called the Biow Agency and asked what it would cost to cancel the "Lucy" contract. He said he found the show "unfunny, silly, and totally boring." Terry Clyne, Biow VP in charge of television, and Edward H. Feldman of the Hollywood office begged McComas to put off his decision until there had been at least one more showing. Slightly swayed by the opinions of the two executives, McComas grumblingly agreed to wait.

The show took off with amazing speed. It instantly went up into the top ten of the national ratings and stayed there. Though there were other amusing comedy sitcoms, many of them expertly produced, the advantage of "Lucy" over the others was the eternal appeal of slapstick. The fun of seeing solemn Lucy in highly embarrassing situations was irresistible. In *Lucy Thinks Ricky Is Trying to Do Away with Her*, Lucy is in a state of extreme nervous tension after reading a murder mystery and learning from Ethel's fortune-telling cards that she will soon die. Convinced Ricky is going to kill her, she dresses up, carries a bullet-proof skillet and brandishes a gun at Ricky. In other shows she was confronted with a long-forgotten "husband" in the form of a tramp, dressed in a lampshade hat to try to join Ricky's nightclub show, impersonated a performing seal, and struggled with Ricky's untidiness in the home. The formula was that Lucy was embattled by circumstances, nervous and threatened, fighting to hold her husband's interest in her, and doing every possible crazy stunt to attract his attention. It was an infallible basis for the series. "I Love Lucy" became a worldwide addiction, and fan mail started to pour in; even the Philip Morris brass crumbled before the onslaught of public opinion. As for William Paley, he was astonished, but happily garnered applause for years to come. The terrific gamble of the winning couple in giving up a combined half-million-dollar income a year to take this plunge had paid off. And all this time, despite seemingly endless hours of work, Lucy was somehow managing to raise her young daughter.

The "Lucy" schedule was rigid and unwavering. Each

show was shot at eight o'clock Friday evenings, in exactly half an hour. A mere four days were spent in rehearsal, planning and fine tuning the scripts. At ten o'clock on Tuesday morning, Marc Daniels, the cast, and the writers sat around a rehearsal table and went over the script for the first time. Rehearsals lasted until 6:00 P.M.; occasionally, an actor would suggest a change, and indeed Vivian Vance became a kind of script editor, toning down some of the more extravagant gags for Lucy because she felt audiences wouldn't accept them. Anything really surrealist was quite ruled out. The team knew how far they could go with the mass audience. Everything had to be tasteful because this was a family show, watched ecstatically by children. If a scene didn't work at all, the writers would produce something not only brand new but often more inventive than before.

On Wednesday, a full-scale rehearsal was held on the actual set. All of the actors memorized the entire script except for William Frawley, who spent the time when he was not called for assiduously studying the baseball scores or sneaking off to listen to them on the radio. At 4:30 P.M. on Wednesday, the first camera run-through was done to time the action to the photography. Karl Freund studied each movement in order to know how to place his cameras in relation to the action.

All morning Thursday, from dawn, Freund and his team adjusted the lighting on the set in order to achieve the correct mood of a New York apartment by day or by night. It was not until twelve noon that the cast appeared, and the rehearsal went on until six in the evening. That same night was the dress rehearsal. Everyone was there as the grueling, meticulously worked-out session went on, with trims, changes, and tightening, often until the small hours of the morning. The pressure did not let up on Friday. Through the morning, the camera team once again prepared carefully for the shots. Extensive final changes were made until four-thirty and then another dress rehearsal took place.

On Friday, there were often parties for visiting performers, and that evening there was a last-minute discussion. At 8:00 P.M., more or less the time Broadway shows started in those days, the actual filming began.

By the fifth or sixth episode, in November 1951, there were long lines outside the studio door as people waited to be admitted. During the filming, various assistants were present with prompt cards on which were written APPLAUSE, LAUGHTER, or CHEERS. Lucy and Desi dared not risk having the audience sitting on its hands, since they had sworn not to use a laugh track, as other shows did. This meant that the audience had to be continually prompted to respond—some audiences were slow to pick up the humor. Others laughed uncontrollably, and great care had to be taken that the sound of the laughter did not drown out any lines. Each night, Desi followed his original routine of introducing the cast and the crew. There was little or no time for retakes. So carefully had the show been prepared that the exact length of the shooting was timed to a fraction. Once the filming had been completed, the footage was rushed to a lab for developing.

The shooting, as it continued throughout the fall, was not without problems. Jess Oppenheimer found Lucy strict and tough at times, and he resented that. She herself had differences with Desi and the others, due to the nerve-shredding tension of the work. She was so thorough and manic, so excited by her sudden power over the public that had been denied her during her screen career, that making the show perfect became an obsession. She knew every light, every cable, every minute detail, and in effect she made herself as knowledgeable about the technique of filmmaking as Papa Fruend himself. Although she tried to be calm, she would flare up, greatly annoyed at any sign of hesitation or incompetence in any member of the crew. She expected everyone to be on his toes, fully prepared, and willing to work unlimited numbers of hours.

Madelyn Pugh recalls that the writing sessions were strongly influenced by Lucy, and if truth be told, Madelyn and

Bob Carroll were really only writing for Lucy, since the other players were simply foils. Ms. Pugh said recently, "Jess, Bob, and I would come up with a one-line idea, a 'What if?' Like, What if Lucy decides to bake her own bread? Then the three of us would figure all of the crazy situations that could emerge from that one premise. Bob and I would write the script during the week and turn it in to Jess on Friday; he would make any additions or changes he thought might improve it; and the script would be delivered to the four stars over the weekend."

Madelyn says, "When Lucy first met you, she tended to be a bit wary, a little challenging. But once you convinced her you knew what you were doing, she would trust your ideas all the way. Some of the stunts we wrote for her could have been dangerous. Yet never once did Lucy back off from any of them, although Desi frequently wanted her to because he was concerned for her safety. She trusted us enough to know that Bob and I had worked out every piece of business ourselves beforehand to make sure it *could* be done. If Lucy had to climb into a barrel, say, then she'd know it was possible because we'd done it ourselves. In one script, we had her working with an elephant. You don't realize just how big and unpredictable an elephant can be until you're standing next to one. If the script called for her to hide dozens of uncooked eggs inside her dress, she knew that I'd tried it myself first to see if it was possible and if it was funny."

Cam McCullough worked as a sound mixer for Lucy for almost twenty-five years. For this technician, it was an almost perfect working situation. He says, "Principally, Desi was the one who set the tone on the set. He was knowledgeable about so many things, and that surprised a lot of people, but he also had the talent of being able to get people to do things his way but with humor. He'd be telling you what he wanted, and he'd also have you laughing at the same time. She ran a tight ship, and seemed fair, but boy, if you goofed she'd let you know it. She didn't pull any punches. There was a coldness there that you didn't find with Desi. Maybe she was afraid people would take advantage.''

Marc Daniels was not as enthusiastic about working on the series as Madelyn Pugh and Bob Carroll were. Much as he enjoyed the work (and he found Desi brighter and more talented than people gave him credit for), he didn't feel close to Lucy. He says, ''I think she was enormously talented, an inventive comedienne, and a great, instinctive, natural actress. There were a couple of times, though, that we clashed during that first season. We had a couple of honest disagreements about how something should be played. But there was never any 'I'm going to do it *my* way.' ''

The team concurs today that the series cemented the rocky marriage of Lucy and Desi. However, the work did take toll of Lucy's health. There was one episode that could have been quite dangerous. Lucy accidentally set fire to her dress with a cigarette in the middle of a rehearsal; she was so obsessed with getting the rehearsal perfect that she began to go up in flames before she agreed to be hosed down. In another scene, she had to jump toward Desi on a balcony, and she fell off it. She got up, injured and limping, but would not stop doing the scene. Nothing would stand in her way of achieving perfection, and as the months went on into 1952, even her sturdy constitution began to give out and she suffered from frequent weakness and exhaustion. The strain was increased because she insisted on entertaining many famous people, old friends and new, who traipsed across the set to see her work or to attend parties that she gave, among them Eve Arden, Rosalind Russell, Jane Withers, and Bing Crosby, who was fascinated by the show and adopted its techniques for his own television appearances.

Roz Russell, one of the great comediennes, was dazzled by Lucy's timing and the expertise of the production, and gave her the compliment of saying that Lucy was far better than Roz herself. By April 1952, 10.5 million households, or well over two-thirds of the entire television viewing audience of that time, were watching "I Love Lucy." The show was top-rated in the nation, and in view of the number of people watching TV, it was estimated that almost 40 million people, just under one-seventh of them children, were addicts of the show. *TV Guide* provided the ultimate endorsement by saying, " 'I Love Lucy' is the season's most popular program—smooth, deft, solidly produced, and funny." And, since the Arnazes owned the show outright, they were already on their way to being very rich. That February, Red Skelton, then at the height of his popularity, who had until that point been just an inch ahead of Lucy in the ratings, received an Emmy. He said, decently, at the Awards ceremony, "I don't deserve this. It should go to Lucille Ball."

However, Desi was not content with simply having the most successful show in the nation. Desilu began to expand. Under Desi's frantic day-and-night guidance, pilot films for two comedy series, starring Eve Arden* and Laraine Day, were launched. Desi ran everything with energy and expertise, even proving to be a very good accountant and business manager who studied budget reports from CBS, and sometimes found errors in their accounting (at one time, CBS had accidentally budgeted an extra million dollars that was not necessary for Desilu). He would also meet frequently with reporters, press agents, potential crew members, and representatives of foreign television corporations, including the BBC from London.

The problems of shooting often had the hilarious awkwardness of the actual routines devised by the writers. One show was entitled *The Ballet*. In this, filmed on February 18, 1952, Lucy decides to obtain a job as a ballerina in Ricky's nightclub revue. She goes to a dancing school to learn technique at the barre. Later, she learns a comic dance routine ("Slowly I Turn") from an old burlesque performer, played by Frank De Mille.

Throwing her leg up while shooting a ballet-school se-

* "Our Miss Brooks."

Lucy, at three and a half years of age.

In *Roman Scandals*.

In *Room Service* with the Marx Brothers.

With Katharine Hepburn and Ginger Rogers in *Stage Door*.

With George Murphy and Desi Arnaz in the 1940s.

With Desi at home in Chatsworth, California.

A Desi-Lucy
Valentine.

Posing as a riveter.

Off-screen
relaxation during
the filming of *The
Long, Long Trailer*.

With Desi, Jr.,
and Lucie.

Richard Burton
and Elizabeth
Taylor,
struggling with
their hostess in
Here's Lucy.

In *Yours, Mine, and Ours* with Henry Fonda and the kids.

Mame.

The Lucy everyone loves.

quence, Lucy accidentally caught it in the practice barre. She was unable to pry it loose and simply made up the dialogue as she went along so that the scene would not have to be reshot. The results were hilarious. In the episode *Pioneer Women*, shot on March 18, Desi had to ride a horse. In the sequence, Desi, trying to be a pioneer, rides home from work instead of taking a cab. The horse had been very carefully prepared. However, the night the filming took place, the horse became startled by the live audience in the studio and refused to move an inch.

Sometimes the writers drew from Lucy and Desi's actual experiences. At other times, they drew from her childhood experiences in Celoron, New York; there were many references to those early days. The Ricardos were married, like the Arnazes, at the Byram River Beagle Club in Greenwich, Connecticut, and Lucy Ricardo, like Lucy herself, went to Jamestown High School.

· CHAPTER 10 ·

*D*espite their grueling schedule, Lucy and Desi made sure that weekends were sacred, devoted to little Lucie. Even at this early age, the baby had a strong character, and they were delighted with her. Lucy worried about the long separations from her child, days in which she wanted so much to be with her. Lucie drew the couple closer than they had been since the very beginning.

They gave costume parties as well as square dances, some of their parties running to over a hundred guests. The ranch at Chatsworth had been added to considerably in recent years. Little Lucie had a wing that was virtually her kingdom, with a large, magnificent playroom. Another part of the house had a refrigerator, washer-dryer, iron and ironing board, freezer, sewing machine, and numerous other gadgets, and also served as a beauty parlor. Lucy could be seen on rare weekdays off or on Sundays slapping egg shampoos on her girlfriends' hair, giving them mudpacks, or putting their hair in curlers. One time a newspaper interviewer came to see her. The reporter's hair resembled that to be found on the average sheepdog. Lucy kept staring at it, unable to answer the questions because she was so mesmerized by the hair. Eventually, she said, "Excuse me, there's something I have to do. Just hold it a minute!" She walked over to her beauty-parlor table, picked up a large pair of scissors, and returned to attack the woman's hair and trim it to her requirements. When she had finished, she announced that she was prepared to proceed with the interview. The woman somehow managed to pitch Lucy the questions, despite the fact that she now had something resembling a crew cut, and was ready to kill Lucy.

Lucy and Desi spent their vacation in Sun Valley that year. They had a long stretch before they had to shoot the next series of shows in the fall. In May, Louella Parsons and Hedda Hopper announced that Lucy was pregnant again. This meant she would be giving birth next TV season, and everybody at CBS began to panic, wondering how they could possibly conceal her increasing size during the fall schedule.

Lucy fretted this could mean the cancellation of the series; and Desi asked Jess Oppenheimer what they could possibly do to overcome the problem. Oppenheimer immediately said that Lucy's pregnancy would be the best thing possible for the show. The audience would be kept breathless for months; Lucy Ricardo would also be pregnant in the series; the delivery would come mid-series, close to airplay. (According to Desi Arnaz, the opposite was true: It was his idea to have Lucy deliver the child as part of the show, and Jess Oppenheimer was worried about it.) At all events, whichever of the two men thought of the idea, it ran into trouble right away. Desi called the Biow Agency to explain the problem and how he intended to solve it. Biow told him the idea was out of the question because pregnancy was never to be shown on TV due to the Standards and Practices rules of the network. Desi called CBS, and they were adamant; Philip Morris refused to allow any such idea to be entertained. The Morris people suggested that Lucy wear clothes that would conceal her pregnancy as long as possible. Desi was furious, but could do nothing. Lucy was equally upset.

Because of the pregnancy the couple was forced to cancel an upcoming New York and London tour at the Roxy and the London Palladium, turning down a fee of $200,000; the officially published reason was they did not want to leave little

Lucie. The press department of Desilu was working overtime
to conceal the baby's upcoming arrival until the matter could
be resolved with both network and sponsor. Everyone was
crushed, feeling that the theme of "I Love Lucy," which was
Lucy wanting to break into nightclub work, to compete with
her husband, would be blown out of the water. Even under
extreme pressure from Desi, Milton Biow would only allow
him to show Lucy pregnant in two shows at most. Desi had no
alternative. He had to go over everyone's head and appeal
directly to Alfred Lyons, chairman of Philip Morris, who had
visited the ranch before and had been shocked to see Lucy
smoking Chesterfields (Lyons insisted she place them in a
Philip Morris pack when she smoked on the show). Desi, in
his letter to Lyons, went over the whole problem very carefully
and said, among other things,

> You are the man who is paying the money for this
> show, and I guess I will have to do whatever you
> decide. . . . We have given you the number-one
> show in the country and, up till now, the creative
> decisions have been in our hands. Your people are
> now telling us we cannot do this, so the only thing I
> want from you, if you agree with them, is that you
> must inform them that we will not accept them tell-
> ing us what not to do unless, in the future, they will
> also tell us what to do. At that point, and if this is
> your decision, we will cease to be responsible to you
> for the show being number one on television, and
> you will have to look to your people, to the network
> and to the Biow Agency for that responsibility.

Lyons received the letter in London. He cabled a memoran-
dum to CBS, Biow, and everybody else concerned in the matter, reading, DON'T FUCK AROUND WITH THE CUBAN! That was
enough. The sponsor called the shots. Nobody at Biow or CBS
dared question the all-powerful Alfred Lyons. However, even

his prompt action didn't solve the problem completely. In order that Lucy would be able to get sufficient rest, CBS would have to start shooting that summer of 1952, and the long season break would be slashed in half.

The writers were retrieved from vacation, and so were William Frawley and Vivian Vance and her husband Phil Ober. The Arnazes returned from Sun Valley. Oppenheimer plunged into script conferences with the team. Feeling somewhat tense about possible adverse reaction from the churches, they began working out all the aspects of humor that could be drawn from pregnancy signs. To cover all bases, a priest, a minister, and a rabbi read every script and oversaw every filming.

The new season's shooting began on July 15, 1952, with a program entitled *Job Switching*, directed by William Asher. As yet, Lucy's pregnancy did not show. It was a role-switching story: Lucy and Ethel went out to get work while their husbands turned into "wives" and did the cooking and cleaning. The two girls found a job making candy in a factory, a hilarious expedition into the blue-collar world. In a classic sequence, they were seen on the assembly line, wrapping candy piece by piece but unable to keep up the pace, forced to eat candies they didn't have time to wrap, hiding others in their bosoms and hats. The reviews were good, headed by Jack Gould in *The New York Times*, who wrote,

> [Miss Ball's] comic artistry can easily be missed because she has a way of making it appear deceptively easy. Perhaps her greatest asset is one of those sublime senses of timing that are instinctive rather than acquired. Whether it is a gesture, a change of expression or delivery of a line, she performs with the split-second assurance that is the heart of real comedy. Mark up Miss Ball as a very regular gal who knows what she's doing. . . . Desi Arnaz, who is Miss Ball's husband both on and off the stage, has improved remarkably as a performer since the debut of "I Love

Lucy" a year ago. He's much more at ease now and an engaging foil. . . . One thing more: The film production is much the best to come out of Hollywood. As an act of simple charity toward the long-suffering home viewer, Miss Ball and Mr. Arnaz should tell the other TV producers how they do it.

Seven episodes were written on Lucy's "condition." Philip Morris didn't want her to smoke while visibly carrying her child. Everyone was jittery filming the first pregnancy episode, entitled *Lucy Is Enceinte*. Monsignor Joseph Devlin of the Legion of Decency, Rabbi Alfred Wolfe, and the Reverend Clifton Moore were given a special stage performance of the show before it was filmed. They didn't want to change anything.

Lucy Is Enceinte, shown on December 8, 1952, was historic: Lucy announces her pregnancy to the Mertzes, who are delighted they will be the godparents, but Lucy can find no way of breaking the news to her husband, so she arrives at the nightclub and sends a note up to the stage. In a contrived twist, Ricky fails to recognize his own wife's handwriting, and announces the coming blessed event from the stage, singing "Rockabye Baby" to the unknown mother. It is only in mid-song that he finds out the happy woman is Lucy.

In the next episode, *Pregnant Women*, there is much discussion about the baby's name. Lucy says, waxing pretentious, that the names should be "unique" and "euphonious." Ricky replies, "We'll call the boy Unique, or the girl Euphonious." Lucy becomes jealous of Ricky's interest in the unborn child, and he makes up to her by giving her a rattle. In the third pregnancy episode, *Lucy's Show-Biz Swan Song*, Lucy is once again trying to crash the nightclub business. She and Ethel go for an audition for a gay nineties revue, croaking their way through "By the Light of the Silvery Moon." Turned down, Lucy manages to join Ricky and the Mertzes in a disastrous comic version of "Sweet Adeline."

In *Lucy Hires an English Tutor*, Lucy, knowing she is "common," tries to learn elegant language from the fancy Percy Livermore, trying to iron out her crude Americanisms so that her child will be master of "royal English." In *Ricky Has Labor Pains*, Ricky becomes jealous of the unborn baby because Lucy is giving it so much attention. Ricky begins to suffer from morning sickness, and Lucy fears he is turning into her, so she gives him a "daddy shower," disguising herself as a reporter and Ethel as a photographer covering the party. In another episode, Lucy decides to become a sculptress so their child will inherit artistic abilities; in still another, Ricky and the Mertzes go bananas worrying about the baby and its delivery.

During the shows, Lucy was shown with all of the eccentricities and obsessions of approaching motherhood, including cravings for such unlikely combinations as sardines and ice cream (when Ricky developed morning sickness, he had a need for special foods). It was understood that Lucy would have to have her second child as she had had her first, by Cesarean section. The child would be born in January, and the show in which she delivered the baby would have to be shot three months before, in the first week of October. The problem was that in those days no one could tell whether an unborn child would be a boy or a girl. It was an unheard-of gamble. If they showed Lucy giving birth to a girl and she gave birth to a boy in real life, it would be a disaster. The show could not be reshot and all the publicity would go down the drain.

Jess Oppenheimer, followed by Desi and Lucy, decided that the baby would be a boy. They risked everything on this wild throw of the dice. In the hospital scene in *Sales Resistance*, the childbirth episode, Ricky was shown the baby, was told it was a boy, and fainted. Desi wouldn't use a double and actually hurt his head in the fall.

During the shooting of the pregnancy episodes, Desi took over the direction. This annoyed his official director, William Asher. Another problem was Vivian Vance. She still suffered from William Frawley's rudeness, and she was tired of having to be twenty pounds overweight, a condition laid down in her contract. Also, she didn't like the ugly dresses she was forced to wear, again not to draw attention away from the star. Despite press-agentry giving the impression of happiness on the set, Vivian frequently argued with Lucy, exasperated by what she felt to be a suppression of her natural attractiveness on the screen. There was an especially ugly moment: Vivian had to make a difficult costume change involving a long trip to her dressing room over complicated cables and light leads. Lucy had her trailer parked right next to the set, which made the change simple for her. According to the show's historian, Bart Andrews, Lucy snapped at Vivian as she appeared, "You almost missed your cue. You're late!" Vivian turned to her and looking at Lucy's pregnant figure screamed, "I'd tell you to go fuck yourself if Desi hadn't already taken care of that!" Lucy glared and stalked off.

Through the winter season of 1952, the country was in a hubbub over Lucy's approaching delivery. Even President Eisenhower's winning of the electoral race of 1952 had to battle for space against the momentous event. On January 14, 1953, reports flew around that little Ricky Ricardo would be born on the following Monday's show. Thousands called the studio and the Hollywood Press Office, demanding to know the details. The nineteenth of January would be a date to be remembered in the annals of television history.

Because the delivery was to be Cesarean, it was possible to time it exactly. Reporters swarmed into the hospital to be with Desi in the waiting room. Lucy entered the obstetrical operating room on cue at 10:00 A.M.; the show, shot in October, was due to be telecast that night. The suspense was unbearable. Desi almost came apart, because if it were a girl, that night's show would have to be taken off the air. At last the tension was broken. Nurses came running into the waiting room and screamed to Desi and the reporters, "It's a boy!"

She, too, had been in a state of agonized suspense as to whether life would imitate art. Desi yelled at the reporters, "That's Lucy for you! Always does her best to cooperate with the show!" Then he called Jess Oppenheimer to tell Jess his powers of prophecy were sensational. Within minutes, news of the birth was all over the world. Hourly bulletins followed, as Desi went on "CBS News" to announce that the baby would be called Desiderio Alberto Arnaz y de Acha IV. There were over a million telegrams, presents, and letters, and truckloads of baby clothes, food, and bedding. Eisenhower's inauguration was pushed off the front pages. Reporter Walter Winchell announced on ABC, "This was a banner week. The nation got a man and Lucy got a boy." That night was the biggest in the history of television. Eisenhower's swearing-in ceremony had an audience of 29 million people, while 44 million watched Lucy Ricardo welcome little Ricky. And there was a bonus beyond that: On February 5, 1953, Lucy received her first two Emmy Awards, for Best Comedienne and Best Situation Comedy on the Air.

· CHAPTER 11 ·

*R*ight after little Desi's birth, Lucy had a nasty shock. The three dogs she treasured most in the world, one of which she had had for many years, all died within one month. It was almost as though she had had to pay a price for her second child. She told Hedda Hopper, "It seems like God waited for the children and then took my dogs." She cried constantly over the loss, and it was impossible for Desi, Sr., to console her.

At the same time, Lucy and Desi signed to appear in a movie for MGM, *The Long, Long Trailer*, after the novel by Clinton Twiss, who had based most of the comical experiences in it on his own while traveling up and down the California coast from Laguna Beach. Lucy's old friend and alleged former love interest Pandro S. Berman was assigned as producer, and Lucy and Desi asked for Vincente Minnelli, father of Liza, to direct the movie. The script was filled with amusing incidents in which a couple faced successive hazards of trying to deal with trailer life. In one funny scene, the wife tries to cook a meal while the trailer is swinging along hairpin bends. It was ideal as an adjunct to "I Love Lucy," and the couple had been aching to make a big feature film. However, they couldn't start right away, because Lucy had to rest, and there was constant work at the studio for Desi.

The couple signed a new $8 million contract with Philip

Morris, the biggest in television history up to that time, for two and a half years more of the program. Arnaz explained ruefully at a press conference, "After everybody gets their cut, we'll wind up with eight dollars and sixty-seven cents saved." The reason for this wry remark was that the $8 million would pay for CBS's network time and provide the show's $50,000-a-week-budget. As Aline Mosby announced in the *Los Angeles Daily News*, the salaries of three hundred people, from directors to electricians, would be deducted from the $50,000 budget. Lucy and Desi had some difficulty paying themselves $3,000 a week each from the residue. Their MGM contract called for $40,000 a week for both with a minimum of $250,000 for both for the run of the contract.

Lucy stayed home for two months to take care of little Desi; the production gap was filled by reruns of the first "Lucy" season. On April 1 she began to film the first episodes involving the actual baby. However, Desi, Jr., was not, the parents decided, to spend his babyhood working in television. Instead, the Arnazes hired twins Richard Lee and Ronald Lee Simmons, who were paid $25 each per show, to play the part of their own son alternately. The reason they had to hire twins was that the California child labor laws forbade any infant to work more than two hours a day. Accompanied by their mother, Mrs. Arthur L. Simmons, their grandmother, and a social worker called for by the City of Los Angeles, the babies relished their stardom, and played with equal expertise under the sometimes flustered direction of William Asher and others, who were not accustomed to dealing on a continuing basis with children as young as that. Jess Oppenheimer wrote in *Look* magazine on April 21 of some of his problems. But the good humor with which he expressed these headaches reflected the delight of the "Lucy" team at the time.

In early April, the Arnazes had Desi, Jr., christened at the location of their religious wedding in 1949, Our Lady of the Valley Church in Canoga Park, near Los Angeles. Father Michael Hurley presided at this Catholic baptism, as he had presided at the earlier nuptials. Further improvements were made to the $22,000 nursery wing of the Chatsworth farm so that the little boy would be surrounded by paintings showing scenes from fairy tales and legends. Lucy told writer Eleanor Harris, "Desi and I don't think we lived until we had children. All of a sudden there's a reason for everything—they're worth every sacrifice, and every deal we make is for them. Before they came, if we made mistakes it didn't matter." Ms. Harris noticed that as Lucy talked, her children were playing happily on the living room floor, while Desi, wearing a frilly apron, was preparing a meal in the kitchen. This picture of domestic bliss was not entirely accurate, however. Weekends were of course crucial to a couple as busy as they were—weekends looked forward to and preciously preserved to spend with the kids. But the fact that all was still not well with the marriage can be understood when it is learned that by now Desi, instead of spending Saturday and Sunday at Chatsworth, was instead on board his yacht at Balboa. This led to constant gossip, confirmed by him later, that he took his mistresses there.

An event in April 1953 was extremely unsettling. About a year earlier, Lucy had been interviewed, much to her dismay, at home by William A. Wheeler, head of the West Coast investigation for the House Un-American Activities Committee which, in the McCarthy era, was probing into alleged Communist activities in Hollywood. Lucy had told Wheeler that she had only joined the Communist party in order to humor her eccentric grandfather Fred Hunt. She had assumed that this reply settled the matter, but occasionally she awakened at night feeling tense, remembering Wheeler, and wondering if it was all over. It was in April 1953 that she received word from various sources that the matter wasn't closed, that the investigators were not satisfied, and that she would soon have to be dragged before a Committee hearing, a thought that was almost unbearable to her.

Here she was, the most famous woman in America, as institutionalized as Mom and apple pie, a symbol of daffy decency in a wicked world, worshipped by practically every adult person alive, adored by children, and now her entire new career, which had barely begun after the dreary decades making bad movies, might end overnight. It was not a question of her being guilty of anything; the mere mention of communism in the time of the Cold War was enough to ruin anybody. By 1953, Hollywood had been decimated, countless members of its writers' and directors' guilds forced into exile, compelled to write under assumed names, unable to obtain work of any kind. Families were disrupted, houses sold, incomes shriveled to nothing. Some prominent actors, most notably John Garfield (dead of a heart attack in 1952), Sam Jaffe, Gale Sondergaard, Larry Parks (who had been sensational in *The Jolson Story*), Will Geer, and Howard Da Silva, had been brought to the edge of ruin by the frenzy of the blacklist. The Committee's rampaging search for so-called conspirators threw the whole movie industry into a paranoid state that today seems beyond belief. Lucy, always embattled, jittery, and on edge, now had to face the worst prospect of her life.

She tried to forget what was coming in the pleasant shooting that summer during the "I Love Lucy" hiatus of *The Long, Long Trailer*. Vincente Minnelli proved to be an enchanter. Warm and sweet, though extremely sophisticated, he had an abstracted air that concealed a keen disciplinarian and a genius with an instinctive grasp of movie rhythm and momentum. His delightful throwaway wit was reflected in the ease, charm, warmth and elegance of the movie as a whole. Lucy's effortless timing had seldom been as clearly exemplified as in the big cooking scene in which all of the food wound up on the floor. Given the luxury of a long, comfortable shooting schedule, a lavish budget, and the opportunity to prepare scenes without the pressure-cooker atmosphere of television, the Arnazes were more or less happy. The only problem was that once more the long hours of making the film reduced the amount of time they could spend with their children. Shooting ended in August, and they happily took off with the kids to their favorite Del Mar for a rest, some sun and swimming, and a chance to collect their thoughts before the beginning of the third "Lucy" season.

What should have been a delightful and dreamlike vacation was rudely interrupted by events Lucy had been dreading for well over a year. The phone rang and she answered it, growing pale and sick with fear as she listened. A cold voice said that she would be called in for more questioning on her Communist affiliations. Desi recalled later that Lucy was beside herself, coming close to hysteria, crying and unable to sleep. Just how the press would handle this was one of her deepest concerns. True, Hedda Hopper and Louella Parsons, the two news hens who ran the Hollywood coop, were quite good to her, and she regarded Hedda as an actual friend. But, as Desi edgily had to agree, these harpies were on the warpath after left-wingers, and it might be the end of the road if either columnist turned against the couple.

Lucy turned up at Room 512, 7046 Hollywood Boulevard, on September 4, 1953, to talk with investigator William A. Wheeler. It was probably the most unpleasant afternoon of her life. In the hot, brown-painted, ugly office, she felt ill with concern as the questions droned on and on monotonously, taken down by a court stenographer tap-tapping away at a small quiet machine, as though Lucy was in court. She gave her birthplace (accurately, for once) as Jamestown, not Butte; asked what her educational background was, she replied, nervously, "Just school, high school." She confirmed she was appearing at Room 512 voluntarily, not under subpoena; she remembered her salaries at Columbia and RKO as $75 and $50 a week in 1936; oddly, she doubted if she had worked in films before that year, quite forgetting her Goldwyn Girl appearances and the films in which she had played small parts. Shown her first registration to vote, she was asked if the signature at the foot of the document was her own, and said that it "looks like my handwriting." Wheeler wasted little time. He said, "You will note that the party you intended to affiliate with at that time was the Communist party." She admitted that she had registered as a Communist, and he asked her the reasons. She said, "It was our grandfather, Fred Hunt. He just wanted us to, we just did something to please him. I didn't intend to vote that way. As I recall, I didn't." She mentioned Fred's admiration for Eugene V. Debs and socialism, his sympathy with the workingman, his subscribing to *The Daily Worker*, and said, "It never meant much to us, because he was so radical on the subject that he pressed his point a little too much." She became incoherent through nerves: "Actually, probably, during our childhood, because he finally got over our heads and we didn't do anything but consider it a nuisance, but [he was our] dad,* and he got into his seventies, and it became so vital to him that the world must be right twenty-four hours a day, all over it, and he was trying his damnedest to do the best he could do for everybody and especially for the workingman; that is, for the garbageman, the maid in the kitchen, the studio worker, the factory worker. He never lost a chance to do what he considered bettering their positions."

Lucy went on: "That was fine, and we went along with it whenever we could. Sometimes it got a little ridiculous because my position in the so-called capitalist world was pretty good and it was a little hard to reconcile the two. We didn't argue with him very much because he had a couple of strokes and if he got overly excited, why, he would have another one. So finally there came a point when my brother was twenty-one, and he was going to see that Freddie registered to help the workingman, which was, in his idea then, the Communist party. At that time it wasn't a thing to hide behind doors, to be a member of that party."

She went on to say that Grandpa considered the family involvement a personal victory at the time, despite the fact that she and her mother and brother privately considered he was

---

* She meant granddad.

wrong because the things he was shouting about didn't seem to be practical for America. She pointed out how confused Grandpa was during the Nazi-Soviet pact of 1940, when Russia and Germany joined forces; he was "very disillusioned by this and didn't know what to say when asked about it." He would "get mad and change the subject." She spoke of his talking to maids or garbagemen and telling them they should not be doing menial work.

Lucy denied she had ever been a member of the Communist party; she was asked whether she was aware she had been a member of the Central Committee of the party of 1936. She said she was not, whereupon Wheeler handed her a document entitled "Appointment of Members of the State Central Committee Meeting at Sacramento in the Year 1936." Three individuals were listed as delegates, including Fred Hunt and Lucy, both at 1344 North Ogden Drive. Lucy said she had no explanation for this document, and said she had not signed it. She had never heard of Emil Freed, who allegedly had appointed her; she did not know if her brother had been appointed; and she blamed her grandfather for putting her name on the document. She denied she had attended the State Central Communist Committee meeting at Sacramento; and said she was "appalled" to learn that meetings of the Communist party had taken place in her home. When the names of those who had attended the meetings were read to her, she denied having heard of them. She repeated again and again that she had only become involved to please her grandfather. She said, "I remember feeling very foxy about the whole thing, because I registered. We had a very bad feeling we had done that. I always felt I would be all right if I didn't vote it just to appease Grandpa." This sentence makes no sense; but it's clear that by now Lucy was hopelessly confused and upset. When Wheeler asked her if she knew the phrase "criminal syndicalism," she replied, sharply, "No, but it is pretty. What does it mean?" Wheeler pointed out that she had signed a document calling for the repeal of the Criminal Syndicalism Act at a time that

Communists were in court on criminal syndicalist charges. Since criminal syndicalism involved sabotage, Wheeler took the fact that she had allegedly tried to have the law repealed very seriously.

Wheeler referred to a mention of her in the Communist paper *Daily People's World* for October 28, 1947, as "one of the high personalities who are sponsoring or a member of the Committee for the First Amendment." The Committee for the First Amendment was set up to oppose the House Committee hearings begun in 1947. Lucy was very upset by this reference. She said, "I can't imagine doing anything for these people. If I was hoodwinked into it, with one of those long democratic souped-up names, that is something else." Reference was made to a broadcast she had given years before in which she had opposed preventing Okies, Oklahoma Dust Bowl farmers, from coming to California. Apparently, the FBI had questioned her on the matter at the time. She delivered a long speech saying that if she had done wrong it was unintentional, that she was not and had never been a Communist, that "at no time in my life have I ever been in sympathy with anything that even faintly resembled it," and that "I thought things were just fine the way they were." She added with a touch of perhaps unintentional humor, "It was almost as terrible to be a Republican in those days." She mentioned her support for Roosevelt and how she had enjoyed helping him with his March of Dimes and War Bond tours. She concluded, "How we got to signing a few things, or going among some people that thought differently, that has happened to all of us out here in the last ten or twelve years, and it is unfortunate, but I will certainly do anything in the world to prove that we made a bad mistake, by, for one week or a couple of weeks, trying to appease an old man." After that statement, Lucy was excused, and, in succession, her mother DeDe and brother Fred were called to give evidence.

DeDe confirmed that the family had joined the party "only to please Fred." Wheeler read to her part of an affidavit by an alleged former Communist, Rena M. Vale, which stated that Ms. Vale had attended a meeting at the house and had been told that those present were guests of Lucille Ball, who was glad to lend her home for the members' class. An instructor had allegedly appeared to give the newcomers lessons in Communist procedure. DeDe claimed she knew nothing of this episode, and, that she had never heard of this woman. She denied any knowledge of signing petitions circulated by one Jack Breger. She denied that Fred was a delegate to the Central Committee of the Communist party. She said, "Fred in fact was the children's [real] father. Their [own] father had passed on, and he had been so good to them we figured to pacify him if it would make him happier—things like that. I am certain in my own mind that neither Lucille Ball, my daughter, or my son, Fred, were connected in any way with the Communist movement." She said she would never have allowed Communist meetings in the house. She said Fred was just "a harmless soul," and she added, "I have said many times, 'Thank goodness, he's interested in *The Daily Worker* instead of getting drunk with the men on the corner or being interested in women,' and things like that. I always knew he was home. I always knew where he was, so if he sat on the corner and read *The Daily Worker* I was happy. At that time it seemed like it was a lucky thing."

Fred Ball gave evidence. He denied membership in the party. He said, touchingly, "I realized, along with the rest of my family, that Grandpa didn't have too many years to go, and what he wanted us to do, as long as it was more or less something that would make him feel that we were with him, we were inclined to do it. He used to talk to all of us and all of our friends by the hour about the workingman, and his *Daily Worker*. We used to listen, not because of the interest we had, but rather because of the courtesy we felt we owed him. And this is the direct result of our attitude toward Grandpa."

Fred described his subsequent problems: how he joined Vega Aircraft on the night shift, only to be fired without warning; how he'd tried to get the job back without success; how doors were closed to him throughout Los Angeles; how he went to Wichita, Kansas. He described going to work for Beechcraft and then G and A Tool Company and the Swallow Airplane Company, and how he had decided to go back to California to join the Army. He had obtained a deferment from Wichita, but then, when he was halfway through the physical, he was told to go home. It was only after a considerable effort that he was able to get into the Army. Eventually he was cleared for service. At last, after the war, he had gone to the FBI to see what was being charged against him, and managed to get work as a result of the further clearance. But for years the matter hung over his head.

Lucy was convinced that nothing more would be heard of the matter. She assumed that it would be buried and that the Committee would on no account release what had been confidential information. However, a bombshell exploded, two days after her meeting with Wheeler, on September 6, 1953.

· CHAPTER 12 ·

*T*hat Sunday, Walter Winchell, who apparently had spoken directly to Wheeler thanks to a leak, announced on his nationwide radio broadcast and telecast that "the most popular of all television stars has been confronted with her membership in the Communist party." Lucy heard the news, and the panic she had been in for the several days before, during, and after her interrogation now overpowered her. Desi heard the news while playing poker with friends in Del Mar. He drove 130 miles at breakneck speed to Chatsworth, knowing that Lucy desperately needed him. When he arrived, Lucy was almost hysterical; with her at the house was Howard Strickling, vice president of MGM in charge of publicity, who was handling the imminent release of *The Long, Long, Trailer*. The group went into a discussion. Strickling read over the transcript which the Committee had provided. Unwisely, he suggested that Lucy and Desi try to duck the issue and not see the press. He was under pressure from Louis B. Mayer to pursue this policy.

Two days passed—of extreme mental anguish for all concerned. Hedda Hopper told me she was in special difficulties because she was known to be Lucy's friend and supporter. She received numerous phone calls from readers, insisting on knowing when she would tackle the issue. Miss Hopper said she was beside herself over this. One of the many things that sold papers was her anti-communism and her tacit approval of the Committee. If there was anything in the charges, if she was found to be defending a Communist, she could be finished herself. On the other hand, she was fond of Lucy, and, after much hesitation, she called Lucy and Desi on that Wednesday at the studio and insisted on having a statement answering Winchell's charges. Desi told her that Winchell's insinuations were "ridiculous," and that Lucy "had never been accused of being a Communist." He added, "The only thing that is red about this kid is her hair!"

Somehow, Lucy managed to struggle through rehearsals for the first show of the new season, *Ricky's Life Story*, to be telecast on October 5. It was a typical concoction in which Lucy, still struggling to break into show business, learns to dance, rehearsing six hours a day for three days in succession. She collapses, exhausted, but then, finding out that Ricky has put her up to this to disillusion her about show business, invades the stage in the nightclub and fools around in a "Lady of Spain" number.

Dealing with the difficult dance routines was always a bugbear of hers, since she was not a talented dancer. Lucy can only have been reminded of the strain she was under when she did Dorothy Arzner's *Dance, Girl Dance*. On September 11, she was supposed to do the afternoon dress rehearsal and film the first day's work in front of the usual live audience. When she woke up, she looked out of the window of her bedroom at Chatsworth and was alarmed to see two men in hats and suits standing outside, looking up toward her. She wondered whether they might be burglars or hit men, and shook Desi awake; he went out and demanded to know what the two were doing there. They told him that they were from the *Los Angeles Herald Express*,* and that they wished to report on Lucy's Communist activities and would like to have a quote from her. One of the two men was carrying a camera; Desi grabbed

---

* Today the *Los Angeles Herald-Examiner*.

him and shook him by the neck, screaming at him. The two men showed their press cards. One said, "The paper has a photostatic copy of an affidavit showing Miss Ball had registered in 1936 as a voter intending to affiliate with the Communist party." Desi managed to calm himself sufficiently to invite the two men in and settle them down while he called the paper's city editor, Agnes Underwood. He told her Lucy would not give an interview to anyone. He also insisted that Miss Underwood tell the reporters to leave immediately. He handed one of them the phone and was pleased to hear Miss Underwood issue the instructions he had asked for. This was a serious mistake. By crossing the reporters, instead of humoring them, he had aggravated them unendurably. That same day, the paper ran a banner headline in red printer's ink, reading, LUCILLE BALL A RED. It also printed Lucy's Communist party card, on the direct orders of top management in the Hearst publishing empire, which owned the paper.

This was a severe blow, and the *Los Angeles Times* coverage was no better. The question was: Would Philip Morris withdraw its sponsorship from CBS for the series? Would the series be able to continue? Would *The Long, Long Trailer* be releasable? And what about public opinion?

Seemingly, the $8 million contract was not cancelable. But no doubt if Philip Morris felt that this political scandal would affect cigarette sales, they could find some lawyer to break the deal.

That afternoon, Lucy and Desi arrived for the 1 P.M. dress-rehearsal call. They ran into a crowd of reporters. Lucy went through the rehearsal, she told me, in a kind of a daze, not knowing what to do, but somehow mechanically managing the dances called for. Meanwhile, Desi rushed to his office and called Frank Stanton, president of CBS, in New York. Desi was terrified. Stanton said he would talk to Bill Paley and get back to him. Then Desi called Philip Morris. Stanton asked their public relations chief, Benjamin Sonnenberg, what the next move should be. Sonnenberg told him that Desi would know how to handle it. Desi sweated out the next two hours until, at 3 P.M., CBS got back to him and Stanton told him, "We're behind you one hundred percent." Desi ran over to Lucy on the soundstage and, tears streaming down his cheeks, told her the good news.

Lucy was still out of her mind with fright. She was petrified by the live audience that night; she feared that they might attack her physically or at the very least hiss and boo her. Desi, though he saw the terrible state Lucy was in, decided not to cancel the live audience, because if he did so, people might take it to mean that she was admitting she was at fault in the matter. As Lucy struggled through the ordeal before 6 P.M., Desi demanded that Donald Jackson of the House Un-Ameri-can Activities Committee immediately hold a press conference exonerating her outright of any guilt. Under pressure, Jackson agreed. Then Desi, still greatly agitated, called his friend Jim Bacon of the Associated Press to make sure the conference got into print all over the world. Bacon promised to do what he could. When Desi brought the news to Lucy, she was deathly pale and feeling faint.

At 8 P.M., a shaking Desi had to confront the live audience as it filed in. Minutes before, Bacon had advised him that she had been cleared at the press conference and all would be well in the morning. But Lucy was still petrified.

Desi said to the crowd, "Ladies and gentlemen, I know that you have read a lot of bad headlines about my wife today. I came from Cuba, but during my years in the United States Army I became an American citizen, and one of the things I admire about this country is that you are considered innocent until you are proven guilty. Up to now, you have only read what people have said about Lucy, but you have not had a chance to read our answer to those accusations. So I will ask you to only do one thing tonight, and that is to reserve your judgment until you read the newspapers tomorrow, where our story will be. In the meantime, I hope you can enjoy the show under these trying circumstances." He added, "And now the girl to whom I've been married for thirteen years and who, I know, is as American as J. Edgar Hoover, President Eisenhower, or Barney Baruch, my favorite wife, the mother of my children, the vice president of Desilu Productions—I am the president—my favorite redhead—even *that* is not legitimate. The girl who plays Lucy—Lucille Ball!" According to Bart Andrews, historian of "I Love Lucy," Desi also said, "Lucille is no Communist. Lucy has never been a Communist, not now and never will be. I was kicked out of Cuba because of communism. We both despise the Communists and everything they stand for."

The inspired speech paid off. Delivered with all of Desi's skill, it electrified the studio audience, which rose to its collective feet and yelled, "We love you, Lucy!" and "We're with you, Desi!" The orchestra struck up the "I Love Lucy" theme and the entire crew and director William Asher joined in the applause. Lucy, in floods of tears, managed to laugh and smile and thank the audience. She ran up into the bleachers, where DeDe was, as usual, sitting, embraced her and Fred, who was seated with her, Desi's mother, Cleo and Ken Morgan, and even the reporters. Then Lucy, without hesitation, pulled herself together sufficiently to open *Ricky's Life Story*. She played the challenge dance, the collapse scene, and the "Lady of Spain" routine with all of her comic skill. Even the most careful inspection of this episode of the series fails to disclose any of the drama that accompanied it. The show was a riot from beginning to end, and the audience gave Lucy another standing ovation.

However, despite this apparent symbol of public response, there were many who continued to object to Lucy's alleged political errors. Hedda Hopper was besieged by angry letters when she sought to clear Lucy's name in her column. M. S. Maloney of Los Angeles wrote to her on behalf of the Gold Star Mothers: "My son didn't vote red to please his grandpa—but he did die in Korea for his Uncle Sam." An anonymous

subscriber wrote, "So now it cán be told. Isn't it just wonderful? The big blame—blame it onto grandpa. Don't you suppose
she also pleased Stalin too?" Another reader snarled, "Always
admired your solid stand for Americanism one hundred percent—but, *et tu*, Brutus! So the only thing RED about Miss
Ball is her hair, eh? Hedda, how can you be so taken in—or
are you TOO all part of this publicity stunt? Certainly convenient to have a dead grandpa, isn't it?" There were many other
letters in this vein.

Ruth Blair, a nurse, wrote, "Do the American people now
have faith in [Lucille Ball]? Speaking for myself and several of
my friends, the answer is no!! . . . I shall *never, never* watch her
show again—I am a hundred percent American!!!" But there
were also a few letters in support, one of which said that this
great star, who had been "taken into the heart of millions of
Americans," was guilty of a "youthful mistake" only, and
"must be forgiven." Convinced now that she was innocent of
any charges, Hedda stood firm in her support of Lucy. Louella
Parsons followed suit in a rare point of agreement with her
arch-rival. Like Hedda, she was inspired less by political en-
lightenment than by fear of upsetting her millions of readers.
But the storm did not cease. The right-wing zealot Westbrook
Pegler, whose column appeared in hundreds of newspapers
across the country, attacked the rest of the press for being "a
dupe of popular appeal" and for clearing Lucy only "because
she is famous and rich." He charged that she had

> not come clean, but had to be tracked down and
> exposed. The proposition that she was only twenty-
> four years old and that her grandfather was a family
> tyrant, a Socialist who made her do this, has no
> value at all with me. . . . This Ball woman knew
> what she was doing when she registered with the
> Communists, and I can tell you that the poor devils
> out there in Hollywood who fought the traitors in
> the movie business took terrible persecution. They

suddenly lost out at the studios, never knowing why. They got threadbare. They got drunk and despondent, and the Reds sneered at them and snubbed them. Their friends were afraid to be seen with them.

They could have done the same thing that Lucille Ball did, but they were too courageous and loyal. Some of them have died. Did Lucille Ball ever send any of these brave, lonely men a note of confidence or encouragement? . . . *Socialist grandfather!* That is a new variant on the whine of the crooked White Sox player who did it for the wife and kiddies!

Columnist Royce Brier angrily rebutted Pegler's charges. He wrote, "Our freedom is in peril if this pillory for the exhibition of peccadillo and casual descent is permitted to stand indefinitely. But it is up to us. The Congress cannot filch our liberty. Only we can from ourselves filch our liberty."

The Sunday after the performance of "I Love Lucy," Lucy and Desi gave a press conference at the ranch. At the end of it, Dan Jenkins of *TV Guide* said, "I think we all owe Lucy an apology." Everyone applauded, and Lucy cried again. Westbrook Pegler was notable by his absence. That night, Walter Winchell announced that Lucy was completely cleared. However, Desi and Lucy never forgave him for his breaking the item in the first place. William S. Paley of CBS, Milton Biow, Alfred Lyons, and Louis B. Mayer talked to each other into the small hours after the Monday night telecast. The ratings people reassured them that "I Love Lucy" was still number one. Everyone more or less breathed again.

However, there was still trouble ahead. War veterans' groups protested against Lucy; members of the American Legion threatened to boycott Philip Morris cigarettes. But when, in a well-timed gesture, President Eisenhower invited the Arnazes, Vivian Vance, and William Frawley to dinner at the White House, few dared criticize. It was a birthday celebration and Lucy, Desi, Vivian, and William Frawley acted out a scene from their series at the banquet. One day earlier, Lucy had been honored by the Jewish organization B'nai B'rith as Woman of the Year.

It was a triumph of popularity over politics. The couple was bound closer now; they were locked into each other by the crisis that had come close to destroying them. Never before had their relationship been so charged with loyalty, affection, and deep feeling.

· CHAPTER 13 ·

*W*ork on the "Lucy" series continued more gruelingly than ever. Inspired, manic, barely able to sit down for a second, Desi worked himself into a lather sixteen hours a day handling all of the countless problems at the studio, producing "Our Miss Brooks," as well as "Lucy," making commercials, and laying out plans for other shows. Everyone who worked with him agrees he was a very good executive, far removed from his empty-headed television image or from that perpetrated by magazines and newspapers, which talked of him either as a former bandleader who had made good or as a mere foil for Lucy's comic talents. It can be said with honesty that it was Desi, and Desi alone, who held the Desilu Production Company together, soothing troubled egos, settling arguments, putting up with temperament, controlling crews, forcing his way through mountains of paperwork, and somehow squeezing in time for investments that made him and Lucy even richer. By 1954, only four years after having a mere $5,000 to their name, he and Lucy were millionaires, and each day Desi engineered business deals that would soon turn them into multimillionaires.

Many benefited from his and Lucy's newfound wealth. Not only was Desi very generous to the staff with bonuses and frequent salary raises, but he also modernized and renovated the studio, so that everybody would enjoy air-conditioned comfort. On the face of it, the atmosphere at Desilu was of a big, happy family. Yet there were still headaches on "I Love Lucy." Vivian Vance and Lucy clashed more frequently, and William Frawley despised Vivian more than ever and made her life miserable now by still refusing to talk to her. Lucy grew edgier, harder to work with; she was beginning to be aware of the crushing responsibilities of being a rich and powerful woman in the industry. A further problem was that people constantly confused her with her on-screen character and she began to have identity problems, trying to convince acquaintances, casual or otherwise, that she was not a daffy, mindlessly ambitious dame.

Further tension arose when Jerry Hausner, who played Ricky's agent in the series, departed in anger and gave a harsh interview to a magazine. This was later repeated in Bart Andrews' history of the show. Hausner's statement illustrated the fact that Desi also, no doubt under the severe pressure, was capable of outbursts of anger.

The episode that caused the rift was entitled *Fan Magazine Interview*. In the story, Ricky's agent informs him that a magazine writer named Eleanor Harris will interview the Ricardos for a "day in the life of" story. Eleanor arrives at 7 A.M., only to find Lucy and Ricky acting out an absurd version of their marriage designed for public consumption, in which Lucy cooks breakfast in an expensive apron, Ricky enjoys the meal in a fancy smoking jacket, the Mertzes are dressed in the height of fashion, and so forth. In one scene, Hausner was to call Desi on a pay telephone. Because the pay telephone was far away from the phone on the main set. Hausner worried that the connections might not work and that it would be impossible to cue the lines correctly. Due to a technical mishap, the phone lines were not connected on the night of the performance; there were awkward pauses and gaps while Hausner asked a question timed to a stopwatch and Desi answered it. Desi was furious, claiming that the problem was Hausner's fault, which it was not, and Desi screamed and raged at Hausner in front of the studio audience and the cast and crew. Hausner told Jess Oppenheimer he would never work on "I Love Lucy" again. And he did not.

February 1954 was a red-letter month for Lucy and Desi. The world premiere of *The Long, Long Trailer* at Radio City Music Hall was a major event. The theater was packed with Lucy's New York fans. She gave an expertly schmaltzy little speech, telling the excited crowd how she had gone to Radio City in the early 1930s, just after it was built, and "in her wildest dreams" had fantasized that she "would one day be on this stage myself." The couple was wined and dined in Manhattan, enjoying the delights of a city that was still clean, bright, and beautiful in 1954. Back in Hollywood, Desi was busier than ever, fighting off headaches and tics caused by pressure. The work was as punishing as before. Desi embarked on "Those Whiting Girls," a television series starring Margaret Whiting and her sister Barbara. He oversaw "Willy" with June Havoc, actress sister of Gypsy Rose Lee (Aaron Spelling, now producer of "Dynasty," "The Love Boat," and the new 1986 "Lucy" was a bit player in the series). Desi also produced "December Bride," in cooperation with CBS itself, starring Spring Byington. "December Bride" was second only in popularity to "I Love Lucy" as a comedy series. Desi never stopped. He made "Make Room for Daddy" ("The Danny Thomas Show"), "The Ray Bolger Show," "The Jimmy Durante Show," and "The Lineup," a crime series that foreshadowed Desilu's later success with the Robert Stack series "The Untouchables." Desi controlled and rode herd on 229 half-hour shows in that year of 1954, or, as he wrote in his memoirs, "the equivalent of about eighty motion pictures." It is scarcely any wonder that his hair went white or that his headaches, violent outbursts of temper, and quarrels with Lucy increased, or that the operation was compelled to move out of General Service Studios to the Motion Picture Center, which had six soundstages adjoining each other.

By 1954, the pressure had increased still further. Guest

stars were more frequently featured on the show. Tennessee Ernie Ford made a two-parter for the spring of 1954. Cornel Wilde turned up on "Lucy," as did the wives of William Holden, Dean Martin, Van Heflin, Alan Ladd, and Forrest Tucker in an episode entitled *The Fashion Show*. William Holden starred in *L.A. at Last*, in which Lucy Ricardo gazes like a fan at Holden at the Brown Derby on Vine Street. There was a scene in which Holden offered to light Lucy's cigarette. She was wearing a false nose to disguise her identity, a nose resembling a large, straggly bean. Holden accidentally put his lighter too close to the nose and it caught fire. Lucy dunked it in a cup of coffee. The scene was retained in the episode. Sometimes, Lucy's real-life colleagues, including her press agent, the very excellent Charlie Pomerantz, were portrayed by actors; once, Dore Schary, head of MGM from 1948 to 1956, played himself in an episode called *Don Juan Is Shelved*. Rock Hudson was the guest star of *In Palm Springs*. (At the time, Lucy and Desi had just bought a weekend home in the desert town.)

Aspects of Hollywood were dealt with in the 1955 season; viewers were given irresistible glimpses of what they believed represented an authentically glamorous Hollywood instead of the tough factory town it really was. Harpo Marx, Richard Widmark, and others added to the steadily increasing list of stars who appeared with Lucy. In one memorable episode, entitled *Harpo Marx*, Lucy dressed up as Clark Gable, Gary Cooper, and Jimmy Durante, effectively deceiving Harpo. She also played a mirror routine with Harpo, in which he is in a doorway and she gives him the impression he is looking in a mirror by not only doubling his appearance, but anticipating his every movement before he makes it.

The basis of this series of Los Angeles episodes was, of course, the fanciful one that Lucy Ricardo was star-struck over the selfsame people the real-life Lucy knew as an equal. Although the concept was somewhat condescending to the audience, it was done with sufficient false naïveté and humor to make it acceptable to all except the severest critics.

Lucy and Desi matched Ricky and Lucy's invasion of the movie colony in real life. In May 1955, at the time the Hollywood shows were on the air, they left the ranch at Chatsworth they had occupied for well over a decade and moved to 1000 N. Roxbury Drive, Beverly Hills, a sprawling, handsome, white imitation Williamsburg colonial house. The increased traffic and overbuilding in the San Fernando Valley had made getting to and from their beloved farm something approaching a nightmare. When they began working on preparations for a new picture, *Forever, Darling,* they realized that the combined stress of this long travel plus making a movie and laying out plans for the next "Lucy" season, not to mention the burden of Desilu itself, would be too much for even their reserves of energy.

The move was traumatic. Lucy and Desi were at their most frazzled and jittery during it; they were worried that the children would not adapt well to a new environment. Packing furniture and mementos of half a lifetime proved to be excruciating, as unnerving a task as any they had embarked on to date. When the last furniture van ground its way through heavy freeway traffic to Beverly Hills, the couple decided that on no account would they ever move again. Lucy lives at 1000 North Roxbury to this day.

Lucy and Desi need not have worried about the children, who adapted well to their new environment. Lucie was a bubbly mimic and extrovert, imitating parrot-fashion everything Lucy did. On one occasion, Lucy was shouting on the phone within Lucie's hearing, "Who does he think he is! What a nerve! I'd like to tell him a thing or two!" Several days later, mother and daughter were standing on a Hollywood sidewalk when the driver who was to pick them up and take them back to North Roxbury was late. Lucille was amazed when her three-year-old child said, in an exact imitation of her mother's voice, "That driver! What a goddamn nerve! Why isn't he here? Who does he think he is?" Some women were passing by and stared at the child in horror, convinced that Lucy was bringing her up with a shocking disregard for proper language. Actually, it wasn't Lucy's fault her daughter was a star-quality junior parrot.

Desi and Lucy started work on a new movie, *Forever, Darling*. A Desilu/MGM production, it was directed by Alexander Hall, Lucy's date of the 1930s. Hall and Desi worked together with her, Desi doubling as producer and actor. James Mason, who appeared in the film in the part of a guardian angel, told me years later that he was conscious of a strain in the couple's relationship throughout the work, but they expertly concealed their differences.

Forever, Darling did not have the charm of *The Long, Long Trailer*. Based on an earlier script, long since abandoned, and planned for Lucy and William Powell in 1942, it was a story about a chemist, played by Desi, and his wife, played by Lucy, whose marriage has deteriorated into constant bickering. Only in two brief sequences, when the couple take off on a camping trip and struggle with a new insecticide, sleeping bags, and a rubber boat, and in a scene in which Lucy imitates the blond vamp Marilyn Maxwell, was there any real charm or wit in the picture. The best thing in it was James Mason's subdued but witty performance as the angel. The couple gave of their best to the movie, but the truth is that it didn't really work. They returned with relief to the series.

At the end of the 1955 season, Philip Morris suddenly dropped "I Love Lucy." No reason was given. Lucy and Desi were in a state of shock. The couple contemplated selling out for several million dollars and retiring from television, disposing of the studio, and only making one movie a year. Desi wondered if they shouldn't devote more time to the children, now that little Desi was two and a half, and little Lucie four. They realized, however, that if they didn't sell out now they would become tycoons; the studio would soon grow until it ranked with MGM or Warner Bros. Lucy debated between having a more leisurely life and plunging into a role of super-colossal Hollywood executive; she made the latter decision—

and lived to regret it. The couple had more than enough money to live the rest of their lives in comfort, but they couldn't resist the challenge.

"I Love Lucy," with a new sponsor and Lucy in Hollywood as its theme, continued, and in one episode Lucy got to meet the great John Wayne. Later, Lucy went to Europe; a precedent was set when several shows of the 1955–1956 season were set aboard the S.S. *Constitution* of the American Export Lines. In *Ricky's European Booking* (No. 137 of the show), Ricky is offered free passage for himself and his band if he will play for the passengers on a trip to Europe; Lucy, Ethel, and Fred go along. Public response to the show was so strong that, despite many critiques by shipping-line executives of the script, which had Lucy stuck halfway in a porthole and in a helicopter landing on the ship's decks (against maritime safety regulations) the episode attracted considerable attention to the *Constitution* and to its owners, the American Export Lines.

In the spring of 1956, Lucy and Desi went to New York for the opening of *Forever, Darling*. They attended a seminar for brides at which, ironically, they answered questions on how to achieve a happy marriage. Their responses pleased the young wives, who left in a cloud of admiration. The couple traveled on to Jamestown, to see several old friends with whom Lucy had lost touch for several years. They walked through Fred Ball's old clapboard house on Eighth Street and attended a party at which Lucy brushed away nostalgic tears. Her sentimental attachment to the past was one of her most attractive features; she had never forgotten her birthplace, never tried to disown it, and gave money in secret to needy former neighbors or acquaintances, making sure that these acts of generosity never leaked into the press.

In the early part of 1956, Lucy again won an Emmy, and William Frawley received his third nomination (Vivian Vance had won the award two years earlier). Desilu now employed 3,300 people and was earning a total of $5 million per annum. Desi began to plan a capital-gains deal in which he would sell five years of "I Love Lucy" to CBS and buy back the 25 percent share of Desilu that CBS bought in 1952 for $1 million and was now worth far more. Desi's price for the five years was $4 million, and at the same time he proposed that, because of the vast earnings for CBS, he pay only $1 millon for the 25 percent, leaving a residue of $3 million in the deal. There was a protracted struggle with William Paley, until at last a settlement was made, the precise details of which have never been made public. At the end of it, the Arnazes were richer than ever.

Vivian Vance got wind of this deal and tried unsuccessfully to secure a substantial increase in her salary. She was so depressed by the feeling of being subsidiary to Desi and Lucy that she spent years in analysis; William Frawley also beefed incessantly about money. He groused, without a break, to everybody, telling all who would listen of Lucy's "generalship" on the set. But neither he nor Vivian Vance ever seriously tried to break their contracts.

By late 1956, even Desi's energy was beginning to fail. He started to fall apart, his nerves shattered from excessive amounts of work. He was distracted temporarily by the matter of finding a three-year-old boy to play little Ricky on the show; he and Lucy never considered for a moment having little Desi do the job. The Mayer twins took over from the Simmons twins. They were well cared for and protected; not only their mother but a nurse, a welfare worker, and their grandmother were with them at all times. However, neither was quite right for the part at the age of three. Desi began a talent search. At last, "Lucy" orchestra leader Horace Heidt came up with a solution. He conducted a TV show for whiz kids, named "Youth Opportunity," which drew the Arnazes' attention to five-year-old Keith Thibodeaux, of Louisiana, who was billed as The World's Tiniest Professional Drummer. As soon as Desi and Lucy saw him tap-tapping away, they decided to sign him to a seven-year contract. He was a near-double of Desi, Jr., and for years to come (and he found this troublesome) he was addressed by strangers as "Desi." His name was changed to Richard Keith to make it more acceptable to the public, and, to make him more completely a surrogate son, he even learned Spanish at the Arnazes' expense. Everyone was pleased with him. He became a good friend of little Desi, almost a brother to him, and the boys spent much time together at 1000 North Roxbury Drive, and at Palm Springs as well. Desi, Sr., found time in his schedule to raise both boys together. He had them swim laps in the pool, taught them to ride and play baseball, and let them go out with him on his yacht to land fish—all by the age of six. Keith's father worked in the Desilu press office for Lucy's cousin, Ken Morgan.

Desi's and Lucy's recurring awareness that their demanding schedules might harm the children persuaded them toward the end of 1956 to terminate "I Love Lucy." But before they did so, they engaged an old friend of Lucy's from the RKO days, Orson Welles, to appear in the series. Lucy told me later that Orson Welles was unusually capricious during the filming of a scene in which he was a chubby Julius Caeser to Vivian Vance's Cleopatra. He proved awkward in a sequence in which Lucy described to him, while dressed in a skin-diving suit, how excellent she had been as Juliet at Jamestown High School. Even Welles' magic act was feeble, and this episode turned out to be one of the weakest of the series.

Exhaustion set in at the end of shooting the sixth season. Desi took off on a mission to see William Paley in New York. He told Paley that finally "I Love Lucy" would have to end. He said he was ill, that he was suffering from problems with his colon and might have to have a colostomy; what was more, he said, he spent long periods of silence or sleep on weekends, when he was deeply exhausted and alienated from Lucy. William Paley was furious with Desi, saying that the show was still hugely successful and it was shocking to think that it would be killed off in its prime. But Desi was adamant.

$\mathcal{D}$esi left the CBS headquarters in a black mood. After considerable discussions, to-ing and fro-ing between executives and lawyers, Paley was forced to yield and agree that there would only be five "Lucy" specials in the 1957–1958 season. This was after Paley's alternative suggestion was turned down by Desi: that Lucy would be on every other week for a full hour, alternating with the "Perry Mason" series starring Raymond Burr. Thousands of letters poured in to Desilu, demanding to know why the series was being suspended. Lucy gave interviews explaining that everyone connected with the show was exhausted, and that "Lucy" was "by no means dead." In desperation, CBS decided to rerun all of the original shows to cover the deficit and calm public fury. For $5 million, Desi, who drove a very hard bargain, sold all the "Lucy" shows to date to CBS outright, and, breaking with tradition, the reruns went into prime time and were shown on Wednesdays at seven-thirty Eastern Standard Time.

The pressure eased, but not sufficiently for Desi. His health grew worse and worse. His stomach pains were so severe he often collapsed. Foolishly, instead of taking some time off and delegating more responsibility, Desi did the worst thing he could possibly have done: He began drinking heavily. By 1957 he was a very sick man, and had to have a colostomy. Yet he

yielded to public pressure and put "Lucy" back on the air as
"The Lucy-Desi Comedy Hour." It began well, with Ann Sothern, Rudy Vallee, Cesar Romero, and Hedda Hopper among
the guest stars. William Paley called at the end of the shooting
and asked "how it had come out in an hour." Desi told him it
was excellent, the best thing he and Lucy had ever done. Paley
replied that all his old doubts had been shelved, and he would
be taking full-page advertisements to announce the expansion
to the new format. However, Desi was forced to break a piece
of bad news to Paley. He told him that the show ran fifteen
minutes overtime. Paley was unfazed by this. He simply ordered Desi to reduce the length to an hour. Desi said that he
had tried that, but it didn't work. Paley was startled, but immediately said, "Okay, we'll expand it to an hour and a half
for the first special, and run the rest in an hour." Desi said
that he had tried that also, but it wasn't possible to expand
the show without making the pace too slow. Paley said that
there had never been such a thing as an hour-and-fifteen-
minute show on television. Desi suggested the unconven-
tional move of asking "The U.S. Steel Hour," which followed
his show, to give up fifteen minutes of their time. Paley hit
the ceiling. He told Desi he was out of his mind. How could
he imagine that Paley would call U.S. Steel and tell them
their show was so lousy it wouldn't hurt if they yielded fifteen minutes?

Desi volunteered to call U.S. Steel himself. Boldly, he told
them that their show was doing badly and that fifteen minutes
cut out of it might help it. In return for this sacrifice, he would
go on at the end of "The Lucy-Desi Comedy Hour" as himself
and thank U.S. Steel for allowing him and Lucy to take fifteen
minutes from them. He would then praise U.S. Steel profusely
and tell his audience of millions not to turn off the set but to
continue watching, as the upcoming series was excellent. The
man was so staggered by this suggestion that he was almost
speechless. Finally, he asked who would foot the bill for the
lost fifteen minutes. Desi, who had already checked with Ford,

his new sponsor, was able to say that Ford would pick up the tab. The steel executive laughed and told Desi he had a deal. Paley gave in and thus the first "Lucy-Desi Comedy Hour" was in fact "The Lucy-Desi Comedy Hour"—and fifteen minutes. "The U.S. Steel Hour" doubled its ratings overnight based on Desi's extravagant commercial for it.

As it turned out, the seventy-five-minute *Lucy Takes a Cruise to Havana* was the best thing she and Desi had ever done. Even Vivian Vance felt reasonably pleased, as she was allowed to wear more attractive clothes on the ship set. The ratings were staggering. Lucy and Desi plunged into the second show with considerable enthusiasm, despite Desi's declining physical condition. It was decided to cast Bette Davis for the second episode, which was to be entitled *The Celebrity Next Door*. Lucy had never forgotten watching Bette from the wings at the John Murray Anderson/Robert Milton School of Theater and Dance thirty years before.

However, Bette was at her most impossible in that period. She asked for the colossal sum of $20,000, unprecedented for a television guest star, and wanted to be billed in equal size with Lucy and Desi; she also wanted her plane fare back to her home in Maine. Lucy was full of admiration for Bette, and would have paid her anything to co-star with her. But Bette was still suffering mentally from a serious accident on June 23, 1957. Bette, who was moving into a new house in Brentwood, had opened a door that had not been pointed out to her by the real estate lady and plunged many feet down a steep cellar staircase onto a stone floor. She lay in agony, her back broken, for hours, unable to move, with no one within reach. Finally, she was rescued by someone who heard her faint cries, and was rushed to the hospital. She was already in bad shape emotionally, having filed for divorce from her husband Gary Merrill; the divorce itself and an ugly, protracted battle for custody of her son were to follow in 1960. And then, in mid-negotiation for her appearance with Lucy, insisting on riding a horse despite her back, she was thrown and splintered her arm in two places. She was, of course, unable to proceed with the show.

Lucy and Desi discussed a possible replacement and finally settled on Tallulah Bankhead, whom many people thought Bette had imitated in her classic movie *All About Eve*. Desi had failed to check on Tallulah's condition, however; she was overfond of the bottle, smoked incessantly, and was in a disgraceful state of health due to these habits. She existed only on the engine of her colossal ego, growling hoarsely at everybody in sight, alternating bursts of affection with bursts of rage, and acting up a storm off the media as well as on, living to the hilt her role of extravagant, melodramatic star. When she arrived, in September 1957, to begin rehearsals for the special, she was drunk from morning to night. She fought savagely with director Jerry Thorpe, was unpunctual, and insulted Lucy, who screamed at her to be more professional and to obey the rule of punctuality in television. Tallulah, suffering from pneumonia, went up on her lines and coughed alarmingly, at one point spattering Lucy in the face. She didn't help matters by giving an interview in which she said that Desi was fat. One day, she was having hair spray put on when she rose unexpectedly and the spray temporarily blinded her as it hit her eyes. She also had a toothache, which contributed to her foul mood. The tooth was capped; then, grinding her teeth in fury over Lucy, she broke the cap.

Matters grew worse. Lucy wanted Tallulah to wear a mustache in one scene like Groucho Marx, and she screamed her refusal. In the afternoon, she would forget all her lines, having had what she chose to call "a liquid brunch." Desi responded to Tallulah by drinking far too much himself. In the mornings, she was groggy, but she read one line with unusual relish to Lucy: "Remove yourself before I pull out the pink hair and expose the black roots underneath!" Amazingly, on the actual night of the filming, Tallulah sailed through the part without a single mistake, acting brilliantly and bringing out the best in Lucy, who had been chain-smoking up to the last second of the performance, terrified Tallulah would blow her lines in front of the audience.

Around the time of the Tallulah special, Dan O'Shea, president of RKO, called Desi to say that General Tire, which had bought the RKO studios from Howard Hughes, wanted to sell the company's assets outright. It had been running at a loss, and for $6.5 million, he could have the whole studio, including the Gower Street and Culver City offices, studios, and sets. Desi called Hughes to ask him whether he should go ahead and make the purchase. Hughes said he should act immediately. Even if the studios had to be torn down to make into parking lots, there were sure to be profits.

Amazingly, because of heavy taxes and loans that had to be repaid, Desi didn't have $6.5 million to spend. He asked O'Shea to give him twenty-four hours ahead of everybody else before the studio was announced for sale. O'Shea told him that there was to be a payment of $2 million down and ten years to pay the rest, with a mortgage at (happy days) 5½ percent. Desi called the Bank of America and asked for the executive who had arranged the loan for the Motion Picture Center purchase. He said he wanted a loan of $2 million on the spot. As soon as Desi explained to him that it was needed to buy RKO, Desi was astonished to hear the man say, "Whom do we send the check to?" Desi said he would call the man back. Then he pretended to O'Shea that the bank was giving him a hard time, and suggested reducing the price to $6 million. O'Shea wouldn't listen. Desi called William Paley and asked if CBS would like to come in with him on a fifty-fifty deal. Paley refused, but said that he would guarantee to rent space at RKO to help Desi out. After some further negotiations, Desi secured a reduction to $6,350,000 from O'Shea. Later, he even managed to squeeze it down to $6,150,000. Dressed in sixteenth-century costume for a scene in the Tallulah Bankhead special, Desi stood at the telephone and made the deal; the Bank of America promised to send O'Shea a $2 million certified check the following morning.

Lucy, also in Elizabethan costume, heard Desi's whoop of delight. She asked him what was going on. He told her, as calmly as he could, "We just bought RKO studios from General Tire." She was staggered. She couldn't believe Desi. Was it possible that the studio where she had toiled so long in the vineyard would now be hers? She was at once delighted and terrified. The investment represented just about all of their assets, and if it backfired on them they could lose all of the carefully constructed pyramid of money they had built. Distracted and worried and at the same time thrilled, she went back on the set with Desi and immediately plunged into a violent fight with Tallulah. That night, neither she nor Desi slept. They went over and over the purchase, arguing, discussing, thrashing out the details of the deal.

At last, Lucy committed herself to the arrangement, pleased by the irony that she would now be the boss of her former workplace. Several weeks went by. Then the sale almost fell through.

Dan O'Shea learned from his advisers that because of tax problems he and the studio couldn't take more than $500,000 in one financial year. Desi was horrified to learn that O'Shea hadn't even cashed the bank's check. Desi told him to forget the $2 million down payment, and he would replace it with $500,000. O'Shea exasperated Desi by saying that in view of the smaller deposit, the figure for the sale would revert to $6.5 million. Desi screamed, "We made a deal for six-one-five-zero. You wanted two million down and you've got it in your pocket. I couldn't care less what Mr. General Tire can or cannot do with his two-million-dollar check. He can cash it, tear it up, or wipe his ass with it for all I care; the sale price is not going to change!" The deal was on again, and concluded rapidly. Now, Desi and Lucy controlled thirty-five movie stages, a forty-acre backlot, and offices, known as Desilu Gower and Desilu Culver, along with the Motion Picture Center, which became Desilu Cahuenga. It was the biggest production facility on earth.

· CHAPTER 15 ·

$\mathcal{T}$he Arnazes moved into RKO at the outset of 1958, and Lucy took Ginger Rogers' former dressing room. She stripped down the pink-and-black walls and changed the somewhat bordellolike atmosphere to subdued pastels dominated by yellows and whites. Now she had a comfortable sitting room, makeup room, bath, and kitchen. Unhappy at home, tortured by Desi's drinking, painfully reminded of what he had once been by the presence of their little son running around the house, Lucy flung herself into an even stricter regimen. She began the Desilu Workshop, run with Maury Thompson, designed to train young actors and actresses and prepare them for long-term contracts in which they would appear in various series run by the studio. She personally chose 22 applicants from the 1,700 who auditioned, chain-smoking as she watched them go through their paces, sucking her cheeks in, protesting to anyone who criticized that she "didn't inhale." Few believed her. She told a journalist, "We don't take money from [our actors]. We pay them sixty dollars a week—the Actors Equity minimum—and they're free to work anywhere they want. They're not tied to us at all. I understand the agency trouble these kids have. It's the same old vicious circle: You can't get a job unless you've acted, and you can't act unless you've had a job. We're just trying to give them exposure."

The Arnaz children were miserable in 1958. Young Desi said later, "I learned pretty early to relate to 'I Love Lucy' as a television show and to my parents as actors in it. I *had* to learn that, because there wasn't much of a relationship between what I saw on TV and what was really going on at home. On TV, my mother was overplayed and my dad was underplayed. Those were difficult years—all those funny things happening each week on television to people who looked like my parents, then the same people agonizing through some terrible, unhappy times at home, and each of them trying to convince my sister and me separately that the other was in the wrong."

Lucy commented, "Sometimes I went out with Desi on the town. But I'm an eight-hours-of-sleep girl, and his hours were a little long for me. He did nothing in moderation. He never does. Naturally, I went through a long period of being positive that I was the one to blame. It was hard to keep working, to keep on being funny, when I was condemning myself. I became so depressed I couldn't go on alone. I had to get advice."

She went to psychiatrists to consult with them on how to save her marriage. They reassured her that the problem was not hers, and she felt better about that. In a desperate effort to avert a divorce, she and Desi and their children took off for a vacation in Europe that summer of 1958. But the rift between them grew wider overseas. According to Lucy, Desi turned on the children and attacked them verbally without warning. On their return, they went to Del Mar to get over the European jaunt. Lucy told a columnist, "One night, the cook was ill, so I prepared dinner. When I called, 'Dinner is ready,' Lucie called back, 'How can dinner be ready when Francis [the cook] is sick?' It was frightening. Although I have always prided myself on being a good cook, my seven-year-old daughter didn't even know I could bake a potato. So I decided to do all the cooking during the first two weeks of our Del Mar vacation. But I was sick with a virus during the first weeks at Del Mar, so Desi did the cooking."

Drinking more heavily than ever, Desi even overworked

when he played golf. He would come home with his hands sore and blistered, bandage them, and then return to the fairway, determined to do a hole in one. If he couldn't succeed in it, he would go on and on until he did.

Desi was preparing "Desilu Playhouse," a weekly hour-long show that he would host. He became obsessed by the idea of obtaining the support of Westinghouse, whose "Studio One" series was faltering. He flew to the Westinghouse head offices in Pittsburgh and pitched the idea to Mark Cresap of Westinghouse. Cresap asked him the budget. Desi told him $12 million. Cresap said that was double what they could afford. He would have to discuss the matter with his directorial board. Desi suggested he pitch the idea based on a simple principle: twice the cost to earn twice the ratings. This inspired optimism worked and the board approved the sponsorship. Desi secured the biggest contract ever negotiated for television, in which Westinghouse supported not only "Desilu Playhouse" but two Desi specials, eight "Lucy-Desi Comedy Hours," and one Lucy special. However, the writers Bob Carroll and Madelyn Pugh said they could no longer stand writing for the Lucy character, and they departed, much to Desi's despair. But he soon wooed them back again with his charming entreaties, and embarked on a series that included stars such as Red Skelton, Danny Thomas, and the great Ernie Kovacs.

A bizarre incident occurred in June 1958. Lucy told me of it in 1972. She was shooting an episode of the Westinghouse "Lucille Ball-Desi Arnaz Hour," *Lucy Goes to Mexico*. In the story, Lucy had to fight a bull in Tijuana, wave a handkerchief at him, and mention that the perfume on it was "Eau de Hamburger." She said, "I was gored by the head of the bull. Just the head. Lucy was supposed to have taken up bullfighting, but they decided it was too dangerous for me to go in a Mexican bullring. They put a bull's head [mounted] on the front of the camera and ran it down a very long track [on a dolly] at me. The damned thing jumped the track and came right at me, with four guys behind it. Thank God Jerry Thorpe, the director, hit me and knocked me down, or I'd have been killed instantly. As it was, I still got gored. Oh, God, the *blood!*"

Screaming in agony, Lucy was taken to the hospital. After a grueling operation, she recovered slowly. The many stitches irritated her, and she was fretful and noisy with the nurses. They were thrilled to have the real-life Lucy in their midst and tended her like a child. "Not since my nose caught fire in the Bill Holden episode had I had so unpleasant an accident," she told me with a glum face. And she reminded me of some of the other mishaps on the series: "Two chimps bit me, and I could *see* the red tooth marks in my arms and legs for weeks. I don't know how I avoided rabies. Or do chimps give you rabies? I can't remember. And I was even bitten by a *bear* on the 'Lucy' show. I'm here to tell you, until you've been bitten by a bear, you haven't lived!"

Lucy has been accident-prone all her life, but never more than in this period of the late 1950s. She told me, "I'm a Leo, so my limbs snap like matchsticks. I've had accidents all my life! See this hand? With four broken nails? Hey, one just went on the floor!"

She was already beginning to develop the symptoms that were to mark her later in life: In her late forties, she grew brittle and fragile, subject to fractures and sudden, unexpected breakdowns of health. Her smoking affected her esophagus adversely, and gave her the rough, recurrently sore throat that made her voice gravelly and deep in those years.

Lucy, whose day began at six A.M. and ended after midnight, delighted in showing columnists around her studio workshop throughout 1958. It was growing rapidly. She would squeeze visitors like Hedda Hopper into an electric golf cart reputedly built by the studio technicians (because she was so thrifty she didn't want to pay for one from a dealer) and drive them around the theater, offices, dressing rooms, and corridors of the building. She insisted that all of the dressing rooms for the Desilu performers be lavishly appointed. Hedda Hopper gushed in her column for September 30, 1958, "Ann

Sothern's dressing room . . . was unbelievably lush and beautiful. More elegant than many homes I've been in." Lucy was always determined that her players would have the best. However, in return, she expected them to give of their best. She was more of a perfectionist than ever, more demanding, more in control. As Desi's health declined further, she clearly realized that she had no alternative but to take over many of the executive duties at the studio. She spent more of her time in his wood-paneled office, which was very elaborate, with a wood-burning fireplace decorated with the family coat of arms of the Arnazes. An enormous desk that occupied one whole side of the room stood in front of a mullioned window overlooking trees. There were trophies and medals on the walls (forty-two in all) and a framed front page of the *New York Herald* for April 15, 1865, announcing the death of Abraham Lincoln. Books, scripts, and more awards were displayed on tables. And there was a private dining room with a piano.

"Desilu Playhouse" began in October 1958 with *Bernadette*, starring Pier Angeli in the title role. Miss Angeli, who was extremely nervous and sensitive, was reluctant to play the part until Desi and Lucy calmed her down. The show was a great success both critically and financially. By now, Desilu was more enormous than ever. In addition to the shows already shooting, "Mr. Adams and Eve," with Ida Lupino and Howard Duff, "Four Star Playhouse," "Trackdown," "Richard Diamond, Private Detective," "Hey, Jennie," and "Goodyear Theatre" were all added that year.

There is an interesting story told by Bart Andrews about Vivan Vance at that time. She was cast in the lead of "Guestward Ho!," a comedy pilot for ABC. When the director called, "Action," Vivian was barely able to move. She remained frozen for some time. Finally, the director found out the reason. She was so used to being in Lucy's shadow that she could barely function on her own; also, in March 1959, she had gone through a painful divorce from her husband Philip Ober.

Lucy and Desi's marriage finally fell apart in 1959. Desi

moved into a separate bedroom. They tried to keep up a front but it was futile.

In that same year, "The Untouchables" was launched. It was first telecast on October 15, 1959, starring Robert Stack and Jerry Paris. Desi, ever restless, ever inspired, despite his heavy drinking, thought of this series as reflecting the true story of a Treasury Department Secret Service man and gangbuster in the Prohibition days of the early 1930s. The show was based on the career of Eliot Ness, who had helped shatter Al Capone's power and had written a book about it. Phil Carlson, a specialist in screen brutality despite his own mild-mannered personality, directed the "Desilu Playhouse" pilot for the series. Van Heflin was first offered the part of Ness, but turned it down, as did Van Johnson; Robert Stack, who was independently wealthy from old California money, a man of good looks, fine physique, and strong presence, was the perfect third choice for the part. His hard-bitten charm and air of self-confidence were ideal for Ness, but it took Desi's manic determination to overcome some of his initial doubts. Stack hated the idea of doing a long-term TV series, not only because of the potential monotony, but because of his feeling that it might destroy his screen career, since he could become typecast in the public mind. But in fact he did go ahead, making one of the most memorable debuts in television history.

When Desi took off to Europe alone in October 1959, the rumors were all over Hollywood that the Arnaz marriage was over. The children were badly affected by what was happening. Little Desi went to kindergarten and turned out, according to Lucy herself, to be a "pathetic, isolated creature" there. She had to take him out of the school, a pattern that was to recur in subsequent years. One night, as Lucy stopped by Desi's room to tuck him in, she heard him whimpering miserably; Lucie was tossing and turning in her bed as well. In agony, Lucy had to tell her children the truth about the marriage. Lucy was astonished when her daughter looked her straight in the eye and said, with amazing precocity, "You wouldn't get a divorce, would you, Mommy?'' Lucy almost snapped back, ''What do you know about divorce?'' The girl repeated her question. Taking a deep breath, Lucy fibbed that she was only planning a separation.

When Desi returned from Europe, he slammed his car into a telephone pole. Matters came to a head again with the 1959 Christmas Day ''Desilu Playhouse.'' Hedda Hopper wrote in her memoirs:

> Lucy asked me to appear on the Christmas show. She was making her bow as director, coaching a dozen or so young players she had been training in her school for over a year. Desi had just returned from a solo trip to Europe. During rehearsals, Vivian Vance and Bill Frawley wanted to take cover with me to avoid the storms between Lucy and Desi. It was dreadful. ''You can't insult him before the entire company,'' I warned her in her dressing room. ''You're partly responsible for this show, too, you know.'' It seemed we were doomed to have a flop on our hands. As director, Lucy was lost without Desi, too mad to see straight, and the show was going to pieces. In dress rehearsal Desi said, ''Lucy, dear, will you let me see if I can pull this thing together for you?'' Lucy snapped back at him with blood in her eye. ''Okay, try it!'' she snarled.

The fact was that, now that she was losing Desi, she was not only unable to take the shock to her ego, she was embittered by the thought of losing the one man in her life who had meant everything to her for almost twenty years. She was a miserable human being; often, even over the most simple matter, she seemed to be on the verge of tears. She overreacted to just about everything, looking for the most part as though someone had just stepped on her face. She seemed humiliated, disappointed, ground down by life. Her immense wealth seemed to bring her no happiness. She had lost the playfulness and antic pleasure in things she once had. Even games became a feverish addiction: Soon, she would acquire a mania for Scrabble, then, tired of that, became obsessed with backgammon. The truth was, she was more like Desi than even she cared to admit. She had the same desire to fill every minute of the day, to work incessantly; she seemed to be fighting a demon inside herself. When the grosses came in at $20 million and up, that year, she wasn't content. Desi wrote in his memoirs, "The economics of the television business began to get ridiculously bad. . . ." He added that out of a gross of $4.5 million, he only made a profit of $250,000 for 1959. He blamed Hollywood corruption for this shocking fact. He began to talk about selling everything and getting out of the business once and for all.

· CHAPTER 16 ·

*I*n early 1960 the couple tried to patch up their relationship for the children's sake. But again Lucy was still convinced that Desi was philandering constantly, often with young women; it is possible that Lucy's increasing coldness, her authoritarian behavior, and the sternness she brought to each day aided in driving Desi once more from her bedroom. But it is much more likely that it was simply his restlessness, his ego, his consuming desire to be reassured and admired, often a problem with men in middle age, that caused a final and inescapable rift in the marriage. It was heartbreaking for both of them to realize that one of the most famous marital relationships in the world was breaking apart a second time. Jess Oppenheimer, who, though no longer with Desilu, kept close contact with the studio, said later, "Desi wouldn't show up for rehearsal on time and when he did he'd be weaving a little, and it was clear that alcohol was affecting his speech and his walk. That's when it was obvious that there were deep problems in the marriage. Until then, they both had at least presented a common front. There was never any serious bickering between the two of them publicly. And when two people who are married are also working together, it's hard to put a false face on things in front of a crew for all those years.

"The only time I ever saw Lucy get really annoyed with

him was when he'd have a few drinks and then start burping. You'd hear her yell 'Desiiiii!' all the way from her dressing room. She had a certain delicacy about her. She hated anything that seemed coarse." The truth, of course, was that the behemoth they had created in Desilu had literally swallowed up their lives. Money, enterprise, and power had wrecked their personal happiness.

Yet, Desi remained as energetic as ever, and Frederick Christian reported in *Cosmopolitan* in January 1960 that he was all over the sets like an unruly schoolchild at recess, squinting through his viewer, shouting orders, conferring with light and prop men and other technicians. His movements were acrobatic; one instant he was up a ladder; the next he was on his hands and knees, showing where he wanted a wall to be built. Sometimes, he would sink into his chair, his chin on his chest, rubbing his fingers through his thinning white hair, or hide his face in his hands in frustration and anguish. Then a second later, muttering to himself, he would get up, flailing his arms about like a windmill. On one occasion, he was so manic in his movements that he rammed his hand into an electric fan, which cut the tops off three of his fingers.

It was as though, since he was losing Lucy, he had to exhaust himself utterly, and he even took over the director's jobs on many series, rushing from set to set, snapping out commands on where players were to walk, irritating them by giving them the exact movements that he made himself, forcing his face into expressions that he wanted them to assume. He would learn the lines of entire scripts of three or four series at once, and, stoked by alcohol, sweep through one dramatic scene after another. He took no lunch break, and Frederick Christian reported, "When the cast and crew knock off . . . Desi races back to his office and absentmindedly eats a sandwich while disposing of various problems. In one fifteen-minute period I watched him consult with his script editor, look through a catalog of performers with a casting-office man, talk to the prop man about a bar for a set, call in the set designer for consultation, and listen to a man who was trying to sell him an electric golf cart."

Whatever his personal problems, the Desi Arnaz of 1960 was still very popular with all his workers. He was said to never have fired one without the gravest cause. Moreover, he was known to be exceptionally generous with bonuses. He always took care of those who were sick or ready for retirement.

As the marriage ground to an end, Desi involved himself more than ever in the big Williamsburg colonial house on Roxbury Drive. He supervised the nurse in charge of Lucie, now eight, and Desi, six, as well as the maid, the cook, and the gardener. He would go with Lucy to Palm Springs on weekends in reconciliation attempts, and take a passionate interest in everything from the accounting to the broom closets of the two hotels he part-owned with her, in Del Mar and Palm Springs. He even found time to go to church, attending mass at the Church of the Good Shepherd in Beverly Hills or at any other location in which he found himself. The two children were raised Catholic; Lucie wore two Saint Christopher medals because little Desi had lost one and was likely to lose anything else that he wore. Desi crammed in visits to the racetrack, baseball games, at which he cheered for the Dodgers, football games, at which he rooted for the Rams, and just about every other sporting event going. He began to take his vacations separately from Lucy, and finally, Lucy actually filed for divorce. She decided to embark on a new move in her career by going to New York to do a musical, *Wildcat*, but first she had to try to put her affairs in order.

According to Desi, the arguments had become more lethal than ever. One night, the couple went to a party at the Dean Martins'. They both tried to put a good face on things; Desi was dressed up in a brand-new tux and Lucy in a designer gown. In the limousine on the way to the party, Lucy said sharply to Desi, "Are we going to be the last ones to leave the party again?" According to Desi's memoirs, he replied, "For chrissakes, Lucy, we haven't even left the fuckin' driveway yet and you're worrying about whether we're going to be the last ones to leave the party. I've got to be the last one to leave the party now. There ain't no way I can miss. You know, in Cuba, when we have a party and it doesn't wind up with everybody having breakfast the next morning, we consider it a lousy party. And now, if I'm having fun and want to stay a little longer than the other people, you consider me an asshole.''

During one of their quarrels, when Desi said, "I cannot keep on living this way," Lucy, according to Desi, replied, "Why don't you die then? That would be a better solution, better for the children, better for everybody!" He replied that he was sorry, but dying was not on his immediate schedule. She screamed, "I'll tell you something, you bastard . . . you cheat . . . you drunken bum. . . . I got enough on you to hang you. By the time I get through with you you'll be as broke as when you got here. You goddamned Spick . . . you . . . wetback!" Desi went to his dressing room and packed up his belongings. He was about to light a cigarette when Lucy came at him with a gun. She pointed it directly at his head and pulled the trigger. But it was a trick gun, an old cigarette lighter that had been lying around. A flame shot out of the muzzle instead of a bullet, and Desi lit his cigarette on it. Desi told her that she could have the divorce as soon as she wanted it.

They still had to do a final "Lucy-Desi Comedy Hour." It was torture for both of them, but they couldn't break up until the Westinghouse contract was completed. It was hard enough to work together, but it was harder still to have to tell the children again. The kids were in Palm Springs when they gave them the unpleasant news. Desi said, "But, Daddy, a divorce? Isn't there some way you can take it all back?" Lucy and Desi looked at each other and she had to fight back the tears.

In *Lucy Meets the Mustache*, the final Lucy-Desi teaming, co-starring Ernie Kovacs, the couple acted with exemplary control in front of the studio audience, but between scenes, Lucy cried helplessly in the wings or rushed to her dressing room and broke down in front of the mirror. Finally, she pulled off the mustache she was wearing and went completely to pieces.

On March 3, 1960, she filed final papers in Santa Monica Superior Court and a press release announced the unpleasant truth to her millions of fans. Talking of what had taken place, Lucy later told Bart Andrews, "Those last five years were sheer, unadulterated hell. I'm afraid I didn't cope too well."

The decision was to have the divorce arrangements completely amicable, with no contest or fights over property. Ken Morgan, Lucy's cousin Cleo's husband, made a statement to *The New York Times* that the couple were equal shareholders in the Desilu stock corporation, their combined holdings amounting to 49 percent. This would be divided equally. They would have joint custody of the children, with Desi given access as much as he wanted. Desilu Productions, Inc., with its seven thousand shareholders, would remain intact.

The divorce was over quickly, as both Lucy and Desi wished. In court, before Superior Judge Orlando H. Rhodes in Santa Monica, Lucy talked of Desi as "a Jekyll and Hyde" who made their marriage "a nightmare for the last three [she meant five] years." She talked of "temper outbursts in front of the children; there was no discussing anything with him. He would have tantrums in front of friends and relatives and we could have no social life for the last three to four years." She mentioned that when the pipes burst in their home, Desi "made himself sick for two days over it. He blamed everybody and everything. By count there were sixteen people he blamed. He was hysterical and screamed and raved about it." Lucy, dressed in a black-and-white-checked silk suit, her hair a brighter orange than ever, cried as she spoke of the miserable years together. Desi at first denied the charges, then confirmed them. But only, he added through a lawyer, to make the divorce go through amicably. The settlement involved Lucy's obtaining half of the $20 million television empire, or 282,800 shares. The children would get $450 monthly support apiece from Desi.

Lucy began work on a movie, *The Facts of Life*, with Bob Hope. This was meant to be therapy as well as a pleasant break in her unpleasant ordeal of loneliness and depression. The picture was shot at Desilu itself; it was the story of two people who have become bored with their separate marriages and decided to have an affair, which is constantly prevented from consummation by a series of comic mishaps. Lucy enjoyed the work, and she was looking forward to going to New York to star in *Wildcat*. Meanwhile, she was fielding questions from reporters like "How does it feel to be the richest woman in Hollywood?" Yet, another mishap occurred during the shooting of *The Facts of Life*. Lucy was climbing into a boat floating in the studio tank when she lost her balance and fell, cutting her face and leg, injuring her back, and knocking herself out in the process. She was rushed to Cedars of Lebanon Hospital and, to everyone's amazement, when she was transferred to her Del Mar beach house to recover, Desi rushed to her side. There was talk of one more reconciliation but Cleo and Ken Morgan told reporters at the door, "They will not be reconciled at this time." Back on the set, Lucy said, "We'll never be together again!"

All through the shooting, thousands of letters poured in, begging Lucy to patch things up with Desi. The public could not endure the shattering of a legendary marriage. Lucy said of this period, "I really hit the bottom of despair—anything from there on had to be up. . . . I hate failure, and that divorce was the number-one failure in my eyes. . . ." She got tired easily, and came down with viral pneumonia after shooting the picture. She turned down several scripts and began seeking to overcome her outright humiliation by pouring herself more and more into preparations for *Wildcat*. She moved to Manhattan along with DeDe and the children, though she was quite sick with a bad virus infection. She took an apartment at the

Imperial House, on Lexington and Sixty-ninth, refurnished it in bright California style, and enrolled Lucie at Marymount and Desi at St. David's. Lucie adjusted well to Marymount, but, Lucy told me, Desi was hopeless at St. David's. "It didn't work out," she told me. "The boys there bullied him, and he couldn't take it. He was crying and miserable, the poor little waif. I guess he just didn't have the strength to handle it all. I had to withdraw him from there."

Lucy invested heavily in *Wildcat*. Perhaps this was just as well, since she could neither sing nor dance and was already pushing fifty. It was a musical about a girl wildcatter in the southwestern oil fields at the turn of the century. N. Richard Nash, who had written *The Rainmaker*, was the author, as well as the co-producer with the director Michael Kidd. It was a very taxing role, calling for highly strenuous routines, and Lucy was at once excited and terrified. It was years since she had done *Dream Girl*, and she had never forgotten how exhausted she had been during the run of that play. She took vocal training under Carlo Menotti (not related to the composer of the same name), because she was determined not to do *sprechsingen*, the technique of "speaking" songs made popular by Rex Harrison in *My Fair Lady*. She told one reporter, "Fortunately, I'll have mostly funny or action or character type songs. That means I'll be doing a lot of cavorting around while I'm singing, and maybe that will keep people from paying too much attention to the quality of the voice." During some of the rewrites, her character was softened a little; she was given a crippled sister to support so that her wildcatter's ambition would not seem to be utterly selfish.

Since Lucy was backing the play with $400,000, she was able to call all the shots. She proved to be as demanding of herself and others as she had been in television. Although her face looked worn because of stress, she had kept her figure, and still had the posture learned when she was a Hattie Carnegie model. But her sore leg, still bandaged from the movie set accident, was a severe handicap when dancing was called for. By the time she was ready for rehearsals after Labor Day, she was well aware that preparing a Broadway musical was far from being a picnic.

Another problem was her feet. She had never been completely comfortable with them since her crippling at sixteen, and had to wear open toes and heels and flat shoes whenever possible. During rehearsals, she was faced with still another headache: a lawsuit for $600,000 filed in Los Angeles. William H. Reinholz contended that he had manufactured and sold a baby walker in 1950, a device similar to a baby carriage that a child could propel and which could not be tipped over. He claimed that Lucy and Desi had appropriated his invention illegally and called it Ricky, Jr. The case was settled out of court.

It was difficult for Lucy to find the ideal co-star in *Wildcat*. He had to be handsome, husky, capable of singing well, and physically correct for a Texas wildcatter. He also should not be too young; his age should not contrast too much with hers. She found the right actor in Keith Andes, who had appeared in films as a muscular blond stud, most notably in Fritz Lang's melodrama *Clash by Night*, opposite Marilyn Monroe. At the time, he was not very well known except from television, and, although he sang very well, had to work hard on the dances.

The show opened in Philadelphia, with rehearsals seven days and seven nights a week. Dressed in black leotards and a purple torso-length sweater, Lucy was tossed around hour after hour by Andes and his husky friends, until she was soaked through with perspiration and nearing total exhaustion. Michael Kidd was a kind but stern taskmaster, and managed to bend Lucy to some extent to his will. But there were still clashes during the preparations.

The Philadelphia audiences were appreciative, but Lucy was wrung out night after night. When reporters came to see her, she was honest about what she was going through. She was overworked and felt the effects of the accident on *The Facts of Life*. Doctors told her she must remain on antibiotics and other medication, and this made her system toxic. If it hadn't been for the two maids, children's nurse, and chauffeured limousine, she could never have gotten through the experience. Moreover, the strain on her vocal cords was severe. Since she still couldn't sing, even after all the training, she had to shout the songs in tune, and this required a taxing degree of concentration. However, she did manage to struggle through the last of the Philadelphia performances and open at the Alvin Theater in New York on December 15.

Right up to the last minute, there were problems and fights. Rewrites went on and on. Sometimes, Lucy would even do the unthinkable, go up on her lines and forget the lyrics of a song; she would stop the performance cold in the middle of a bar, announce to the audience that she was all at sea, and start the song again. The audience was with her every minute, and applauded her. She fought over costumes, makeup, and hair. When she went to a local restaurant, she was notably testy; a friend reported later that she said, "Goddammit, why don't they make tables so you can put your legs under them?" She put her feet up on another chair and ordered wine on the rocks.

The opening-night audience was ecstatic, and the play was set for a long run. But the reviews of the show were poor, with only Lucy escaping general condemnation. Walter Kerr of *The New York Times* wrote, "Miss Ball is up there, doing all of the spectacular and animated and energetic and deliriously accomplished things she can do. . . ." Her legion of fans poured into New York from New Jersey, New York State, Connecticut, and Rhode Island on the bus packages that formed the basis of Broadway business. Desi came to see the show twice, and that was encouraging, as Lucy was still in love with him, but part of her wished he hadn't come, waking up feelings she would rather leave dormant.

Lucy was ill through most of the run. Snowstorms swept through New York in late January and early February 1961, and Lucy had to leave the show again and again, suffering from viral pneumonia, physical exhaustion, emotional depression, bursitis, and recurring infection in her injured leg. The play closed for a full two weeks while she went to Miami to get some sun. She was in terrible shape when she returned, but still was determined not to let the public down.

Early in April, after a grueling March, she felt another virus infection coming on. She was doing a dance routine with Edith King, entitled "Tippy Tippy Toes," when she felt faint and her breath started to go. Undoubtedly, her constant smoking and lack of sufficient rest and exercise had broken her down. Without warning, she blacked out and fell right across Edith King, who tried to catch her, breaking a wrist in the process. Many in the audience let out screams of shock, and the curtain was rung down. In order to keep the performance going, Sheila Hackett, assistant choreographer, gamely assumed the role and, dressed in a replica of Lucy's clothes, somehow managed to get through the performance. Lucy was absent several times after that, and in May, for almost a whole week, her understudy, Betty Jane Watson, took over. Lucy fainted again, right in front of the audience, during a matinee, and there was some talk of closing the production because of her condition. Finally, in June, *Wildcat* did close, with an announcement that it would reopen on August 7, following a nine-week suspension. It did not. In a joint statement, Michael Kidd and N. Richard Nash said that the reason the play would not reopen was the action of Local 802 of the Musicians' Union, which had made what they called an "exorbitant demand" for payment of regular salaries for twenty-six musicians in the orchestra over the layoff period. This, the producers claimed, would cost Lucy $50,000 and up. The union had refused to lessen its demands and therefore the play would not be reopened. It had lost a total of five weeks due to the illness problem, but it had never failed to do good business because of Lucy's name.

Lucy flew to London and Italy with the children for a rest. One of her consolations in this ordeal had been Dr. Norman Vincent Peale, proselytizer of the power of positive thinking;

indeed, she later claimed that she could not have done *Wildcat* at all without his spiritual support. She had little good to say for anyone else at that time, but she did feel very good about him. Reminiscing about her experience with *Wildcat* after her return to Hollywood later that year, Lucy growled, "Ugh! . . . I hired the best people in the business, I thought, to do what they do, and they didn't do it. I should have shouted some* and maybe it would have been a better show, but I was tired. . . . *Wildcat* was never more than a female *Rainmaker*, but nobody told me how bad it was. Except the gypsies in the chorus. They knew everything. . . . I was fixing and changing *Wildcat* up to the night I closed. When I left the show, I was so sick they almost carried me out in a coffin. I had to give back $165,000 out of my own pocket for ticket refunds—the most money ever refunded, they said. Now I don't think I'll ever do another play. The loss of the days and contact with the outer world is terrible. I learned something good, even from a horrible experience like *Wildcat*. I learned that people came to the theater to see the Lucy they knew and I didn't give it to them."

One of her few good memories of *Wildcat* was a funny episode in which the Lucy the world knew did emerge. Mousy, a Yorkshire terrier in the show, deposited its doings on the stage in the middle of a scene. Without breaking her number, Lucy made a face at the audience, grabbed a mop from a supporting actress, a pail from another, and cleaned up the mess. Talking to the audience directly, breaking out of character completely, she said, "It's in the small print in my contract. I have to clean up the dog shit!"

* She did.

· CHAPTER 17 ·

$\mathcal{U}$ppermost in Lucy's thoughts at the time of *Wildcat* was a man in whom she was beginning to develop a romantic interest. Gary Morton, born Morton Goldapper, was a moderately talented comedian who had been working at Radio City Music Hall when they met briefly during the preparations for *Wildcat*. They had dated each other on and off, seeing each other as much as possible during the run of the show, while Morton played the Copacabana. Morton had proved to be supportive during Lucy's struggle with exhaustion and nervous breakdown. He was very much the opposite of Desi. A self-contained, cheerful, uncomplicated man, heavily built, with huge shoulders, he was forty-two at the time he met Lucy. He had the qualities necessary in all successful husbands of motion-picture stars: He was unselfish, unshakeable, sturdy, deferent when that was needed, and good at countering insecurities, fragility, and self-doubt. He could shrug off Lucy's temper; he was not, like Desi, volatile, nervous, and passionate. He was a medication for Lucy following the long, tormenting sickness of her previous marriage. He could offer her a shoulder to cry on; she needed someone like Gary Morton.

Above all, Morton, with his Jewish borscht-belt humor and background, could kid Lucy, cheer her up, bring her out of herself. And he had an additional advantage: He was a New

Yorker. Since Lucy was born in New York State, that gave them something in common.

Oddly, Lucy decided that she wouldn't make up her mind to marry Gary until Desi approved of him. She brought him to meet Desi rather in the way that most people would bring a prospective mate to meet their parents. When Desi approved of Gary, she told the columnist Earl Wilson, "Desi has been very sweet and very nice about the whole thing—he certainly has given his approval." The final decree of divorce from Desi was obtained on May 17, 1961. By August, Lucy had committed herself firmly to Gary, and wedding plans were made for November. When Gary was playing Lake Tahoe, she visited him, busy studying a script (which she did not finally approve) of James Kirkwood's *There Must Be a Pony*, in which she was to have played a character based on the silent-screen mother of the author.

The same August, Lucy put Desi into St. John's Military Academy in Los Angeles. But once again, she had to withdraw him almost immediately. She told me in 1973, "They held him on weekend detentions for eight hours a day—he had to sit bolt upright the whole time. He was having nightmares. He couldn't sleep. I said, 'What's the matter with you?' And he said, 'They gave me detention for tying a shoelace during drill when I was supposed to be at attention.' I said, 'Oh, come on!' And he told me that thirteen-year-old 'generals' were giving these bullying orders! I took him out of school again."

It is clear that Lucy was coddling Desi, and, at the same time, she was unwittingly causing him anguish by mentioning his withdrawal from school to others, particularly the press.

Gary tried to secure young Desi's happiness by being a new father to him. The incongruous religious atmosphere at 1000 N. Roxbury Drive—with Lucy following Norman Vincent Peale's brand of WASPish uplift, Desi insisting that the children be raised as Catholics, and Gary retaining his Jewish convictions—made for an exceptionally complicated household. Lucy decided that she and Gary should marry in New York, in church on a Sunday, with Dr. Peale officiating. She was busy during the preparations for the marriage, rehearsing for a TV special entitled "The Good Years," in which she appeared with Henry Fonda. She rushed around Manhattan buying her trousseau on November 15, announcing, "I want something beautiful to be married in, and I want something gay to go dancing in." She snapped up a blue-green sleeveless silk windowpane dress with a tulle headdress for her wedding gown, as well as a tweed suit trimmed with red velvet, a mauve suit with a matching chiffon blouse, and a black wool cocktail dress. Always mindful of her support among the columnists of the press, Lucy burst into Hedda Hopper's suite at the Waldorf Towers to announce the details of the wedding.

The marriage took place on November 19, 1961, at the Marble Collegiate Church on Fifth Avenue and Nineteenth Street. DeDe was present, along with Fred Ball, Cleo and Ken Morgan, young Desi, and Lucie. Paula Stewart was matron of honor, and comedian Jack Carter was best man. One thousand five hundred fans milled outside the church, chanting, "I Love Lucy." So vast was the crowd of well-wishers that policemen had to form a flying wedge to allow Lucy and Gary to enter. As the couple left the church in the bitter November cold, Lucy said (and meant it), "I'm happy! I'm happy!"

In an interview with Earl Wilson, held at the Imperial House, where Lucy retained her large apartment, Lucy said, "I won't be going to Gary's nightclub openings. I'll frequently be busy, but even if I weren't I wouldn't go. Because if you go, people mistake the reason. They don't think you go because you want to be with somebody you like. They think you go to help business!" Morton said to Wilson, "Lucy lives in Beverly Hills, and we'll lead a suburban life. And you can park your car out there!" Gary also said, "I keep thinking of the laughs we had the first time Lucy cooked dinner for me. The steak tasted like hockey pucks. I kept smiling with the whole thing in my mouth. I couldn't get it out." Lucy said, "I'm very good at cooking for twenty people." "Yeah," Gary commented.

"She's great for a restaurant, but for one person—forget it!" Wilson also asked Lucy if she ever made any effort to coach Gary in his work. She replied in the affirmative. "Yeah, I'm guilty of that. I heard him do his act one night at the Concord. One word bothered me. I didn't say anything about it for weeks. Then he did it again and I said, 'Guess I'll tell him about the one word he's dropping.' "

Gary commented, "Criticism of that kind is like coming from the queen. And it worked. I wasn't pronouncing one word clearly. When I corrected it, what was a snicker became a scream!"

The couple stayed on in New York so that Lucy could complete her television show. Then they took off for Palm Springs, where Gary had a nightclub engagement. Later, they took off for Acapulco for a delayed honeymoon. At the age of fifty, Lucy, who jokingly told Earl Wilson she only married once every twenty years, had again discovered romance. And her marriage, this time, was built to last.

If Gary had had a stronger ego, it could have been a disaster; certainly, he never took off as a television comedian, and even his nightclub career was to be short-lived.

That Lucy was as big as ever was confirmed by the fact that she was on the cover of *Life* magazine in January 1962, with the heading LUCY'S BACK ON TV. And, suddenly hungry for her old acclaim, and depressed over Desi's disaster at military school, Lucy reconstituted "I Love Lucy" as "The Lucy Show," rehiring Bob Carroll and Madelyn Pugh, luring them back from retirement. CBS made a deal with her and Desilu; Desi, still suffering from declining health, sold her his share in the studio for just over $2.5 million, and retired to raise horses in Corona Del Mar. In 1963, he married a divorcée, Edith Mack Hirsch, an extroverted woman of great charm who resembled a more stable, less volatile Lucy. Friends said that he still loved Lucy.

Lucy became extremely busy once more. She was now the head of Desilu, undertaking responsibilities with great expertise, but still under tremendous pressure, as Desi had been. She proved to be an able executive, a TV tycoon of no mean ability. When I first met her in 1962, I recall, she sat in her white-walled three-room suite, red hair flaring, munching a Cobb salad, taking endless phone calls, tapping long-nailed fingers impatiently. With "The Danny Thomas Show," "The Untouchables," "Ben Casey," "Lassie," "The Andy Griffith Show," "The Dick Van Dyke Show," "My Three Sons," and "My Favorite Martian" on her slate, and her new "Lucy" series firmly launched, she was clearly in a nervous frazzle, snatching up the telephone to answer awkward questions with barely concealed impatience. Although she looked remarkably well, her figure slim and youthful for her age, she was challenging, severe, and hard to please. An innocuous remark could easily upset her, and at the same time a question about somebody whose name was associated with hers could provoke her to tears and a long discussion of this or that retired or dead executive. She told me that she attended all stockholders' meetings, supervised budgets for all pilots, was preparing twenty-six hour-long shows based on John F. Kennedy's *Profiles in Courage*, and could tell to the last penny (and did) how much Desilu had made in the previous two quarters. It turned out that the gross income for the first quarter of 1963 was a staggering $840,875, over $70,000 more than it had been in 1962, the last year of Desi's regime.

She was tough, no question of it, but at the same time more vulnerable than ever. A workaholic, she barely had time for her children between office and sleep. It was clear from talking to her colleagues that they were nervously respectful of her, and had great admiration for her. Edwin E. Holly, Desilu vice president of administration, and attorney Milton (Mickey) Rudin,* both very able men, couldn't speak highly enough of her seriousness of purpose. Indeed, at a board meeting in August of 1963, she proved to be quite spectacular. Listing the company's massive new profits, as she read through horn-rims

* Also Frank Sinatra's lawyer.

a large sheaf of prepared notes, she contradicted the informality of her purple-flowered summer dress. She explained how the red ink in the ledgers had resulted from $1.8 million of deferred show-cost write-offs; she talked of the firm's "hard, conservative policy"; and she even brought a laugh when a stockholder asked vice president Edwin Holly to repeat the last first-quarter results. "You speak right into that gadget, honey," she said as she gave the vice president the microphone.

She turned sharp when another executive began to list some of the Desilu productions playing on foreign TV screens. Not content with half a dozen countries' names, she insisted on hearing the complete list. At the end, she informed him briskly that he had neglected to mention Canada and Australia, where business was very good. Just to rub in her point, she had the entire board sit through a "Lucy" show in Japanese, which not a single person understood.

· CHAPTER 18 ·

$\mathcal{L}$ucy was constantly busy throughout the early 1960s. In 1962, she received $100,000 for guesting on "The Danny Kaye Show" (an NBC–General Motors special). That same year she fielded a lawsuit which charged that she had failed to pay the balance of a debt owed for the purchase of the Coconino Equipment Company of Flagstaff, Arizona; and she was briskly working on her new "Lucy Show." She gave her best interview ever to Hedda Hopper, describing some of her accidents: In addition to the alligator that bit her in the old Goldwyn picture, she mentioned that she had been attacked by a monkey on "I've Got a Secret." She described an episode while making an early (unnamed) film: "I had to ride in the car with a Great Dane, and eat off his plate. We were at Malibu Lake. It was muddy, smelly. I had to slop around in five feet of ooze and pretend I was drowning while shouting, 'Help, help! Please help me!' I was yelling for all I was worth when a man in a tree, who was part of the crew, spotted a water moccasin and everyone went wild but didn't do anything. When I heard the word 'moccasin,' I thought someone had lost a shoe. Then someone yelled, 'Snake!' That got me going; I tried to get out and the dog, excited by the commotion, plunged into the water and grabbed me by the wrist, trying to save me. But he darn near drowned me because his big paws kept banging my head under water again. Between us we scared the heck out of that snake."

Lucy was queen of a rodeo, co-starring with Jimmy Durante, at the Los Angeles Memorial Coliseum. She got caught in traffic on the freeway on her way to the show and she arrived late. When she got there, she didn't wait to park her car but made her way headlong into the ring. A horse was brought to her; she stepped into the stirrup only to discover that her matador pants were so tight that if she threw her leg over the saddle they would rip. Two men had to lift her onto the horse. As she took the reins, she realized she didn't know the name of the horse. Therefore, she wouldn't be able to give it any instructions. She screamed to everyone in sight, quite disregarding the television cameras, "What's his goddamned name?" A man screamed back, "Bessie!" And the horse heard it and suddenly began galloping around the arena out of sequence. Lucy was almost thrown in its headlong flight until at last she coaxed it to a trot. Finally, the time came for her to give a speech. Her pants were too tight to allow her to dismount, so she was compelled to say to the vast audience of people watching, "I'd be happy to get off this horse, but my pants are too tight!" She brought the house down.

Lucy made a new movie, *Critic's Choice*, in which she yet again co-starred with Bob Hope. It was drawn from a play by Jean Kerr, wife of the critic Walter Kerr, and dealt with the struggle of the wife of a prominent theater critic to create a play of her own. Lucy wasn't happy during the filming, despite her great regard for Hope. She found working in feature films tedious and slow compared to television. She missed learning fifty-two pages of dialogue in two days; she missed the long hours of hard work and resented the endless preparations in film-making which resulted in the inspiration fading out by late afternoon when the company finally got around to the actual shooting.

In November 1962, Lucy was in New York, staying at the

Plaza and enjoying Gary Morton's first anniversary gifts of a gold evening bag and a tiny gold wristwatch. The Mortons spent Christmas with the children at the Franconia, New Hampshire, ski resort. She and Gary often laughed at each other's behavior. Morton told *The New York Times* on December 9: "Lucy's funny without realizing it. She got out of her shower this morning, walked into the bedroom still wet, and shook herself like a dog. . . . I laughed my head off."

Back in Hollywood, Lucie and Desi, Jr., converted the garage into a little theater where they put on plays and fooled around with costumes, makeup, and lighting. Lucy declined the job of producer but insisted on their polishing the show before it was shown to the neighborhood children. She proved to be quite strict in her supervision.

She was equally strict at Desilu. She built the studio's profits still further and Gary always provided a sympathetic ear. She had six pilots going out in the 1964 season, including Donald O'Connor in "The Hoofer" and Dan Dailey in "Papa G.I." It was in that year that Gary made his debut on Lucy's show. The episode dealt with golf, and Gary of course was obsessed with the sport. By March, Lucy had been offered a record $90,000 per half hour for her series. The deal was for twenty-six first-runs and repeats the next season, with an overall budget of $2,300,000. The new series had been consistently in the top ten since 1962. All of these announcements came after Lucy's statement that she would be retiring. She had been arguing with CBS over the terms.

The year was marked with a certain number of problems. Not least of these was an article by Goodman Ace in the *Saturday Review* for May 16, 1964. Ace reported that he had written an hour-long special comedy program for Lucy, who was to appear with Jack Benny, Danny Thomas, Gary Moore, Andy Griffith, and Phil Silvers. Lucy was to play herself as president of Desilu Productions. In Goodman Ace's story Lucy would be petrified she was losing her job to Phil Silvers. She insisted the writer make a change showing that she was not in the least afraid of losing her job. She then insisted on a further change in which she would not receive a pie in the face. Nor would she pretend to be an old scrubwoman. Stories like this gave the public the impression Lucy was becoming more and more fussy about the way she was portrayed on television.

When Lucy made her dramatic debut on TV in the Desilu series "The Greatest Show on Earth," the show flopped. Critics didn't like her doing a sentimental story in which she played a lonely circus performer falling for an orphaned boy whom she tries to adopt. She was unable to get two series, "The Hoofers" and "Mr. Hammond and the Little People," off the ground. She was also upset because the network dropped her beloved "Glynis," starring Glynis Johns. The frustrations always made her overreact strongly; she wasn't a person who could take defeat lying down.

There was another problem at home. Both children missed their father, and went to see him at his homes in Palm Springs on weekends as often as possible. It had taken them a considerable length of time to get used to Gary Morton, for all of his determined efforts to ingratiate himself with them, and despite the fact that he was utterly warm, charming, and outgoing. They demanded Lucy see the film *The Parent Trap* again and again; in that picture, twins played by Hayley Mills try to bring their parents back together after they have separated. In the summer of 1964, Lucy and Gary were in New York, where a steamy August 31 was declared Lucy Day at the World's Fair. An immense crowd of hysterical well-wishers greeted her; nobody had ever drawn such a crowd at the fair before. Accompanied by DeDe, Gary, and Hedda Hopper, Lucy put her handprints in concrete at the fair's Hollywood Pavilion. All expenses were paid by her TV sponsors, General Foods, the CBS network, and the fair; the $500-a-day penthouse was rent-free courtesy of the New York Hilton Hotel. She could easily have afforded it herself; in the past twelve months Desilu had grossed $24 million. In interviews conducted at the hotel, Gary was expertly modest, talking of his pride in Lucy and his lack of envy.

Not content with all of her other work, Lucy embarked on a daily radio talk show, lasting ten minutes, in which she chatted with various friends, including Danny Kaye, Bing Crosby, the Dean Martins, Red Skelton, Bob Hope, Agnes Moorehead, and Hedda Hopper. The show was called "Let's Talk to Lucy." Informal and lighthearted, it caught on instantly, but it stretched out Lucy's energies still further. In her fifties, it seemed that her manic desire for work had not decreased.

At twelve, Desi, Jr., made his debut in show business. He formed a trio with the handsome thirteen-year-old Dino (Dean Paul) Martin, son of Dean Martin, and Billy Hinsche. The trio was known as Dino, Desi, and Billy. Frank Sinatra gave the boys a recording contract on the spot. When they made their TV debut on "The Hollywood Palace," and on Dean Martin's TV show, they received $4,000; they again earned a decent sum on "The Ed Sullivan Show." Soon, they had their own music publishing company, and naturally looked to Lucy for approval. Lucy told reporters she had mixed feelings about the boys' success, because they had "achieved it too quickly" and hadn't had to earn their rewards. She fussed over Desi's weight, noting how pudgy he looked on television.

There were some stormy events in 1965. At the annual meeting of shareholders in August, John Gilbert, who owned one hundred shares of stock, demanded to know why Lucy was earning $500,000 a year when the profits had fallen $455,000 compared with 1964. Gilbert harangued Lucy until she lost her temper and called upon attorney Milton Rudin to take over. Rudin told Desilu security chief John Reeves to expel Gilbert from the meeting. Gilbert fought with Reeves so violently that his reading glasses fell to the floor. The two men were rolling around in a struggle on the carpet when Lucy screamed, "Leave Gilbert alone! Let him go back to his seat!" There was a screeching match between the stockholders present, as Lucy joined in the fray, glaring angrily at Gilbert but following every word he said. Rudin tried to explain that Lucy was "underpaid in relation to other stars," while Lucy told the disorderly crowd that she plowed her own money back into the company. Finally, so loud was the argument between all concerned that Lucy felt compelled to break the tension by saying, "Mr. Gilbert, do you mind if I go to the ladies' room?" When he snapped back his permission, she walked out in a fury. Returning, she smoked one cigarette after another, breaking off only to throw down two tablets with the words "Bufferin and water on the house!" When someone piped up with, "Why don't you just take a dollar a year?" she replied, "This isn't World War Two, it's the TV business!"

It was an unpleasant day. And at the end of it, Gilbert and other stockholders filed a lawsuit against Desilu, charging outright that Lucy had been excessively paid, and that she should not have allowed her salary to escalate from $175,000 to $490,000 in four years. She was charged with having "engaged in a plan and scheme to use her control and dominance over the corporation to obtain for herself excessive and illegal compensation." The case fizzled out, but it left Lucy even more embittered. The truth was that she was well worth the $390,000 as a actress and $100,000 as president of Desilu that made up her income. However, there is no doubt that she was drastically disturbed by this division within the ranks of the shareholders.

In the summer of 1966, Lucy was in London. She still enjoyed great popularity in Britain. In "Lucy in London," she appeared with Anthony Newley, then at the height of his fame following the spectacular success of his song "What Kind of Fool Am I?" She looked wonderful and enjoyed the swinging delights of Carnaby Street, but inevitably ran into one of her recurring pratfalls. In a sequence shot on the Thames, she succeeded in rocking a rubber boat so violently that she wound up in the river. She whizzed about on a motorcycle, filmed a scene at midnight in the Chamber of Horrors at Madame Tussaud's Wax Museum, and also filmed at the Tower of London on the site of Ann Boleyn's execution on the block. The British loved the show, which was released as a Chemstrand special on October 24, 1966.

Just three weeks earlier, an incident had taken place that deeply distressed Lucy. Desi, Sr., was arrested at Del Mar for allegedly firing a .38 caliber revolver at two beach youths who, he claimed, had driven up and down in front of his house, cursing him loudly as he, comedian Jimmy Durante, and Edith's daughter were building a bonfire. His version was that he had taken his gun, a gift from the cast of "The Untouchables," walked up to the two boys, and asked them what they were doing there. When they didn't reply, he said, "This is private property. I've got a gun, and I'll shoot your tires and car." Then, he said, he shot into the ground and the boys disappeared. However, the boys accused him of trying to kill them, and he was arrested by the sheriff and booked on suspicion of assault with a deadly weapon. Desi was released on bail, and the case was later dismissed. Lucy's concern was so intense that it was clear she still cared deeply for him.

Lucy was under pressure at the time to sell Desilu to Gulf and Western Industries, which had just bought Paramount. The plan was to incorporate the Desilu operation in the Paramount complex. Certainly, this possibility was tempting. After the tremendously successful first years under Lucy's guidance, Desilu had begun to slip. "Mission Impossible," "Star Trek," and other series had been sold to networks because of ratings problems. Many shareholders and even Mickey Rudin felt that Lucy would be best advised to sell because the conglomerates were taking over everything and resented even the smallest independent, let alone a giant like Desilu. Lucy was very uneasy about the corporate takeover. She was much opposed to the whole idea of giant corporations swallowing up Hollywood. But Rudin was determined. He correctly and decently felt that Lucy shouldn't fight the inevitable or risk ruining her health by continuing to battle on alone when profits were falling and overheads increasing daily.

Lucy was in Miami in February 1967, visiting with Jackie Gleason at his home there to discuss a possible movie in which she would co-star with him as the legendary actress Lillian Russell, with Jackie as the portly millionaire Diamond Jim Brady. A second motive for her trip was to avoid reaching the painful decision that she would have to sell her beloved one-woman studio. She hated the very thought of the sale, and perhaps in Miami she could sort out her thoughts on the subject more satisfactorily. She even avoided Rudin's phone calls, compelling him to fly to Miami to confront her with the matter head-on. He laid it on the line. She must sell. Lucy burst into tears. He told her that she had twenty-four hours or the whole deal would be blown. Finally, it came down to one hour left. Still hesitating, she said that she hadn't even met the all-powerful Charles Bluhdorn, head of Gulf and Western. Rudin asked her if she would talk to him on the phone. She agreed at last. Bluhdorn said craftily to her, "Miss Ball, one of the things that I am prepared to like about you is that you care." Touched by this cunning compliment, Lucy sobbed again and agreed to the sale. The shareholders one and all voted for the merger. Suddenly, overnight, Lucy was bereft of Desilu. She later told me she was at once horrified, depressed, and relieved. The millions she made from the sale certainly were a salve to her ego, and the release from pressure, even for a workaholic like herself, cannot have been entirely unwelcome. But she had to work again immediately, or she couldn't have borne the excess freedom that was thrust upon her. She agreed to make what would turn out to be the most enjoyable movie of her career.

· CHAPTER 19 ·

$\mathcal{T}$he picture was *Yours, Mine, and Ours*. It was based on the experiences of Frank and Helen Beardsley, a Northern California couple. When they married, Helen had eight children from a previous marriage and Frank had ten, and they went ahead and had more children of their own. Lucy had read the story in *Life* magazine and found it cute; she desperately wanted to make a family picture, since she was deeply offended by what she thought to be the crassness and crudity of contemporary Hollywood movies.

At first, she had difficulty getting the project off the ground. Even though she was still one of the top television stars, she was scarcely bankable at the box office as a movie actress. She had been a complete flop in *Critic's Choice* through no fault of her own, because the film simply hadn't worked; both she and Bob Hope were miscast as New York sophisticates, and the public couldn't identify with writers as screen heroes. Also, people were afraid that she wouldn't take direction since, like Desi before her, she had become known as someone who directed the directors, and who was accustomed to being a tycoon, present on every set at Desilu and running interference on everybody.

None of the screenplays she had had written for *Yours, Mine, and Ours* was quite right. They had been done by screenwriters who were simply trying to mimic the broad, low comedy of the "Lucy" shows. Finally, she decided to ask the very skillful Melville Shavelson to help her direct the picture and put it together. He hit on the excellent idea of calling in Frank and Helen Beardsley themselves as technical advisers. Lucy was fascinated by the couple and a new script was pulled together based upon their real-life experiences with their children. The result was a fresh, truthful, very identifiable comedy for middle America.

She cast her old friend and former date Henry Fonda opposite her. She had never forgotten him in *The Big Street*, and remained a fan. She asked Shavelson to test her own children, not insisting they be cast, but Desi was making too much money with his band and Lucie was overweight and her test didn't work. Unfortunately, Lucy didn't hesitate to "direct" Shavelson once the picture started. Shavelson said later, "I recall that one day she said, 'Cut. Let's do it again. There's a shadow on Hank's [Fonda's] chin. Mel, move that light three inches to the left. Now stay where you are, Hank.' "

Thus, the picture was codirected by Lucy. The scenes in which a false eyelash wandered up onto Lucy's forehead, in which the children got her drunk, and in which she laughed and cried at the same time under the influence of the bottle were admirably played. *Yours, Mine, and Ours* was a hit, grossing $17 million. However, instead of being delighted, Lucy was upset. She blamed Shavelson for not telling her the movie would be a success in advance, expecting him to have had the power of prophecy. The reason she was so annoyed was that she hadn't tax-sheltered her profit-sharing agreement and lost most of the $2 million she made from the picture to the IRS.

In the late 1960s and early 1970s, Lucy grew more and more Victorian and puritanical. She hated the contemporary violence and sex that permeated the screen; she was exasperated by even such harmless adventures as the James Bond pictures, and would turn them off in the event that they started to be shown in her living room. When *Thunderball* was shown at 1000 North Roxbury, and she saw blood spurting, bullets flying, and sharks biting, and a bare-chested Sean Connery climbing on top of a pretty girl, she had had enough. Much to the annoyance of Lucie and Desi, she screamed, "Stop the movie! What the hell kind of picture is this?" and stamped out. She also hated *Blow-Up*, Antonioni's mod-erotic movie set in swinging London. Once the sex started, and David Hemmings' bare buttocks were shown, she again stopped the screening and fled. She asked to see a Western. She grew hysterical as a girl tore her clothes off, made the sign of the cross, and mounted a cowboy. She said later, "They were crawling over each other in bed like there was no tomorrow. Ugh!"

She was torn between her workaholism and her obsession with her vacation home in Snowmass, Colorado. She was as obsessive about vacations as she was about work. When she was at Snowmass she longed for the studio, and when she was at the studio she longed for Snowmass. Her children were driven as hard as or even harder than anyone else when she employed them in her show. When they went home with her at night, she would (Desi, Jr., claimed later) remind them of their mistakes until they fell into bed exhausted. They were told never to show any emotions in public, especially to neighbors. Even cooking dinner became a major operation for Lucy, as though it was the most important thing in the world. One night, both she and Desi, Jr., each determined not to be outstaged by the other, after an unseemly quarrel as to who should cook for the guests, cooked the dinners separately. Embarrassed, everyone had to eat two meals and pretend they were equally well cooked.

Desi said later that when he was out at night, Lucy would pace the floor until he came home. If he was very late, there would be a drastic scene. Often, he would skip dinner without telling her he wasn't coming home. That would infuriate her.

Lucy complained about students at Beverly Hills High School who drank and took drugs, convinced he himself was smoking pot. When he brought boys home, she disliked them intensely. She claimed some of the girls at the school were pregnant. She pulled him out of school again and he had to continue with private teachers. Then she pulled Lucie out of the Immaculate Heart School. She said later, "A lot of girls who boarded there were unhappy misfits. All the friends she brought home were among the rejected."

Lucy insisted her children be immaculately dressed at all times. She constantly fought with Desi, Jr., to make him cut his hair, which in 1969 and 1970 was tantamount to making him an outcast among the young. She hated to see him in jeans with his shirt hanging out or wearing love beads. One magazine described Lucy as "a terrifying superwoman, over-protective of her children and herself."

In 1970, the trio, Dino, Desi, and Billy, began to slip a little, and there was talk of their breaking up. Their tours grew less frequent. Partly because of this, and his fears about his future career, but also because of his fights with his mother on the set and his other insecurities, Desi became, by his own confession, a chronic alcoholic and drug user. He told columnist Vernon Scott, "I started drinking as an alternative to dealing with my fears and resentments from childhood. Most of my friends were drinking heavily, too. It was socially acceptable—but that didn't mean it was right." He was miserable, confused, and depressed in private, while seeming cheerful, husky, and handsome in public.

There was a ghastly scene on "The Dick Cavett Show." Lucy appeared with her daughter and Carol Burnett. Carol told Lucie she hoped her daughters would grow up to resemble her. Cavett asked Lucy whether she would model her son on anyone. Lucy said she wished Desi, Jr., would learn lessons from Cavett. It was typical of her many harsh and wounding public criticisms of her own child. She told me years later, "Desi, Jr., didn't take to my show like Lucie, because he didn't understand comedy the way she does. He was asleep on the sidelines when we'd call him and I was ready to smack him. When he said he wanted to do dramatic things, I said, 'Oh, really?' " She pointed out to me that both Desi, Jr., and Lucie worked for scale on the show, a fact she seemed to find appealing. For a while, Desi, Jr., gave up his musical career completely to appear on "Here's Lucy."

She still treated them like babies. She told a writer for *Coronet* magazine, "Both my kids are inclined to settle for just getting by. Desi was grounded for two months, no phone, no television, no one over after school, no going anywhere even on the weekends. I wrenched my back disconnecting all his electrical equipment because he'd gotten two D's in his grades!" She told a reporter that Lucie, who received her driver's license on her sixteenth birthday, wanted a good car. Lucy gave her a Jeep someone had just given her. Her daughter decided she wanted something better. Lucy told her she could have a good car as soon as her grades went up. They didn't.

Raging at hippies, Hell's Angels, drug addicts, teenybopper sexpots, and free-love enthusiasts, Lucy told *Coronet*, "In our home, it's school and homework; early to bed, and not so many dates, just on weekends. I know where [my children] are every minute. They must cue me in on wherever they're going and with whom. And the Sunset Strip is out—I don't care whether places are especially advertised or not for the young crowd."

They were forbidden to go to certain homes. Lucy forced her daughter to break with her best friend because she felt the other girl was dominant and the only reason they were friends was because they had been in neighboring bassinets at Cedars of Lebanon Hospital. She said she slapped her children if they were rude. She added, "There have been times when I could have cried my eyes out because they wouldn't let me do all the things I would love to do for them. But at least we've gotten past the no-communication barrier."

Desi, Jr., hated to be ordered to bed by ten P.M. She told a reporter for Earl Wilson why: "D is failing. You'd think in view of his father he'd have a little aptitude for Spanish, wouldn't you?" This remark found its way into Wilson's column all over America.

Even though Paramount was running her operation, she was as fierce as ever on the set of "The Lucy Show." It was reported that she would storm into the script-reading, with producer, director, writers, and series regulars present, and growl, "Things have sure changed since Charlie [Bluhdorn] took over. Why aren't the pencils all sharp?" She once moaned, "This script is all exposition! I kept hoping there'd be a joke coming up, not just a lot of words! You, Milt Josefsberg [one of the writers], don't you just sit there with your chin in your expensive hand!" Gary Morton nervously suggested a one-liner. Lucy rejected it immediately.

When she watched replays, she would say, "Get the sound man on this! We lost three lines there!" She was annoyed one night when Mrs. Vincente Minnelli insisted she go to the Garson Kanins' wedding anniversary party at Chasen's. She went, but she fumed all evening because she was missing the run-throughs, and when Denise Minnelli asked her why she didn't go to parties, she replied, "Don't you realize that people who come to parties are people who don't work?" When a player would grumble about reading a line, she'd say, "If you want to stay friends with Mr. Bluhdorn, you'd better say it!" She said to Carol Burnett one night, "Carol, you were marvelous! I always said you'd make it, if only you'd pay attention to me!" She growled at one of her writers, who asked her if she would like to hear some gags, "There's no time now. Give them to me for Christmas. You never know what to give me."

She was again tough with Desi, Jr., over his friends. When he complained that he only had one pal, Keith Thibodeaux, the TV Ricky, she demanded to know why. He brought home some friends. After they left, she snapped, "Now you have to make a choice. Some are too old, some too young, some just come to see the house. Whittle it down!" He did, to three.

She was at it again when she presented the newly renamed "Here's Lucy" with her children on location at the U.S. Air Force Academy in Colorado Springs, where, like her character in *Best Foot Forward*, she made a real-life hit with the cadets.

She told a reporter there, "Lucie and Desi are either spoiled or stepped on. Mostly, they're spoiled. Things aren't easy in this business, and that's what I'm trying to have them discover." Soon after that she was telling *Photoplay*, "Women's lib? I don't know the meaning of it. I'm tired of the ugly. Give me Fred Astaire and Ginger Rogers any day."

"Here's Lucy" was huge in 1970. There were no signs of her name flagging in the least. But her personal behavior didn't change. She called the girls Desi dated and Lucie's boyfriends "a bunch of fishheads." Resilient, sturdy Lucie took her mother's critiques in stride. More sensitive and vulnerable, now heavily into drugs, Desi, Jr., did not.

At the beginning of 1970, Desi was chemically dependent on drugs, and his mother once again went overboard. Lucie began dating an actor-director, Phil Vandervort, and decided to get her own apartment. Lucy watched the clock when her daughter went out with him, cautioning her constantly not "to go all the way." One night, when the couple came home very late, Lucy got violently upset. This provoked her daughter even more strongly to move out. Desi, Jr., said later, "Things got pretty tense. There was a big scene when my sister left. . . ." Lucie had been secretly buying up bits of furniture over several weeks from her earnings on the show.

Also in the spring of 1970, seventeen-year-old Desi began seriously dating twenty-three-year-old Patty Duke. He met her in a Hollywood recording studio; they were immediately attracted to each other. Desi asked Patty if she would go to The Daisy with him that night, one of the places Lucy had strictly forbidden him to visit. They discoed until close to dawn. Soon after that, they were involved in an affair.

Patty Duke was the brilliantly talented star of *The Miracle Worker*, in which she won the Academy Award as the young Helen Keller. Later, she was equally impressive on television in *My Sweet Charlie*. She had had a sad childhood. Her father left the family and she was raised by a drama coach who put her on the stage as a child. She chewed gum in enormous quantities, chain-smoked, bit off her false fingernails and then devoured the real ones to the quick. She almost lost her career because she appeared to terrible reviews in the disastrous *Valley of the Dolls* playing Neely O'Hara, a pill-popper and emotional wreck. The director, Mark Robeson, described her accurately when he gave the reasons for casting her in the picture: "I wanted to have a girl whose nerve endings were exposed and ready to fly out before your eyes."

She had married Harry Falk, pleasant, easygoing assistant director of her "Patty Duke Show," when she was sixteen and he was thirty. Within two years, they had separated. When she met Desi, Patty was in the process of obtaining a divorce, which was finalized on May 1, 1970.

At the funeral of her discoverer and mentor John Ross in Palm Desert that same week, Patty told a reporter through floods of tears that she was going to have a baby. She was wrong, but conceived that same month. Later she asserted—and he did not deny it—that Desi, Jr., was the father. Lucy was furious at the relationship. She could just about cope with Phil Vandervort, but she certainly couldn't cope with Patty. The fact that Patty was not divorced when the affair began and was several years older than Desi drove Lucy into anger and sad frustration. Moreover, a tug-of-war developed between his mother and his lover when Patty demanded he leave home, be a man, marry her, and accept responsibility for the baby. Lucy demanded he stay at North Roxbury Drive. Finally Desi, like his sister, left the house.

Night after night Desi and Patty went discoing. Finally, it became clear that Lucy would never give her blessing to a marriage of her still-underage son. Patty and he unexpectedly arrived in Hawaii to join Lucy, who was there on vacation. Lucy remained adamant.

To try to ease her mind and perhaps find a husband, Patty flew to Chicago, where she announced she would appear in a play but in fact did not. Just before she left, she sublet her apartment to a young and handsome Las Vegas promoter,

Mike Tell, son of a Las Vegas newspaper publisher, Jack Tell. There was a strong mutual attraction. While Mike lived in her apartment, he phoned her every day in Chicago and wooed her with gifts of flowers. Finally, he proposed marriage to her on the phone. Although they had only met once, in the lobby of her building, she accepted him. He was physically appealing to her, and she felt he would make a good father for her child.

She flew back from Chicago, and Desi turned up without warning at the apartment. Mike was furious. He drew her aside, afraid of her attraction to Desi, took her into the bedroom, sank to his knees in front of her, and insisted she accept his hand in marriage immediately. She agreed again. Then, while Mike returned to the living room, Patty asked Desi into the bedroom and told him of her decision. Desi walked out in tears.

This melodramatic scene took place at four P.M. Six and a half hours later, Patty Duke married Mike Tell in Las Vegas. Jack Tell, her father-in-law, said, "My wife and I haven't lost a son. What we've done is gained an Academy Award— winner." Patty said, "I'm going to have a Duke baby. It will have my last name only, not Mike's."

Desi immediately began dating actress Kim Darby. The day after the wedding in Las Vegas, June 25, 1970, Patty and Mike moved into a $450-a-day suite at the International Hotel in Las Vegas. According to Patty, who later made a statement under oath in divorce court, the marriage was never sexually consummated. According to Mike, it was consummated five days later in the heated pool of the hotel at four A.M., where he made love to Patty in the water. Later, he was to claim that the baby with whom Patty was already pregnant was the result of that experience. But she was over a month pregnant when they wed.

During the nineteen-day honeymoon, Patty flew her Saint Bernard dog from Chicago in a Lear jet because she didn't want it to be in the cargo hold of a normal airplane. She chartered another jet to take her and Mike to his grandmother in New Jersey. This cost a total of $30,000. Another $30,000 was spent during the nineteen-day frenzy of spending. By this time, the couple were thoroughly sick of each other. Mike Tell was so run down with nights without sleep and the constant traveling that he was stricken with hepatitis and was rushed into Sunrise Hospital in Las Vegas.

The couple's attorney, David Licht, was swamped with thousands of dollars of bills they had run up. After just a few weeks, when Mike came out of the hospital, the couple met at Licht's office in Los Angeles to sign the divorce papers. Patty burst into tears but agreed to sign. Mike refused. A quarrel over property followed, when Patty tried to fight Tell over $30,000 he was demanding as a settlement. He returned to Nevada and refused to receive divorce papers. Patty threatened to put ads in the Las Vegas newspapers to announce that he was avoiding legal documents. Tell hired lawyer Melvin Belli to act as a go-between and to win Patty back, and persuade her the marriage could be saved. When he realized his cause was hopeless, he finally gave in and took off to a mountain cabin in Colorado not far from Snowmass to write a manuscript entitled, "All I Want to Do Is Make People Happy."

That fall, at a court hearing, Judge Edward Brand declared that Tell was not the father of Patty's unborn child and agreed to annul the marriage.

At Christmas 1970, with the baby due in January, Lucy decided to whisk her son off to Snowmass. She didn't want him to have any part of the child. She was already annoyed with Lucie, who had become friendly with Patty, for going shopping with Patty for the baby's wardrobe. She refused to believe the child was Desi's. She told me she said to Desi, Jr., " 'You feel responsible? Boy, you're all of sixteen and a half [actually he was older]. You want to spend the rest of your life with this *person*? Are you really the father?' He wanted the baby to be his; it made him feel very manly. I said, 'You have six more years of school. You haven't even started college,' and he said, 'I want the responsibility. I'm a man now.' "

Lucy also told me: "It was ghastly . . . I was so put-upon; I couldn't believe what was happening. There were a hundred stories in a hundred magazines, and they all made me sick. It was 'They did, they didn't, she didn't, he wouldn't, she didn't, I never did, he never did, they wouldn't, they won't, they did too much, they won't do anything.' It was the silliest bunch of crap I've ever read!"

As soon as Patty called Desi to say (incorrectly) she was in labor in January, he rushed to Los Angeles. She was still locked in litigation with Tell and was on the verge of having a breakdown. As it turned out, the baby wasn't born in January or even in the first half of February. One wag said that when the child was finally born it would "be in possession of a high school diploma."

Patty wanted the baby to be born in Lucy's home. Lucy was determined it would not be. "Until I see it, I won't know for sure if it's his," Lucy told one writer.

She stayed on at Snowmass until March 1971. The baby was born on February 25. Lucy was so nervous during this period that scenes took place at Snowmass quite similar to those in her "Lucy" series. At one stage, the hose broke off the washing machine and wound around the room like a snake, spewing water all over the apartment while Lucy tried to grab it. She was equally annoyed with Lucie for planning to marry Phil Vandervort. He was now described as an actor-producer. The couple would frequently visit with Desi, Sr., and play chess with him at his estate in Baja California. Finally, Lucy relented and hired Vandervort as an assistant to Gary Morton in her production outfit. She had to admit that he was very attractive and charming, but she would constantly call friends and ask them obsessively, "What do you think is gonna happen? Huh? What do you think?" And then, still obsessively, "Do you think they're gonna get married?"

The birth of Patty Duke's child brought about as many headlines as Desi's own birth. The baby, born by Cesarean section, weighed a mere five pounds. His name was Sean Patrick Duke.* Lucy was furious because Gary Morton actually visited Patty at St. John's Hospital in Santa Monica; it was only under extreme pressure from everyone that she was forced to supply a crib, bassinet, and knitted garment.

As for Desi, Jr., he accepted that the baby was his. He fought his mother constantly over this. At the same time, Desi, Jr., gallantly told reporters that Patty and his mother got along beautifully. Patty told the newspapers, "Sean was two months old before I ever even spoke to Lucy—and then the only reason I was at their house was because Desi had begged me to come. . . ."

Desi gave out huge blow-ups of photographs of the baby to friends and put them all over his house and Patty's apartment. When she got home from the hospital, he cleaned the kitchen and helped prepare the baby's bottle. When she fired a nurse, he took over the nurse's duties. He cooked for Patty like a housewife and fought with her over her chain-smoking. One time, he was trying to change the diaper when the baby vomited all over his new suede jacket. This did not faze him. He gave Patty as much money as he could afford from his earnings in a picture, *Red Sky at Morning*, that he had recently shot in New Mexico. He gave Patty twin crosses that his mother had once owned. Lucy was very upset about this too, since she had given them to her son to wear.

Patty bought a house in Beverly Hills; she spoke to *Photoplay* of Lucy's disinterest in her child, "I don't need her. Not accepting Sean is her loss, not mine. She's always wanted grandchildren, according to Desi. Now she can have one. I guess she'll never be a grandmother unless she lets herself." That same month, May 1971, at the time of a special tribute to Lucy at the Dorothy Chandler Pavilion in Los Angeles, an anonymous woman announced she was the mother of Desi's newborn daughter, Julia Desiree. Nothing more was heard of this.

---

* As Sean Astin, he appeared recently in *The Goonies*.

In July, Patty met John Astin, a successful young actor, and Desi, Jr., and she finally broke up. That same month, Lucie married Phil Vandervort. Desi, Sr., was present at the wedding, which took place at dusk in the garden of Roxbury Drive, with a full orchestra, hundreds of guests in white chairs arranged in rows on the lawn, yellow and white streamers, and latticed pillars draped with flowers. The couple stood under an arch of yellow carnations, yellow chrysanthemums, and white daisies, with the Reverend Ray Harris, director of UCLA's Department of Spiritual Care, officiating. Among the guests were Jimmy Durante, Buddy Hackett, Lloyd and Beau Bridges, Olivia Hussey and her husband Dino Martin, and Jack Carter. It was Lucie's twentieth birthday. Lucy was greeted with applause and a standing ovation as she arrived.

· CHAPTER 20 ·

In the wake of the wedding, Desi, Jr., began dating an actress named Judy Brown, whom he met at a screening of *The Sicilian Clan*. The couple drove to La Costa, near San Diego, where they spent the weekend with Dino and Olivia Martin. After the party, Desi and Judy drove over to Desi, Sr.'s house in Corona Del Mar and stayed there overnight. All through the weekend, Dino, Olivia, Desi, and Judy played mixed doubles. They were followed by photographers everywhere. Judy, a beauty, had already dated Warren Beatty, Ryan O'Neal, and Christopher Jones. The next weekend, Judy became Desi's weekend guest at the La Costa Tennis Tournament; soon afterward, they broke up. Late in 1971, Desi, Jr., enrolled at the California Institute of the Arts, to study music arrangement and composition; but he dropped out quickly because he couldn't devote enough time to his studies. While at the institute, he agreed to appear in *Marco*, a musical about Marco Polo, to be shot in Japan the following summer.

In January 1972, Liza Minnelli, who had been friendly with Lucy from the time her father, Vincente Minnelli, directed her in *The Long, Long Trailer*, met Desi, Jr., again after several years. On the set of *The Long, Long Trailer* she, aged seven, had dandled Desi on her knee. Liza had come to like Lucy and they had almost a mother-daughter relationship over the years. In no time, Liza replaced Judy Brown in Desi's affections. The new couple exchanged friendship rings that month.

Kaye Ballard, well-known nightclub and stage performer and star of "The Mothers-in-Law," another Desilu production, recalls an interesting incident from that year. She and Lucy were bicycling in Palm Springs when a mad dog jumped out of a bush and snarled at them. Kaye fell off her bicycle, but Lucy turned on the beast and screamed, "Get back in those bushes, you son of a bitch!" The son of a bitch did.

Lucy had yet another mishap—this time at Snowmass. It was variously described as a skiing accident while she was coming down a slope, and a fall when someone skied right into her. The exact circumstances of this episode remain obscure. At all events, she proved, by her own admission, to be a handful when she was taken to the local hospital. She told me in 1973, "I was in the hospital five times; it took weeks of bed rest and a whole year to get over that accident. I did twenty-four shows of "Here's Lucy" in a cast. I wouldn't have massages and I wouldn't lie in bed one second longer than I had to. I suffer from claustrophobia. Dreadfully. I can't even stand to relax. If I do, I doze off. I wake up screaming DAAA! like that. I feel my arms are tied down by some guy. Tight and stifling! And the plaster cast! Forget it! At first they had me right up to the waist in it. I took the heaviest thing I could find, which was the handle used to raise and lower the hospital bed, and I broke the damned cast all the way down to the calf. Three times in a row. Finally, they gave me what I wanted: a cast I could move in a little. I still screamed! But I kinda got used to it. Then I'd fall asleep and wake up and still be encased! I'd pound at the cast and cry out like a maniac, and they'd come running in.

"It was hell. Of course, things always happen to me like this. All my life it's been arms legs arms legs arms legs."

Lucy, back at the house in February but still in the cast, stir-crazy and grumbling at everyone, was happy to be with Liza. Liza was full of fun, giggly, daffy, yet with a steely professionalism underneath. She was always giving Lucy remedies: at one stage, she whipped up a concoction of banana, orange juice, and coconut in a blender, informing Lucy that she must drink it if she didn't want her hair to fall out. Lucy became addicted to it. Of course, she saw a problem with Desi, Jr.'s, relationship with Liza, who was still married to Peter Allen. The slender, slight, almost excessively energetic Allen came from Australia, where he and Chris Allen had formed a duo. He and Liza, and Judy Garland and Judy's husband Mark Herron, had formed a bizarre quartet in Japan during Judy's prolonged visit to the Orient following a disastrous Australian tour.

After she was divorced from Allen, Liza had dated the charming, amusing Jim Bailey, one of the best known and most talented of "illusionists" (his own term) evoking major female stars on the stage. And it was now Jim Bailey who, to Lucy's increasing surprise, began dating her daughter.

The fact that Lucie would be interested in a man who wore a dress on the stage and who recreated constantly on stage and TV the mother of her son's present date was a puzzle she couldn't quite cope with.

She had first met Bailey early in 1972. She plagued her friend Kaye Ballard to arrange for her to meet Bailey since she hated dealing with agents and managers. She was determined to have Bailey on her show to do an "illusion" of Phyllis Diller.

Lucy was frantic and restless waiting for Bailey to come to Palm Springs for a meeting at her house. She plagued Kaye continually for hours. Finally, Bailey arrived. He told me he found Lucy sitting on a chair with her leg in the cast, puffing away at a cigarette and wearing a housecoat. With her were the TV actor Ross Martin, Martin's wife Olivia, Gary Morton, and Lucy's maid, Willie Mae. All through the conversation, Bailey couldn't take his eyes off Lucy's sleeve. He was astonished to see that a price tag was still dangling from it. Every time she would wave her arms around, chain-smoking furiously, sucking in her cheeks and pretending she didn't inhale, the price tag flew through the air on the end of its string.

Lucy suddenly caught Bailey's eye staring at this object. She followed his eye to the sleeve and screamed, "What the hell is this? Willie Mae! Get in here!" Lucy was struggling with the price tag and it refused to come off. She struggled and struggled, while everybody became hysterical with laughter. She was furious. Finally, Willie Mae ran in with a huge pair of scissors and snipped it off.

Later that night, driving back from a restaurant, Lucy badgered Bailey ceaselessly on what he would do on the show if he could come on in July. Mae West? Judy Garland? Streisand? Finally, she got to the point and mentioned Phyllis Diller. She snapped, "Well, do you want to do it or not?" He thought that all she would have had to do was call his agent and she could have avoided the lavish canapés, the dinner out, and the drive. But he wasn't rude enough to say so.

When Bailey first met Lucie, he told me, she was still married to Phil Vandervort. But after just a few months, the marriage was already falling apart. One night, at a party at Bailey's house in Beverly Hills, Lucy came with Gary, and Lucie with Vandervort. At another party, at the Century Plaza Hotel, where Bailey was appearing, Lucie stayed long after the guests had gone; Vandervort didn't want to stay, but she did. There was a fight when Vandervort again wanted to leave and Lucie didn't. She threw the car keys down the hall after him as he stood at the elevator pleading with her to leave and screamed, "If you're going, you're going without me!" And she stayed with Bailey very late.

From then on, according to Bailey, Lucie and Bailey were not merely dating, they plunged headlong into an affair. Bailey says, "Lucy liked me very much. But when I started my involvement with her daughter she told me she used to lie awake nights trying to figure it all out. She kept asking herself, "Isn't he? Is he? Is he gay? Isn't he? If he wears a dress, which is he? How could he be having an affair with my daughter?"

While Lucy was trying to figure this out, Desi and Liza

moved into Lucy's house and lived there without benefit of wedlock. This again was a great deal for Lucy to handle. The couple lived in the guest house by the pool, and one time they didn't come out for three days and nights. Lucy would tug at Bailey's sleeve anxiously and say, "Do you suppose they're all right? Do you suppose they're sick?" Once again, Bailey was amazed at Lucy's naïveté and told her he was quite sure the couple was perfectly all right.

Bailey was fascinated by Lucy. He observed her endless smoking, her obsessive interest in Pouilly-Fuissé (to which he introduced her), her fascination with Scrabble which later turned into an obsession with backgammon, and her fondness for an obscure word game called Let's Take a Trip. Julie Andrews had taught it to Carol Burnett, who taught it to Jim, who taught it to Lucy.

At the Riviera Hotel in Las Vegas, Lucy arrived with Gary, Lucie, DeDe, Jim Bailey, and Gary's cousin, the comedian Sid Gould, and his wife Vanda Barra to see Liza Minnelli's opening. Lucy won money hand over fist at every game she touched; she had funds from her entire staff to bet because she was almost incapable of losing. When a Keno ticket stuck to her foot, she won $2,500 with it.

That summer, Desi, Jr., left for Japan to make *Marco*, for which he had composed many of the songs and some of the music. It was the story of Marco Polo as a youth, who wins the affection of the Chinese emperor Kublai Khan, played by Zero Mostel. There were three months of shooting in the rainy season, and even when Liza arrived, Desi was on edge, according to news reports. He screamed at a photographer who took too many pictures of him, fought savagely with the director, and proved to be a problem on the set.

Back in Hollywood in July, Bailey was set to appear on Lucy's show. The premise was that Phyllis Diller had been booked to do a charity benefit, run by Lucy, and she had canceled because she had laryngitis. Lucie, looking in the paper, had seen Jim's picture as Phyllis, and called him up to take over. She didn't tell her mother, and the fun would arise from that.

The day before they shot the show, Bailey, by a peculiar irony, was stricken with laryngitis himself. He had rehearsed a song, "Fever," to be performed by him and Lucie, so often that he lost his voice. Hysterical at the news, Lucy called him in the middle of the night. She woke him, saying, "How do you feel? How do you feel? Do you feel any better? You have to gargle. . . . You *must* gargle!" He croaked, "I'm trying to sleep!"

Exhausted from being awakened by Lucy, Bailey rose at dawn, drove to the studio (Lucy was now running her operation at Universal), and called the doctor for some cortisone. When he came in for the dress rehearsal, Lucy told him anxiously, "Now rest your voice. Don't use it any more than you have to!" Of course, he had no voice to use. When he became speechless during the Phyllis Diller routine, Lucy played both herself and Phyllis Diller vocally to help him.

She was determined to go ahead with him. When she found his guest dressing room was not air-conditioned and the heavy July heat was relieved only by a tiny fan, thus threatening to melt his makeup, Lucy put him in her air-conditioned dressing room and got made up in her office. His voice came back for the actual show because of the cortisone pills, and he breezed expertly through it. Bailey Says, "I will never forget Lucy's professionalism and her graciousness to me during the week we worked. I had been told she was difficult. She wasn't. I learned much from her."

Finally, Lucie and Vandervort were divorced, and then Lucie's relationship with Bailey also fell apart. Jim and Lucie traveled the country together while he was on tour, but there were frequent separations and finally, Lucy, who had never been at all comfortable with the relationship to begin with, told Bailey, "You know, kid, it's never going to work." She told him, "You have a career. This girl wants a career. Where are you going to have this marriage? In airports?"

"I knew she was remembering her own marriage to Desi, Sr.," Bailey says, "and I knew she was right. I knew what I wanted if Lucie and I got married. I guess I was a male chauvinist! The wife makes the home, in my eyes. It took us a while to split. I didn't quite know how to break it to Lucie. Finally, we talked it through. We went our separate ways. I loved her very much and still do. We had a wonderful time together. But it couldn't last." We are very good friends today.

Bailey holds one special memory of Lucy. It was a night at her home when there was a screening of Woody Allen's *Everything You Wanted to Know About Sex But Were Afraid to Ask*. In the movie, a character goes to bed with a sheep in a hotel suite, another man, with a wife, children, and a bristling mustache, spends an evening in a dress, and an enormous breast appears on the horizon. Lucy muttered, "Am I seeing a man making love to a *sheep?* Am I seeing a man who is married with children wearing a *gown?* Am I seeing a *breast* appearing over the horizon? Has civilization come to an end? Take this picture off! Now! Immediately! This is filth!" She picked up her handbag and said, "I'm not watching this. I'm going to bed!" And she did.

Back from Japan, Desi, Jr., continued dating Liza. A psychic predicted that they would break up, saying they would never get married because they had been wed in a previous life as courtiers of Louis XIV [sic] and Marie Antoinette.

By the outset of 1973, Lucy had plunged into the shooting of her first feature film in some time, *Mame*. The picture was based both on *Auntie Mame*, by Patrick Dennis, and on the stage production, which starred Angela Lansbury on Broadway. Preparing for what would be a terrible movie was yet another Lucy nightmare. She told me, "Up to *Mame* my only exercise had been sitting down for two seconds, running around constantly. For *Mame* I had to learn not only to walk again, but to dance again. I hadn't danced in a movie for thirty years or more. Now I was up at five every day. I worked with Onna White, the dance director who did *Oliver!*, for months on end for ninety minutes every morning, stretching and bending. Jesus! It was hell. I thought I'd die. It's a miracle what Onna White did with me."

I vividly recall visiting Lucy on the set. It was nine A.M., early in a rainy February, and the director Gene Saks and Onna White were driving her relentlessly through her paces. Wearing a red Santa Claus cap, she mouthed the words to her prerecorded, throaty croaking (she still couldn't sing) of "Need a Little Christmas Now," following Mame's ruin in the Wall Street crash. Right in the middle of a take, the cap fell off. Un-Mameishly, Lucy stalked off angrily for a grim consultation with her milliner, whom she insisted on calling the Mad Hatter. Fuming, furious, she strode over to me and grabbed my arm, grinning starkly. She whispered, and I didn't believe her, "You see this cigarette? I *don't inhale it. I daren't!* Last night my *esophagus* gave out. I went *blue from head to foot* and lay there on the floor, *as though I had been stung by a thousand bees.* That's just the way I'm going to die, with my esophagus giving up on me. I'll stifle, I know it, and most of the time, day and night, I feel I'm *stifling.* Do you know what I mean?"

I didn't have a chance to reply. Like most stars, Lucy wasn't interested in a response, taking for granted in advance what it would be. She limped back on the set, croaking instructions. Grim, concentrated, she reminded me that making a musical was about as much fun as mixing cement. Like a lady wrestler, she charged into her scenes, nostrils flaring, ready to trample anyone who crossed her. But as soon as the camera turned, she sparkled like a young girl, kicked up a still-shapely leg, charmingly crinkled her clown's face, and hung on to her cap. She finished the scene in a Santa Claus mask, arms flung wide, mouth bigger than a mailbox slot, wanting to scream with tension but instead grinning from ear to ear for the close-up until the director screeched, "Cut!" Then, frowning deeply, she collapsed into a chair.

Mame took nineteen weeks of grueling shooting during which Lucy was in constant pain. She told me during the production, among other things, about a strange obsession she had. When she got on an airplane she would be driven to clean the toilets, and when she had finished with the one she was in she would wait for the others—in line if need be—and clean them as well. Often, she would spend much of the flight in the bathrooms! And if she saw a cigarette stub or a crumpled-up paper carton on the floor, or a piece of newspaper or a glove, she would get on her hands and knees, to the stupefaction of the other passengers and pick the litter up.

She said to me on a later visit, "Why am I doing this? I must be out of my mind. Dancing for a whole hour, exercise, the vocal coach, Jesus. Movies! The *hours!* It's like running backward!"

She talked about Liza and Desi. She said, "I hope it lasts. I don't care if they never get married. They don't have time to settle down in a house. And they have seven dogs to take care of between them. They say, 'Can we leave them with you?' And I reply, 'One cotton-picking minute! Once in a while, I'll take your dogs, and the puppies. But every time a dog drops a litter, you can't dump the pups on me. We've got five god-damned dogs already!' Liza! I feel like a mother to her. I don't think she'll ever settle down. She doesn't know what settling down is. She's never had a home. Liza took on all the respon-sibility long before Judy died. She helped her half-sister Lorna Luft go out on her own. Now she has the responsibility of her half-brother, Joey. He's a poor little guy and very lonely. She's too generous. She kills herself working and throws thousands here, thousands there. She told me she's trying to settle her mother's residue of financial problems. I said, 'Fine! But make sure she really owed them!' Monsters took Liza for over a million and a quarter more than her mother's debts, just for openers. I tried to be a mother to her!"

Lucy was furious at repeated reports that she had tried to prevent Bea Arthur from playing Mame's friend, Vera. She said that she had insisted on Ms. Arthur in order to have two fog-horn voices on the screen at once. She was also incensed that people were criticizing her for not being able to sing. She said, "Mame drank and stayed up all night. Was she supposed to sound like Julie Andrews? *Come on!*" *

There were many difficult episodes during the shooting. When an electrician put two phones in her dressing room, she screamed, "Two phones! Who do you think I am? The President? Is the second one the hot line to Moscow? Put the second one in the john!" To the annoyance of the Warners publicity department, she constantly told reporters that she "hated making movies." She missed her live audience. Her leg annoyed her every day. The heavy makeup irritated her skin. Articles about her upset her continuously. She was extremely nervous about the fox-hunt scene in *Mame*. She told me, "With my luck, I'll get thrown. And I have to catch the fox, turn it over on its back, and tickle its belly. Just leave me with this thought: When I turn the fox over, how can I stop the damned thing from scratching me half to death?" I told her it would probably be a mechanical fox. And she said, "Suppose it bites me with its metal teeth?" I told her, "You'll be perfectly all right if you don't use the tail as a lever!" She looked at me in astonishment, innocently believing every word. "Ohhhh. . . . Really? I'll certainly avoid the tail then!"

She told me, quite inconsequentially, that there was one thing worse than making pictures and only one: It was your house catching fire. She asked me if mine had. I said I lived in an apartment and it had not been on fire, but I'd once been in a hotel that began to blaze and I had had to walk down fifteen flights of stairs. She didn't hear me; she was off again. "My house caught fire *twice*," she said. "I was *desperate*. And you know, after I got all the dogs out, I thought, what shall I save next? And I ran into the smoke and got the kids' photographs." With that, she made her way back onto the set.

Unfortunately, *Mame* proved to be less than a hit. Not all of the concentration in the world, not all of the hard work, nor

---

* In fact, she sounded like Julius Tannen.

Scrabble or backgammon games, nor fights with everyone, could make her feel more comfortable. Angela Lansbury should have played the part. Arid and dreary, the movie did not do well. (She had put money in it.) And at the same time, Desi, Jr.'s, *Marco* was a disaster, albeit on a smaller scale.

Desi, Jr., continued to see Liza. While Lucy was making *Mame*, he was shooting *Billy Two Hats* in Israel. Once again, Liza crossed the world to be with him. But eventually, the relationship fell apart. When Liza was in London, she became mesmerized by Peter Sellers. Even though he quite lacked Desi's physical attraction, Sellers was so talented that Liza found him irresistible. Desi was appalled, depressed, and plunged back into heavy drugs. But he was consoled by meeting and falling for Victoria Principal.

· CHAPTER 21 ·

$\mathscr{I}$n part because she owned a big piece of *Mame*, Lucy took off on an extensive coast-to-coast promotional tour for the picture in the fall of 1974. She told a reporter for the *Los Angeles Herald Examiner*, "I'm out pushing this picture because I don't want the industry to go down the sewer—and I mean *sewer!* There are too many lines around the wrong movie houses these days. *Last Tango in Paris*, for instance. I don't know why Marlon Brando would lower himself to do a film like that. I think there are a lot of dirty old men making a fast buck—and confusing young people."

In interview after interview on the tour, which was as grueling and exhausting as only talk-show tours can be, Lucy constantly kept up an attack on violence and sex in pictures. She said in one interview, "I am here to entertain and make you forget reality as much as possible."

It was in 1974 that she started to think of ending "Here's Lucy." She had grown more delicate and was frequently overtired following *Mame*. Her health habits didn't help; endlessly smoking cigarettes, chewing hard candy, and downing Pouilly-Fuissé was scarcely a recipe for a strong constitution and vigorous health in old age. It was quite a wrench to her to have to admit that her television career was nearing its end. The *Mame* promotional tour left her very drained.

She was as feisty as ever. When she found out Liza Minnelli was planning to marry Peter Sellers, she was heard to scream, "Peter *Sellers?* Who's kidding who? Liza must be *crazy!*" She saw Desi, Sr., now and again. She was pleased for him when he, at fifty-seven but looking ten years older, embarked on a pilot for a show entitled "Dr. Domingo," about a small-town doctor doubling as local coroner. The pilot figured as an episode in Raymond Burr's "Ironside" series, but didn't make it into the network season. Desi told a reporter, "I quit the business in 1960 because it got to be a monster. At the beginning it was fun, but when you're in charge of three studios, with three thousand people and thirty-five soundstages working all the time, the fun is long gone."

When Lucy weakened in her resolve to end "Here's Lucy," talking of "perhaps six more years of product," the CBS executives decided against it. The reasons for this are obscure, since the show was doing well, but possibly Lucy's shaky health and increased reputation of being hard to work with encouraged them. However, from William Paley down, there were the warmest possible feelings for her at the network. Everyone was aware of her still-extraordinary popularity and fame in 1974, and it was decided to embark upon various specials with her over the years.

She didn't adjust well to the sudden leisure that was imposed upon her by the change, but at least she was able to spend a good deal more time with her down-home, lively DeDe, who was now over eighty. DeDe was never fazed by Lucy's tension and nervousness, slapping her down cheerfully when she got out of hand; through the years, she almost never missed the filming of a single show, and always led the cheering, laughter, and applause in the studio audience. She told a reporter, Barbara Sternig, "I'm not a demandin' mother. I'm not cryin' all the time. I don't ask for anything, and I'm self-sufficient as far as taking care of myself. I do all my own work and all my own cooking. I live my own life . . . I don't go to

Lucille's house or anyone's unless I'm invited. Not that I sit and mope and wait until I'm invited, either. I go places on my own. Lucille knows I have my friends and she has hers."

Lucy gave interviews constantly in the mid-1970s, possibly in part to allay the boredom. She was explored carefully by a piece in *TV Guide*, written by Terrence O'Flaherty, who made a summary entitled "The Lucy Book of Records." He disclosed that she had made 495 TV shows, including 179 episodes of "I Love Lucy," 156 of "The Lucy Show," 144 of "Here's Lucy," and 16 specials. Run end-to-end, the total viewing time of these would last for ten days and nights.* She had used up two tons worth of paper for the total number of scripts. She had worked with lions, tigers, sheep, goats, penguins, chimpanzees, porpoises, horses, bears, cats, birds, pigs, and dogs. Among other things, she had played an Indian, a bricklayer, a grape trampler, a fight manager, a sax player in a band of nuns, a Martian, an astronaut, a pool hustler, a kangaroo, the front end of a horse, and a pickle. She had used a total of 7,500 yards of cloth, or enough to wrap several mummies. The author was at pains to say that "no personal slur was intended." In the shows she had been coated with chocolate, starched, soaked, plunged down stairs on skis, had slid down a fire pole, been locked in handcuffs, and been "crowned"—with a loving cup on her head. Unfortunately, he added, no statistics were available on how many times her teeth had been blacked out or she had received a custard pie in the face.

Lucy put a brave face on her semiretirement. She told a writer for *Modern Screen*, "I've learned you don't rake more leaves than you can get into a wheelbarrow. I would never give up my career entirely, but I think the time has come when Gary and I can have more home life by my tapering off a little."

There was no question that her marriage to Gary Morton had been a success. His devotion to her, the way in which he never showed his ego and allowed her to call the shots, was

---

* Actually, this was only the total running time of the half-hour shows.

noted by everyone. Asked how it felt to be married to a woman so much more successful than he was, a question fairly typical of show-business reporters, he replied, "I've never thought about it." He had never hesitated to come and watch her work but had never intruded. Now, he was glad to see her under less pressure at her age. But he also had to feel her frustration at being out of the spotlight, and that cannot have been easy for him. The truth was that the break with television was traumatic for her and there was no getting over that.

A pleasant change of scene occurred when Lucie Arnaz opened in 1974 with John Gavin and Tommy Tune in *Seesaw*, directed by Michael Bennett, a musical based upon William Gibson's *Two for the Seesaw*. Lucie had done *Cabaret* twice, in Flint, Michigan, and in California, and *Once Upon a Mattress* on a tour through Ohio, but *Seesaw* was a new and bold adventure for her. The show had been on the road for six months before it opened in L.A. It received excellent reviews from the critics; the *Los Angeles Times'* Dan Sullivan said that in the role of Gittel, "the young, tough Jewish broad of the musical, Lucie 'lights her up from underneath.' " Her dance numbers with the tall, spindly Tommy Tune were exceptionally charming, accentuated in many ways by their great difference in height. Sullivan wrote,

> It could be argued that Miss Arnaz, while perfectly at home with Cy Coleman's and Dorothy Fields' songs, and Michael Bennett's dance numbers, doesn't have as much "electricity" as a harder-edged personality might. But then neither does she seem on the edge of shorting out. It's an agreeably life-sized, normal-temperature performance with far more attention to what Gittel is like inside than you would get from one of the electric people.

Ron Pennington wrote in the *Hollywood Reporter*, "Arnaz proves to be an effervescent young performer, and she sails

through the role with a great deal of energy and fun spirit."
Phil Vandervort was present at the opening; they were still not
divorced, and it was said that he wanted to come back to her.
However, this was merely columnists' talk. Lucy sat completely motionless throughout the show, petrified her daughter
would make a mistake. Desi, Sr., was also there, making the
disconcerting remark, "I'm not saying she's the greatest singer
and dancer in the world, but she's so honest!" As for Desi, Jr.,
his date, interestingly enough, was Olivia Hussey, who had
just separated from Dino Martin.

A curious episode took place at the Emmys on May 19,
1975. Lucy was there to present an award to the producer of
the best series of the season. Just as she was preparing to go
onstage, an usher told her she must take a phone call. She said
it was out of the question. The usher said it was a matter of life
or death. Gary Morton picked up the phone for her. A woman's voice said, "I am a nurse at UCLA Medical Center. Miss
Lucille Ball's son, Desi, Jr., has been critically injured in an
automobile accident and we are not sure if he will recover.
Please tell Miss Ball to come at once." Gary looked up from
the phone in horror. Lucy was standing there. She said, "Wait
a minute." Then she went to the phone herself and placed a
call to Desi, Jr., at his home. He answered, asking if anything
had gone wrong; he was enjoying the telecast. The hoaxer's
name was never discovered.

Lucy continued to make provocative remarks to reporters
in those years. She said more revealingly than she intended to
one paper, "Women's lib doesn't interest me. I've been liberated all my life. I'm so liberated that my husband does everything for me!"

Lucy formed a friendship during the 1970s with Sammy
and Altovise Davis. Altovise in many ways felt out of place in
show-business circles; she was quite the reverse of Sammy,
who was enormously extroverted and somewhat hyperactive.
Lucy invited Altovise frequently to her home, plunging her
into Scrabble games, followed by her new craze of backgam-

mon. In the periods when Davis was on the road, and during a clash between husband and wife on the issue of President Nixon's administration and the Watergate affair, Lucy stepped in to save the marriage.

Lucy's problems with Desi, Jr., did not decrease. While Lucie's career flourished, young Desi suffered from severe fits of depression. He failed to get assignments, and, despite his pleasure in Lucie's success, was painfully aware of the difference in their talents. Insecure as always, afraid of his mother, dreading her private criticisms of him and appalled by her remarks about him in print, he plunged deeper and deeper into drugs. On January 25, 1979, he was admitted to Cedars Sinai Medical Center in Los Angeles for narcotics abuse, depression, and an upper-respiratory infection. He apparently was on Thorazine, a powerful medication, when he left the hospital on February 6. This whole matter was extremely tormenting to his mother.

That same year, Lucie opened on Broadway in *They're Playing Our Song*, book by Neil Simon, with music by Marvin Hamlisch, and lyrics by Carole Bayer Sager. She played Sonia Walsk, a lyricist in love with a pop composer, played by Robert Klein. *Time* magazine said of Lucie, "Arnaz . . . sings her lyrics in depth, with Streisand's gift for matching feeling with meaning. She hurdles the barricade of being the daughter of Lucille Ball and Desi Arnaz by imitating neither, but she has inherited their incomparable comic timing."

In June, Lucy announced that she would be heading a new production company to develop programs and talent for NBC, and would also star in entertainment specials. Fred Silverman, president of NBC, confirmed this new development at a press conference at the Century Plaza in Los Angeles on June 24. Although she had exclaimed in response to the announcement, "Boy, am I ready for this!" plans dragged from the beginning. Instead she began lecturing in various places, and she was hired as an assistant professor, of all things, at California State University, Northridge, growling responses to the students' well-meaning but often uninformed questions. Asked why she bothered with teaching at this stage in her career, she said, "I try to teach the practical, get-you-through-the-day basics of survival in the TV and film business. Students are thrown out with what they think are all the ingredients, but they sometimes have to start from scratch. I emphasize self-preservation. These classes are intended to be survival kits. I try to teach them the art of taking care of themselves in every way so someone else doesn't have to. I believe in a positive attitude, self-improvement, and assertiveness."

That year, Vivian Vance, who had so often fought savagely with Lucy on the set, but for whom Lucy retained great affection, was stricken with cancer. She was forced to back down from a March of Dimes fund-raising campaign because of her illness. Lucy flew to San Francisco to be with her, and cried uncontrollably on the plane. She ran in and hugged Vivian, shocked to see her condition. Later, on "Good Morning, America," Lucy sobbed right on camera, something quite unheard of for her, when Vivian's name was mentioned; Vivian's protracted death was a painful ordeal for Lucy.

In January 1980, Lucy opened the Helen Bonfils Theater Complex in Denver with Henry Fonda. Fifteen days later, Desi, Jr., married the actress Linda Purl, who had appeared with him in the TV movies *Having Babies* and *Black Market Baby.* One month after that, the NBC plans, embarked on several months earlier, emerged. The name of the show was "Lucy Moves to NBC," with Lucy listed as executive producer. The special was singularly clumsy and awkward. Directed by her old friend Jack Donohue, it had Lucy in retirement being lured back to show business by Fred Silverman, followed by Lucy moving into her new offices at Burbank and being welcomed by Johnny Carson, Gary Coleman, Bob Hope, and Jack Klugman. Gale Gordon, so often a stalwart of "Here's Lucy," appeared to do some comedy routines. It could have been put together by a computer, and was a waste of everybody's time. The only relief in it was the obvious affection Lucy clearly felt for the delicate young Gary Coleman, whose survival on a dialysis machine she found utterly amazing and touching; she was deeply impressed with his talent.

She rather liked Linda Purl, saying with her usual lack of discretion to *People* magazine, "[She is] organized. If there's anyone in the world who isn't organized, it's my son. I hope she rubs off on him, and he doesn't rub off on her." These harsh words must have been excruciatingly painful for Desi, Jr., to read. She claimed to one interviewer that because of treatments with steroids for her deteriorating bone marrow, her feminine cycles were restored when she was close to seventy. She was very busy hosting backgammon benefits, emphasizing her passion for the game. Then, on June 26, 1980, Lucie was married in an outdoor ceremony at Mount Marron, New York, to actor Laurence Luckinbill, who at forty-seven was twenty years her senior. They were wed at the seventy-acre estate of Don Farber, Luckinbill's attorney. Lucy bestowed her blessing on the wedding despite the great age difference, and was very touched when Desi, Sr., sang to Lucie at the ceremony a number he had composed in her honor. She hugged and kissed him, and it was clear to many that she still loved him. Both she and Desi, Sr., were in tears when Luckinbill put the ring on Lucie's finger. Lucy cried even more when the couple recited lengthy vows of their own composition, Luckinbill saying, "I cherish you more than I can ever put into words." After the ceremony, Desi, Sr., and his wife Edie, and Lucy and Gary Morton, joined the grand buffet. They all enjoyed themselves enormously as they sat on the grass on red-and-white tablecloths under the apple trees.

In August, 1980, Lucie and Luckinbill opened at the Wilshire Theater in Los Angeles in Brian Clark's play *Whose Life Is It, Anyway?* Lucie was already expecting her first child when the show premiered. Both she and her husband were very good in the play. During the run, they changed roles: Lucie began as the patient who fights for her right to die, with Luckinbill as the doctor; then they switched parts. Dan Sullivan in the *Los Angeles Times* was complimentary about both the first and second incarnations of the show. Of the second, he wrote, "The actress has no trouble at all with the role's toughest physical demand, to lie under those sheets for two hours without moving a finger. We are touched by the contrast between the still body and the mobile face. And we are delighted by the feisty spirit." Unfortunately, this acting triumph was not followed by an equivalent film success when Lucie appeared with Neil Diamond in *The Jazz Singer*, released that same winter. The movie, a second remake of Al Jolson's pioneer talkie, made little or no impression, was badly reviewed, and sank without a trace.

In September 1981, Lucy's net worth was listed by *Los Angeles* magazine as between $50 million and $100 million. However, it cannot be said that she was a happy woman. The box-office disappointment of *Mame* and the many bad reviews that greeted her performance in it still smarted. Out of touch with everything, her house piled high with scripts that she couldn't bring herself to produce or appear in, still alienated from her son, she took consolation only in the birth of her grandchild, the Luckinbills' little boy, Simon, named for Neil Simon, who introduced Luckinbill and Lucie.

Lucie told an interviewer for the *Star* magazine on April 9, 1985, that her mother had furnished an apartment in New York. It had a great deal of glassware. Simon, and later his little brother Joseph, were not allowed to go there very often because they would break things. She added, "My mother will say, 'Don't touch this! Don't touch that! Don't sit on that. . . . Take off your shoes in front of the door!' When Mom and Gary come over here, I say, 'Watch out for your cigarettes! Don't put them on anything.' "

The 1980s were in many ways easier years for Lucy, whose consolations were the Luckinbills. At least Lucy seemed to have mellowed to the point that she was respectful of her daughter even when they collided, far more so than of her son, and she found at last a kind of peace and comfort in her old age. She was extremely careful about the lighting when she did make an occasional television appearance, but she avoided face-lifts and other attempts to fend off the inevitable, and stuck only to her red mop of hair, still dyed after some forty years, now contrasting oddly with her complexion. Her retaining it was probably as much a desire to keep her trademark as anything else.

She had many plans. Incredibly, in view of her previous experience, she talked of a return to the theater, and while in New York in 1982 she called Morton ("Teke") DaCosta, a director she admired, asking if he could find her a play for a cross-country tour. She even considered briefly appearing in a version of the life of Tallulah Bankhead, commenting to DaCosta, "Where are you going to find another Tallulah with as deep a basso as mine?" But nothing came of this.

She appeared on five segments of "Good Morning, America" in 1983, rushing through some of the superficial facts of her career. She sat bolt upright as she always did, clearly tense despite her apparent good feelings for the host, David Hartman. There was talk that she would appear with Lucie in a play, *I Never Loved My Daughter*, about an entertainer stricken with a fatal illness. Again, this turned out to be a false rumor. Lucy spent more and more time in New York in 1983 and 1984, leasing an apartment in the East Sixties to be nearer her grandchildren. She would arrive at cocktail parties with snapshots of the children and call columnists, including her ultimate fan, the columnist Radie Harris, to discuss the growing infants. Miss Harris gushed on January 11, 1983, in the *Hollywood Reporter*, "It hardly seems thirty-two years ago that I sat on Lucy's bed at Chatsworth, while she and Desi awaited the birth of little Lucie, and no two parents ever anticipated their first-born with such joy."

Lucy received the inevitable round of honors in those years. She was given special recognition for her outstanding accomplishments as a great entertainer at the March of Dimes Jack Benny Memorial Award ceremony at the Century Plaza

Hotel in Los Angeles on June 3, 1983, with Carol Burnett, Dean Martin, Gregory Peck, Jack Lemmon, and Bob Hope among the people present. Yet at the same time she was the recipient of bad news: Desi, Sr.'s wife, of whom Lucy remained fond, was stricken with cancer and had a protracted struggle before her death in 1984. According to some sources, Lucy was so sorry for her first husband that she gave him use of the pool guest house once occupied by Liza Minnelli and Desi, Jr.

On February 26, 1984, Lucy, along with Milton Berle, Paddy Chayefsky, Edward R. Murrow, David Sarnoff, Norman Lear, and William S. Paley, was among the first to be inducted into the Television Academy Hall of Fame.

In April she was honored by the Museum of Broadcasting in Manhattan. Now seventy-two, she still had enormous public appeal; fans waited in icy, rain-swept weather in order to be able to meet Lucy for a discussion in person. According to *People* magazine, when the discussion began, a small woman asked if she could shake her hand. Lucy declined. The woman begged her. Finally, Lucy reluctantly did accede to the woman's request. At that moment, the woman grabbed her in a tight hug and wouldn't let go. Lucy broke free, gasping, "She scared the hell out of me!"

That evening, Lucy told the museum audience she would never work on television again. She said, "I'm not going to try alone now what I've done with my partners in the past. And my partners are in heaven." (William Frawley had also died.)

DeDe died finally at a very advanced age and Lucy told one reporter, "I rely on the guidance of my mother from beyond the grave. When I have a problem, I dream, and she gives me the answer."

Lucy and Gary Morton found some solace in running Lucille Ball Productions, which presented the movie *All the Right Moves*, a rather mediocre picture starring Tom Cruise, about a high school athlete who tries to escape life in a small town.

The film was quite popular, but was not a huge success. Lucy wanted to make it because it was "clean."

Desi, Jr., emerged with distinction in that period. He took his courage in his hands and decided to devote his time to touring various cities to lecture on the dangers of drug abuse and talk about ways to overcome forms of addiction. Both he and Lucy remained grimly silent about each other; all attempts to draw him out on the subject of his mother failed, and clearly his early suffering was something he couldn't bear to think about. Although his marriage to Linda Purl had collapsed, and he had now apparently retreated into a monastic existence, his looks seemed to improve, if anything, with age, and certainly he had now come to the point of assuming his most useful role in life.

· EPILOGUE ·

*L*ate in 1984, despite saying she would never work in television again, Lucy planned a comeback in a dramatic role. She was to play the character of a bag lady in the teleplay *Stone Pillow*, made by Schaefer/Karpf Productions in association with Gaylord Productions for a fall 1985 airing on CBS. George Schaefer would direct from a script by Rose Leiman Goldemberg. Lucy very much liked Rose Goldemberg's script, but felt it needed some fixing, and the rewrites were delayed by the sudden and shocking death of Mrs. Goldemberg's daughter in an accident. Also, Lucy was somewhat anxious about shooting in the brutal winter of New York, and it was decided to make the film in the spring. This presented an unexpected problem. The filming didn't begin until May; there was an early heatwave in Manhattan, and Lucy had to wear heavy layers of clothing since Florabelle, the bag lady, was supposed to be suffering from the cold. Never particularly robust in recent years, undermined by her addiction to smoking and her fondness for Pouilly-Fuissé (though she was never intoxicated), Lucy was scarcely in the best of shape to deal with the grueling thirty-one-day shooting schedule. She acted the part of the feisty, defiant, and unbeatable bag lady with considerable skill, particularly in the scene in which Florabelle leaves the rest home and makes off in a temper into an exceptionally bleak and harshly ugly building site, where the sheer emptiness and glaring indifference of the city drive her in desperation back to the shelter again. Allowing for the sentimentality of the story, and the fact that few bag ladies in history have had either the vocal energy or verbal fluency of Florabelle, it was a creditable portrait of an embattled woman at the end of her tether; and in the clashes with the shelter staff, Lucy's quality as an actress really came through. It was the first chance she had had to play a dramatic role in many years.

The experience took its toll. Hungry to work again, like most stars who have been unemployed for a time, yet as sensitive as ever when it came to the daily setbacks and ordeals of shooting anything for the screen, Lucy grimly set about her task of making the whole production work. She lost twenty-three pounds she could ill afford to lose and became painfully thin and weak, collapsing with dehydration because of insufficient liquid intake in the heat; also, weighed down by her heavy clothes and by exhaustion, she fell and ripped a tendon in her arm. She continued doggedly to the end of the shooting, and, when she returned to Los Angeles, was admitted to a hospital. To those who met her afterward, she seemed frail and quite aged.

The show had mixed reviews. The trades were respectful, as one might expect, but several papers deplored the show, and she was greatly depressed by some of the adverse comments. One critic charged that her fingernails were not black as they should have been and that her face looked as though it were shot through sixteen folds of pink gauze. Yet certainly she had a good chance for an Emmy nomination, and she told many friends in her grating baritone voice that she was proud of George Schaefer's work and of her own.

The pain from her injured arm caused her great periods of depression in the late fall of 1985. She recovered speedily, appearing at Bridges Auditorium at Claremont College in California to answer questions from students on a Saturday night —Halloween. The evening began with about half an hour of clips from "I Love Lucy," including scenes in which she stamped on grapes, assembled chocolates on a candy belt, concealed eggs in her blouse, and gaped at William Holden in the Brown Derby. For a full ninety minutes and with remarkable energy, not showing a trace of her injury, she fielded the questions of a young and hugely enthusiastic audience that still clearly loved her, proving even to her that she was as famous as ever to the younger generation. Showing little or nothing of her depressed and gloomy side, she acted up a storm, only letting loose her temper when someone asked her, "How do you feel about being an American institution?" When she snapped back, "What the hell does that mean?" she did it with a growling laugh, and the audience laughed with her. She replied, "I'm sure you meant that as a compliment. Let's just say anything I can be that's American is okay with me. Let's leave it at that. Next question!"

She paced the stage, puffing at cigarettes, never sitting still for a full hour and a half. She spoke of Vivian Vance, saying that she had told Vivian how much she meant to her just before Vivian died; and of Henry Fonda, who, she said, didn't know who she was when they made *The Big Street*, but with whom she loved making *Yours, Mine, and Ours;* and also of Joan Crawford, who was "so tiny." She didn't mention that Miss Crawford, arriving at the studio for one of the "Lucy" shows, was carrying with her a bag containing 100-proof vodka and was so small and insignificant looking that she was mistaken for an intruder on the set and very nearly had to leave until she identified herself. Lucy said of *Stone Pillow,* "Because of it I learned to have compassion for the homeless. And I hope you will buy it. I hope you people will let me do something besides 'Lucy.' If you think 'I don't want to see her do that; I want to see her be funny,' I can buy that. But I hope you'll think [*Stone Pillow*] has some merit." It proved that she is still a very great star in her seventies.

But soon afterward she was preparing "Lucy" again.

"Life with Lucy" was launched in the fall season by ABC

in 1986. Lucy worked desperately hard with members of her long-standing team of writers, but the formula failed to work. She was very saddened when she received the news that due to bad ratings the show would be suspended as of November 15. But she had a consolation prize. On December 17, 1986, she was honored by President Reagan with an award for a life-long achievement at the Kennedy Center in Washington, D.C. along with Yehudi Menuhin, Jessica Tandy, Hume Cronyn, Anthony Tudor and Ray Charles.

Despite the rift with her son, the tragedy of the loss of her first marriage, the difficult life she had led, her dislike of sex and violence today, and the surprising, disturbing moments when her darker side has emerged, Lucille Ball is still one of the most popular and impressive Americans alive. The fact that she would scowl at such a description and take another deep puff on her cigarette says a great deal about her and illustrates why, unpretentious and honest, abrasive and likable, discontented, difficult and desirable, she is in a sense her own creation and will always be loved by all generations.

In those films marked with an asterisk, Lucille Ball was an uncredited "bit" player.

*Broadway Thru a Keyhole. 1933.
*Blood Money. 1933.
*The Bowery. 1933.
*Roman Scandals. 1933.
*Moulin Rouge. 1934.
*Murder at the Vanities. 1934.
*Nana. 1934.
*Bottoms Up. 1934.
*Hold That Girl. 1934.
*Bulldog Drummond Strikes Back. 1934.
*The Affairs of Cellini. 1934.
*Kid Millions. 1934.
*Perfectly Mismated. 1934. (Short)
*Three Little Pigskins. 1934. (Short)
*Broadway Bill. 1934.
*Jealousy. 1934.
*Men of the Night. 1934.
*The Fugitive Lady. 1934.
 Carnival. 1935.
 Roberta. 1935.

Old Man Rhythm. 1935.
Top Hat. 1935.
The Three Musketeers. 1935.
I Dream Too Much. 1935.
Mary of Scotland. 1936.
Chatterbox. 1936.
Follow the Fleet. 1936.
The Farmer in the Dell. 1936.
Bunker Bean. 1936.
That Girl from Paris. 1936.
Winterset. 1936.
Don't Tell the Wife. 1937.
Stage Door. 1937.
The Joy of Living. 1938.
Go Chase Yourself. 1938.
Having Wonderful Time. 1938.
The Affairs of Annabel. 1938.
Room Service. 1938.
The Next Time I Marry. 1938.
Annabel Takes a Tour. 1938.
Beauty for the Asking. 1939.
Twelve Crowded Hours. 1939.
Panama Lady. 1939.
Five Came Back. 1939.
That's Right, You're Wrong. 1939.
The Marines Fly High. 1940.
You Can't Fool Your Wife. 1940.
Dance, Girl, Dance. 1940.
Too Many Girls. 1940.
A Girl, a Guy, and a Gob. 1941.
Look Who's Laughing. 1941.
Valley of the Sun. 1942.
The Big Street. 1942.
Seven Days' Leave. 1942.
Du Barry Was a Lady. 1943.
Best Foot Forward. 1943.

Thousands Cheer. 1943. (Cameo)

Meet the People. 1944.

Without Love. 1945.

Abbott and Costello in Hollywood. 1945. (Cameo)

Ziegfeld Follies. 1946. (Sketch)

The Dark Corner. 1946.

Easy to Wed. 1946.

Two Smart People. 1946.

Lover Come Back. 1946.

Lured. 1947.

Her Husband's Affairs. 1947.

Sorrowful Jones. 1949.

Easy Living. 1949.

Miss Grant Takes Richmond. 1949.

A Woman of Distinction. 1950. (Uncredited cameo)

Fancy Pants. 1950.

The Fuller Brush Girl. 1950.

The Magic Carpet. 1951.

The Long, Long Trailer. 1954.

Forever, Darling. 1956.

The Facts of Life. 1960.

Critic's Choice. 1963.

MGM's Big Parade of Comedy. 1964. (Contains a sequence from *Meet the People.*)

A Guide for the Married Man. 1967. (Cameo)

Your's Mine and Ours. 1968.

Mame. 1974.

That's Entertainment. 1974. (Contains a sequence from *Ziegfeld Follies.*)

That's Dancing. 1984. (Features Lucille Ball in a montage of sequences from M-G-M musicals.)

THE TELEVISION APPEARANCES
OF LUCILLE BALL

"I Love Lucy." CBS, October 15, 1951—September 24, 1961.

"Westinghouse Desilu Playhouse." CBS, October 13, 1958—June 10, 1960. (Lucille Ball was not featured in every episode, but did appear on a regular basis in this series.)

"The Danny Thomas Show." CBS, January 5, 1959.

"The Ann Sothern Show." CBS, October 5, 1959.

"Lucy in Connecticut." CBS, July 3, 1960—September 25, 1960.

"The Lucy-Desi Comedy Hour." CBS, July 2, 1962—August 31, 1967.

"The Lucy Show." CBS, October 1, 1962—September 2, 1974. (Initially broadcast as "The Lucille Ball Show;" retitled "The Lucy Show," November 1962; retitled "Here's Lucy," September 1968).

"The Good Years." CBS, January 12, 1962.

"The Danny Kaye Special." NBC, November 11, 1962.

"The Lucille Ball Comedy Hour." CBS, April 19, 1964.

"Lucille Ball in London." CBS, October 24, 1966.

"The Ed Sullivan Show." CBS, March 17, 1968.

"Swing Out, Sweet Land." NBC, April 8, 1971.

"A Man and a Woman." NBC, September 16, 1973.

"Happy Anniversary and Goodbye." CBS, November 19, 1974.

"Dean Martin Celebrity Roast: Lucille Ball." NBC, February 7, 1975.

"A Lucille Ball Special Starring Lucille Ball and Dean Martin." CBS, March 1, 1975.

"The Emmy Awards." CBS, May 19, 1975.

"A Lucille Ball Special with Jackie Gleason." CBS, December 3, 1975.

"Gypsy in My Soul." CBS, January 20, 1976.

"What Now Catherine Curtis?" CBS, March 30, 1976.

"The Practice." NBC, October 13, 1976.

"Texaco Presents Bob Hope's World of Comedy." NBC, October 29, 1976.

"CBS Salutes Lucy: The First 25 Years." CBS, November 28, 1976.

"Dean Martin Celebrity Roast: Danny Thomas." NBC, December 15, 1976.

"The Second Annual Circus of the Stars." CBS, January 10, 1977.

"All-Star Tribute to Vaudeville." NBC, March 25, 1977.

"The Lucille Ball Special." CBS, November 21, 1977.

"The Barbara Walters Special." ABC, December 6, 1977.

"Gene Kelly—An American in Pasadena." CBS, December 15, 1977.

"TV: The Fabulous '50s." NBC, March 5, 1978.

"The American Film Institute Salute to Henry Fonda." CBS, March 15, 1978.

"CBS: On the Air." CBS, March 26, 1978.

"A Tribute to 'Mr. Television' Milton Berle." NBC, March 26, 1978.

"Dean Martin Celebrity Roast: Jimmy Stewart." NBC, May 10, 1978.

"Happy Birthday, Bob." NBC, May 29, 1978.

"Lucy Comes to Nashville." CBS, November 19, 1978.

"Photoplay Hall of Fame." ABC, November 21, 1978.

"The Television Annual" '78–'79. ABC, May 14, 1979.

"Lucy Moves to NBC." NBC, February 8, 1980.

"The Steve Allen Comedy Hour." NBC, October 18, 1980.
"Bungle Abbey." NBC, December 5, 1980.
"Good Morning America." ABC, May 17–21, 1982.
"The Best of Three's Company." ABC, May 18, 1982.
Stone Pillow. CBS, November 5, 1985.
"Life with Lucy," ABC, fall 1986.

Famous Lives
from St. Martin's Press

LIBERACE: THE TRUE STORY
Bob Thomas
_____ 91352-4 $3.95 U.S. _____ 91354-0 $4.95 Can.

THE FITZGERALDS AND THE KENNEDYS
Doris Kearns Goodwin
_____ 90933-0 $5.95 U.S. _____ 90934-9 $6.95 Can.

CAROLINE AND STEPHANIE
Susan Crimp and Patricia Burstein
_____ 91116-5 $3.50 U.S. _____ 91117-3 $4.50 Can.

PATRICK SWAYZE
Mitchell Krugel
_____ 91449-0 $3.50 U.S. _____ 91450-4 $4.50 Can

YOUR CHEATIN' HEART:
A BIOGRAPHY OF HANK WILLIAMS
Chet Flippo
_____ 91400-8 $3.95 U.S. _____ 91401-6 $4.95 Can.

WHO'S SORRY NOW?
Connie Francis
_____ 90386-3 $3.95 U.S. _____ 90383-9 $4.95 Can.

Publishers Book and Audio Mailing Service
P.O. Box 120159, Staten Island, NY 10312-0004

Please send me the book(s) I have checked above. I am enclosing
$ _____ (please add $1.25 for the first book, and $.25 for each
additional book to cover postage and handling. Send check or
money order only—no CODs.)

Name _____

Address _____

City _____ State/Zip _____

Please allow six weeks for delivery. Prices subject to change
without notice.